Stalking the U-boat

Smithsonian History of Aviation Series
Von Hardesty, Series Editor

On December 17, 1903, on a windy beach in North Carolina, aviation became a reality. The development of aviation over the course of little less than a century stands as an awe-inspiring accomplishment in both a civilian and military context. The airplane has brought whole continents closer together, at the same time it has been a lethal instrument of war.

This series of books is intended to contribute to the overall understanding of the history of aviation—its science and technology, as well as the social, cultural, and political environment in which it developed and matured. Some publications help fill the many gaps that still exist in the literature of flight; others add new information and interpretation to current knowledge. While the series appeals to a broad audience of general readers and specialists in the field, its hallmark is strong scholarly content.

The series is international in scope and will include works in three major categories:

Smithsonian Studies in Aviation History: works that provide new and original knowledge.

Smithsonian Classics of Aviation History: carefully selected out-of-print works that are considered essential scholarship.

Smithsonian Contributions to Aviation History: previously unpublished documents, reports, symposia, and other materials.

Advisory Board: Roger E. Bilstein, *University of Houston;* Horst Boog, *Militärgeschichtliches Forschungsamt;* Emmanuel Chadeau, *Université de Charles de Gaulle;* Tom D. Crouch, *National Air and Space Museum;* John Greenwood, *historian;* Terry Gwynne-Jones, *author;* R. Cargill Hall, *Center for Air Force History;* Richard P. Hallion, *Air Force Historian;* James R. Hansen, *Auburn University;* Von Hardesty, *National Air and Space Museum;* William M. Leary, *University of Georgia;* W. David Lewis, *Auburn University;* Donald S. Lopez, *National Air and Space Museum;* Air Vice-Marshal R. A. Mason, CBE MA RAF (Ret.); Colonel Phillip S. Meilinger, *Maxwell Air Force Base;* John H. Morrow, Jr., *University of Georgia;* Richard J. Overy, *King's College, London;* Dominick A. Pisano, *National Air and Space Museum;* E. T. Wooldridge, *National Air and Space Museum.*

Max Schoenfeld

Stalking the U-boat

USAAF Offensive Antisubmarine Operations in World War II

Smithsonian Institution Press
Washington and London

This book was edited by Initial Cap Editorial Services.
Production editor: Jack Kirshbaum
Designer: Alan Carter

Library of Congress Cataloging-in-Publication Data
Schoenfeld, Maxwell Philip, 1936–
    USAAF antisubmarine operations / by Max Schoenfeld.
    p. cm. — (Smithsonian history of aviation series)
    Includes bibliographical references and index.
    ISBN 1-56098-403-1
    1. World War, 1939–1945—Aerial operations, American. 2. Anti-
submarine aircraft—United States. 3. World War, 1939–1945—Naval operations—Submarine. I. Title. II. Series D790.S38 1994
    940.54'516—dc20   93–41041
British Library Cataloging-in-Publication data available

Printed in the United States of America
99 98 97 96 95   4 3 2 1

To Ronald and Johanna Warloski

Contents

Preface and Acknowledgments

Readers are entitled to know what they are getting. I have endeavored to do two things in this narrative. First, I have sought to provide an account of the primary overseas activities of the USAAF's Antisubmarine Command. This organization existed for barely a year, from September 1942 until August 1943. Its operations in the eastern Atlantic, which constituted the bulk of its offensive achievement, were entirely the work of two units, the 479th and 480th Antisubmarine Groups. To the best of my knowledge nothing has been published on the work of these two groups since the chapter on the Antisubmarine Command appeared in volume 2 of W. F. Craven and J. L. Cate, eds., *The Army Air Forces in World War II*, published in 1949. Four decades have since passed, and this interesting episode in the development of modern air power, with its varied lessons and experiences, has remained largely ignored.

It is not difficult to understand why. The USAAF gave up its claim on a role in antisubmarine warfare in 1943 and has only occasionally looked back. This was surely a correct decision within the context of the times, and the modern-day USAF has not felt a need to recall an episode that was out of the mainstream of its development. Most of the personnel of Antisubmarine Command went on after 1943 to other units and other activities. When the war ended, their loyalties had thus also moved on, and only a few seem to have felt a strong desire to see recorded this part of their experiences. The U.S. Navy, which took over all responsibility for antisubmarine warfare (ASW) in 1943, has never felt a need to look closely at the USAAF experience. The USN has its own history of ASW air operations, which that service has seen as a sufficient base of past experience. The USN also has traditionally looked on ASW as an integrated type of warfare, requiring the participation of both fixed wing and rotary aircraft, surface ships, and in modern times, also fixed underwater arrays and ASW submarines. Thus there was no incentive to look at the singular USAAF experience of World War II. So this chapter in the development of American aviation had remained unwritten.

I came to the subject late in the day, so to speak, when I discovered that this topic had languished in a historical limbo, and that there was much of interest in the USAAF ASW experience. My chief regret is that many of those who could have contributed from their experiences to making this story more complete are no longer alive. Even a decade earlier, a good number of additional sources would have been available. This fact underlines something all students of World War II now find pressing upon them: the generation that fought the war is beginning to leave us in large numbers, and the living sources available to us will contract rapidly in the next decade. Many members of the 479th and 480th Groups preserved significant amounts of materials from their World War II days. These have been greatly valuable in verifying oral testimony and filling in gaps in official records, which for USAAF Antisubmarine Command are not always as comprehensive as one might wish. I fear that as the World War II veterans depart, most of these personal records will become dispersed, if not destroyed. It will be a substantial loss.

The second goal of this account is to give a reasonably comprehensive picture of the experience of the two USAAF antisubmarine groups that were deployed overseas to Europe and North Africa. This has been easier to accomplish for the 480th Group, which existed from January to November 1943, than for the 479th Group, which existed only from July to October 1943. I have examined every attack on a submarine by these two groups, for example, in order to capture some picture of the average achievement in ordinary circumstances. Perhaps too often accounts of military performance focus on outstanding events, the highlights of operations. This can convey a false image of what was, for those in the ASW business at least, an often tedious and frustrating activity. By looking at failed as well as successful attacks one gains a better understanding of the average experience of the aviators. This focus should not mislead the reader into underestimating the accomplishment of the USAAF fliers. Their record compares favorably with what was achieved in the same time period by other Allied ASW units, whether Royal Air Force (RAF) or USN. I have endeavored to set the experience of the two groups within the context of antisubmarine warfare as it developed during World War II in order to provide a basis to allow readers to judge for themselves what was accomplished by these units.

A writer of some experience once offered sound advice to others through the voice of one of his characters: "An honest tale speeds best being plainly told" (*King Richard III*, IV, iv, 359). I have tried to take that advice to heart. My tale is a straightforward one. It could not have been written without the help of many others; there are substantial debts which it is my obligation and pleasure to acknowledge. The United States Air Force Historical Research Center (or Agency, as it has now been renamed) awarded me a grant that enabled me to use the resources of the center at Maxwell Air Force Base, Montgomery, Alabama, as a research associate. The staff there contributed generously in making my stay a rewarding and pleasant experience. The School of Graduate Studies and Research of the University of Wisconsin–Eau Claire provided funding for a summer research trip to work in British archives as well as underwriting the costs of photographic reproduction and the drawing of maps by the UW–EC Media Development Center.

My good friend and gifted colleague, Prof. Richard H. Marcus, gave up time from his work on the Fifteenth Air Force to perform the thankless chore of reading my initial manuscript, which greatly benefited from his extensive knowledge of military aviation and acute eye for a clumsy phrase or poorly developed paragraph. I regret he did not live to see the benefits he bestowed on my narrative. My good friend and former student, Prof. William A. Jacobs of the University of Alaska–Anchorage, similarly performed the task of critical reading with his customary thoroughness and thoughtfulness. His suggestions and insights greatly improved the final product. I also wish to thank Mark Rose, who read his way through reels of microfilm to compile data found in the appendixes. Jan-Bart Taminiau brought his expertise in computer programming to my rescue in an hour of need; I am in his debt. Scott Riphenburg labored over formatting the final manuscript. Therese D. Boyd was a constructive editor, who saved me from both errors and infelicities of expression. The dedication of this book acknowledges a debt beyond repayment. It should finally be said that the remaining defects of this work cannot be laid against those whose help made it a better book than it would otherwise have been.

Stalking the U-boat

1

A Strategic Antisubmarine Force

The "Battle of the Atlantic," as Winston Churchill christened it, was the longest military campaign of World War II. It ran from the first days of September 1939 until May of 1945. So long a campaign went through a series of stages. A new stage opened when the United States was catapulted into the war by the Japanese attack on Pearl Harbor. Hitler and Mussolini supported their Tripartite Pact partner in the Far East by declaring war on the embattled American democracy. Hitler followed his words of war with deeds. In January 1942 German submarines began to arrive in American coastal waters. They found defenses unprepared, and enjoyed a "merry massacre" until midsummer. But an earlier stage of the U-boat campaign in British coastal waters had made clear than once coastal convoys were set up and protected, it was very hard indeed for the U-boats to operate successfully so close to hostile territory. By the middle of 1942, this also became true of American coastal waters, and the German submarines moved away to find more productive hunting at lower risk.

By the late summer of 1942 Adm. Karl Doenitz, the German U-boat commander-in-chief, had recalled most of his submarines from American coastal waters to mid-Atlantic anticonvoy operations, which left the growing American antisubmarine air forces with few potential targets to find in their coastal waters. The Army Air Forces leadership, in particular, was anxious to test the doctrine of a "strategic offensive" against U-boats by seeking out the submarines where they were numerous.[1] On September 14, 1942, the Chief of Staff of the U.S. Army, Gen. George C. Marshall, sent a letter to his naval equal, Adm. Ernest J. King, in which he observed that experience indicated that "effective employment of air forces against submarines demands rapid communications, mobility, and freedom from the restrictions inherent in command systems based on area responsibility." In order to achieve these desired characteristics, Marshall informed King, "I am . . . directing the organization of the . . . Anti-Submarine Army Air Command. This unit will be charged with submarine destruction as its primary mission." Control of the new organization would be centralized in the War Department "in order that it may be promptly dispatched, in whole or in part, to the scene of current enemy submarine activities."[2]

Behind this letter lay significant differences of opinion within the American military establishment regarding the appropriate use of air power. In the view of the War Department, the issue was "whether the extended antisubmarine war should proceed on essentially offensive lines, carrying the battle to the enemy as briskly as resources would permit, or whether it should consist primarily of extended convoy coverage."[3] As one member of the Army Air Forces staff put it: "It seems apparent that persistent offensive measures afford the *only hope* of effectively dealing with the submarine menace" (emphasis added).[4] The first commander of this new Army Air Forces command, Brig. Gen. Westside T. Larson, described his organization, charged to hunt out hostile submarines wherever they may be, as "the Strategic Air Force employed in submarine warfare."[5] This strategic force's operations, Larson warned, "must not be restricted to any area or areas." The proper relationship between this force and the USN's antisubmarine organization, Larson wrote, should be one of co-equals, conducting antisubmarine operations jointly. But the air force, he stressed, should not be under the operational control of the Navy's command.[6] "Co-equal" was, indeed, the critical word here. The implication was clear enough. A co-equal partner deserved co-equal status. The ultimate claim was for the Air Force as an independent service, a point not lost on the USN hierarchy, which was fiercely opposed to the concept of an independent air force.

The immediate challenge confronting advocates of a strategic antisubmarine air command was that the newly born organization possessed in late

1942 very limited resources for accomplishing its task. By year's end, the anti-submarine command would have only 19 squadrons operating a total of 209 aircraft. Of these, just 20 were B-24s, "the type already recognized as the best weapon then available for the purpose" of strategic antisubmarine warfare (ASW).[7] These preferred aircraft were concentrated in two squadrons, the 1st and 2nd Antisubmarine Squadrons, and earmarked for the Twelfth Air Force, which was to be set up in North Africa to support the American forces landed there in the TORCH operation of November 1942.

But even to get these two squadrons equipped with B-24 Liberators, and the aircraft with 10-centimeter (shortwave or S-band) radar for submarine detection, stretched available resources. Crews were dispatched directly to the factories to pick up the Liberators as they came off the production lines and fly them to Wright-Patterson Field at Dayton, Ohio, to have the radar equipment installed, and thence to Langley Field, Virginia, for departure for North Africa via the northern route through Newfoundland and the United Kingdom.[8] In the end it was only possible to deploy nine aircraft of the 1st Antisubmarine Squadron in late November and early December 1942; by then the North African landings were already completed, and the most critical period of U-boat danger to those landings was past. Events had outrun the ability of the antisubmarine command to get organized, equipped, and deployed. Indeed, the USAAF strategic antisubmarine force would become based in North Africa only in March of 1943. First, it would operate in the United Kingdom, something the American aircrews discovered only when they arrived in that country, thinking they were en route to French Morocco. This had not been intended by anyone in Washington, but came about as a result of direct British intervention.

Allied Intervention

If the peak of submarine activity off the northwest coast of Africa had passed by late 1942, there still had to be a steady passage of U-boats across the Bay of Biscay, to and from the five submarine bases the Germans had established along the western coast of France. By late 1942 roughly 90 percent of all U-boats operating in the Atlantic sailed from these bases. Here the Royal Air Force's (RAF) Coastal Command was already endeavoring to interdict the passage of the German submarines.

In late 1942, the British were faced with an increasingly serious problem in ways and means. In the first half of 1942, German U-boats wreaked havoc off the East Coast of an unprepared United States. But by the end of the year they had receded into the mid-Atlantic to prey upon the transatlantic convoys that were Britain's wartime lifeline and essential to any hopes of an eventual Allied offensive in Europe, a goal central to the prosecution of the Anglo-American alliance's war strategy. Clearly, adequate resources had to be committed to the antisubmarine campaign if the grand strategy of the war was to be achieved.

Unfortunately, many in the British leadership saw ASW as an essentially defensive activity, and one that demanded the long-range aircraft that they wished to deploy instead in the strategic bombing of Germany. Throughout 1942 a contest had raged between the Royal Navy and RAF over allocation of these prized long-range aircraft, a contest in which the British prime minister, Winston Churchill, was more than a passive spectator.[9] British resources of these aircraft were so limited, the production so sought after, and the potential for conflict between the British services so serious that there was good reason to seek outside relief: let the Americans contribute air units for the antisubmarine campaign.[10] Here was a principle around which the entire British political-military leadership could rally, led by their formidable political chief.

It was, indeed, Mr. Churchill who launched the campaign in a letter to Harry Hopkins, the chief confidant of Pres. Franklin D. Roosevelt and a leading expediter of the American war effort. In mid-1942 Coastal Command had been able to attack U-boats in the Bay of Biscay at night with aircraft equipped with radar and the powerful Leigh Light. But in the early autumn the Germans had deployed on their U-boats a device that could detect the emissions of the British metric or long-wave radar, nullifying the night campaign in the bay. Centimetric radar would restore the initiative to the Allies until such time as the Germans could detect it also. That, it turned out, would be quite a long time. As the RAF wished to give its Bomber Command first call on British production of centimetric radar in order to improve bombing accuracy, American aircraft equipped with U.S.-built shortwave radar were greatly desired for the antisubmarine campaign.

Churchill explained to Hopkins how the British antisubmarine campaign had been crippled by the German development of a receiver that could detect metric radar emissions, and the prime minister noted that the German

U-boat bases along the Bay of Biscay lay directly athwart the main convoy routes between Britain and the newly established battlefront in Morocco and Algeria. Churchill then asked Hopkins for an American force of thirty Liberators equipped with centimetric radar, to operate under RAF Coastal Command to intercept the German U-boats crossing the Bay of Biscay. Thus the USAAF aircraft, Mr. Churchill concluded, "could be put to work immediately, in an area where they would make a direct contribution to the American war effort."[11] The prime minister had certainly not erred on the side of caution; he had asked for all the long-range aircraft equipped with centimeter radar that the USAAF possessed, and then some.[12]

As early as November 24, the War Department indicated a readiness to have the American squadrons work "in co-operation with the British Coastal Command."[13] The British wanted rather more than this, however, and their Chiefs of Staff appealed to the American Joint Chiefs, observing that "some" of the USAAF Liberators en route to North Africa "might more profitably be operated in the Bay of Biscay from bases in the United Kingdom."[14] The combined British political-military effort to obtain the American aircraft achieved a measure of success. On December 2, 1942, Hopkins informed Churchill that Washington would allow Gen. Dwight D. Eisenhower, the Supreme Allied Commander in North Africa, to determine whether he immediately needed the twenty-one Liberators of the 1st and 2nd Antisubmarine Squadrons in North Africa, or if they might be employed elsewhere. The British then appealed to Eisenhower in Algiers that the Liberators be deployed to operate from the United Kingdom over the Bay of Biscay, and this he agreed to.[15] A delighted Churchill minuted to the Chief of the Air Staff and First Sea Lord regarding Eisenhower's message: "Surely this is very good!"[16]

The prime minister had cause to be pleased. Basing the American squadrons in England for antisubmarine operations relieved a serious strain within the British political-military establishment. The coordinated effort that establishment had put forth to secure the American assets for their Biscay operations commands respect, and helps to explain why the British weight in World War II policy decisions at times exceeded the resources that the United Kingdom could bring to bear on the conduct of the war. However impressive, the British victory was incomplete. By late 1942 the Americans had gained sufficient experience in the nature of inter-Allied politics to guard themselves toward the future. Churchill would have done well to note a line in Hopkins's letter, where the presidential adviser observed that "the assignment to the European theatre [of these aircraft] must necessarily be temporary."[17] But for the moment, at least, the destination of the two American Antisubmarine Command squadrons was set.

The State of the Art, September 1939–November 1942

When the first American antisubmarine aircraft lifted off for the long transatlantic flight to the United Kingdom to join the antisubmarine war in the eastern Atlantic, the British were far advanced of the Americans. Great Britain had been at war for three years and three months by November 1942, while its American ally had been engaged in World War II not quite a full year. The character of war works to concentrate the mind; cumulative experience comes to count. Although much had been shared by the British, and much had been learned by the Americans in the first year, there remained areas where the newcomers would have some catching up to do. What had the British learned in over three years of war?

In September 1939 relatively little consideration had been given to the role of aircraft in ASW. Although airplanes had operated in this role in the latter years of World War I, it attracted little attention between the wars. In that period, the RAF was intent on development of its strategic bombing doctrine and capabilities, and later on in the thirties, the problem of defending the home island against an attacking bomber force. ASW was the natural business of the Royal Navy, which felt it had a sovereign remedy for the U-boat threat in the form of asdic (what Americans call sonar), which detected submerged submarines by sound. With the outbreak of war, the limitations of sonar and the need for aircraft to aid ships in the business of antisubmarine warfare quickly became apparent. It was evident that the RAF would have to play a large role in ASW.[18]

The RAF had in 1936 reorganized itself along functional lines. The names of the organizations revealed their roles; for example, Bomber Command, Fighter Command, Coastal Command. To the last would fall the ASW role. The bulk of Coastal Command's squadrons in late 1939 were designated General Reconnaissance (GR), their primary tasks to seek out the location of enemy ships and to scout for the fleet. But as early as mid-November of 1939, Coastal Command recognized ASW as equal in importance to its reconnaissance work. Soon, ASW would become the command's overriding priority. This, in turn, required an assessment of what means were available to prosecute the war against submarines from the air. The short answer was not much. The basic GR aircraft of 1939, the Avro Anson, was a comfortable twin-engine plane that was forgiving and easy to fly, but for ASW work it lacked both range and a useful weapons load.[19]

The weapons available at the time also were limited in capability, chiefly 100-pound bombs that normally had to hit a submarine to do any harm, and this was notoriously hard to do.[20] These bombs also had the nasty habit of skipping on the surface of the water, allowing their timed fuses to explode them in midair as they rebounded off the sea's surface. This could render them more dangerous to the attacking aircraft than to the U-boat being attacked. As early as September 5, 1939, an Anson was lost to damage inflicted by its own weapons. In this case it was perhaps just as well, since it was a British submarine that was attacked.[21] Distinguishing friendly submarine from foe was a problem for ASW aircraft throughout the war or, perhaps more accurately, a problem for friendly submarines.

As the normal weapons load for an Anson was four not very useful 100-pound bombs, its patrol range was short, and a doctrine or technique for attack had yet to be developed, it was clear that the main accomplishment of airplanes early in the war was in forcing U-boats to submerge, thus greatly limiting their mobility, and in attracting the attention of patrolling warships to the submarines' presence.[22] Helping antisubmarine ships find the U-boats, which they could then destroy, was the primary useful role for ASW aircraft for some time, although there were a few isolated cases of submarines being sunk from the air.[23]

But the weapon was too weak; even a direct hit with the 100-pound bomb did not guarantee the sinking of a U-boat if its pressure hull was not breached. Thus the search began for more powerful weapons. The best available was a 450-pound naval depth charge, which was so powerful that a near miss could sink a submarine. In RAF use, with a rounded fairing on the nose and a fin to stabilize it in flight, this became the Mark VII depth charge. Equipped with a simple hydrostatic exploder, it largely ended any threat to the aircraft that dropped it. Its chief drawbacks were its weight, which limited the number that could be carried, and the need to release it from a low altitude (not over 100 feet) at a relatively slow speed (not over 115 MPH) or its thin casing would break up on hitting the water. By late 1940 a much better weapon was available, the Mark VIII depth charge; since it was a 250-pound weapon, more could be carried, and it could be released from 200 feet and at speeds up to 200 MPH without breaking up.[24]

Early Radars

To attack a U-boat, it first had to be located; the seas are broad and submarines small objects to spot from the air. The great advantage of the aircraft over the surface ship in ASW is the plane's much greater search capacity. That is, a plane flying at 125 knots covers or sweeps an area five times greater in length than a ship moving at 25 knots. As area constitutes breadth times length, it was important to expand a plane's vision to its sides as widely as possible to increase the area swept. A further problem was that lookouts in the submarine were more apt to see the plane before the airplane saw the submarine; indeed, statistical evidence indicated that, two times out of three, the sub saw the plane first and submerged to safety before the aircraft could see it.[25] By the end of 1941 the lower surfaces of ASW aircraft had been repainted in a flat white, which reduced their visibility about 20 percent on average.[26] But this was not enough; science was called on to do better, and science in this case meant radar.

Radar developed very rapidly in the late 1930s and in the 1940s, but at the outbreak of World War II there was no such thing as a radar-equipped aircraft. (Airplanes had in a few cases been equipped with radar for test purposes, but nothing more.) The weight and fragility of the early radar equipment did not encourage such development. However, war is a great catalyst of technology, and the need to intercept German bomber aircraft at night led the British to press ahead with airborne radar. The problem was that this same imperative led to most such equipment being allocated to equip night fighters against the German bombers; ASW aircraft would have to wait their turn. Nonetheless, their turn did come. The British designated such ASW radars as air-to-surface-vessel (ASV) radar. In the case of submarines, it was, of course, a matter of air to surfaced vessel. Radar waves are reflected by the water's surface; submerged U-boats were safe from it. In fact, for all practical purposes, so were surfaced U-boats, for the early ASW radar, ASV Mark I, had drastic limitations.

While British tests revealed that a plane at 3,000 feet equipped with ASV Mark I could detect a surfaced submarine at 5½ miles, the target was lost in the reflections from the water's surface ("surface clutter") at a range of 4½ miles. Flying at very low altitude, 200 feet, still allowed a U-boat to be detected at 3½ miles, and surface clutter did not obscure the target until only one-half mile away. This was quite good, but flying at 200 feet off the water for any length of time was very demanding, especially in bad weather. And the optimums achieved in tests were hard to duplicate, or even approach, in normal operations. Nonetheless, by early 1940, Coastal Command had twelve Lockheed Hudsons fitted with ASV Mark I.[27] The appearance of this airplane, an American product, as a replacement for the Anson, is worth commenting on, as it began something of a World War II tradition for Coastal Command.[28]

It quickly became apparent that Bomber Command and Coastal Command of the RAF were interested in the same type of aircraft, those able to fly a long distance with a large weapons load. But British production facilities, which had to build large numbers of fighters for the air defense of the island nation, as well as for support of ground forces, were hard-pressed to supply enough larger aircraft to meet the goals of the strategic bombing program, much less support the antisubmarine effort. Soon enough Bomber Command would have to give up whole squadrons of its planes to Coastal Command to help cope with the U-boat menace, but for the RAF this was the worst possible solution. A much better solution was to equip Coastal Command with American-built aircraft. While the Hudson was the first, it would have many notable successors, including the Consolidated PBY Catalina, Boeing B-17 Flying Fortress, and supremely, the Consolidated B-24 Liberator, which emerged as the Allies' chief ASW aircraft of the war.

ASV Mark I in practice proved almost useless in detecting submarines. However, it was a great boon to Coastal Command aviators flying in the typical weather of the Atlantic approaches to northwest Europe. It was also helpful in finding the convoys that the planes were assigned to escort, for a large convoy gave a significant return on the ASV Mark I scope. So, too, the coastlines of large land bodies showed up well enough to help aerial navigation in poor visibility. But the need for something better was understood early on, and led to the development of ASV Mark II. Like ASV Mark I, it was a metric wavelength radar, but it possessed a more powerful transmitter and a more sensitive receiver. But also like Mark I, it was plagued by production delays, and first allocation was to Bomber Command. By October 1940 only forty-five ASV Mark II sets had been delivered to Coastal Command.[29]

A significant virtue of ASV Mark II was the ingenious aerial system devised to go with it, which greatly increased the sweep-width of a searching aircraft. Planes were equipped with two sets of aerials, only one of which could be used at any time. When the side-looking aerials were in use, an ASV Mark II–equipped airplane could sweep a swathe roughly 10 miles either side of the plane's flight path. At 120 MPH an area 20 × 120 miles, or 2,400 square miles, could be covered in an hour. When something worth investigating was detected by use of the side-looking aerials, the plane turned 90 degrees toward the target and switched to its forward-looking aerials in order to close and investigate. Still, sea clutter was a problem. At 1,000 feet, a U-boat was detectable at ten miles using the side aerials, and at seven miles ahead, but became lost in the sea clutter at three miles.[30]

Continuing Radar Developments

The British understood in 1940 that something much better was possible, centimeter wavelength radar. British scientists had solved the chief problem in its development, getting sufficient power into an equipment of reasonable size and weight. But British technical and production facilities had great difficulty designing and manufacturing reliable centimeter radar equipment, and the first units built went to Fighter Command and Bomber Command. The British had not kept their scientific achievement to themselves, but shared the development with the Americans in 1940. Thus it was that the first centimeter radars to see use in Coastal Command were those in the planes of the USAAF 1st and 2nd Antisubmarine Squadrons. British ASW squadrons would have to wait until 1943 for their own equipment. From mid-1941 to the end of 1942, the metric ASV Mark II was the prime search tool (other than the Eyeball Mark I) for submarine search and detection.

The British had gotten their ASV radar airborne well ahead of comparable American equipment. It was not a case of deficient American science and technology. With the notable exception of the resonant cavity magnetron, which proved the key to centimetric radar, American scientific progress was similar to that of Great Britain (and, for that matter, Germany). However, the Americans lacked the pressure of belligerent status to accelerate their efforts. The U.S. Army Signal Corps had developed equipment much like the British ASV Mark II, which flew from Wright Field over Lake Erie for the first time on November 4, 1940. The first equipment, the SCR-268, picked up an ore boat at 17 miles. However, when the British turned over their own, battle-tested equipment to the Americans, the decision was made to use these as the basis for further work in the United States, which thereafter went forward rapidly.[31]

Like the ASV Mark I, the improved metric equipment failed to produce results up to the expectations engendered by tests. It was in mid-1941 that Air Chief Marshal Sir Philip Joubert de la Ferté became Air Officer Command-ing-in-Chief (AOC-in-C) of RAF Coastal Command. Joubert, a man of con-siderable talent, came to Coastal Command in no small part because of the pressure to get better results from its radar equipment. His investigation quickly revealed numerous problems impeding the best use of the available equipment. Quick design and manufacture under wartime pressures had pro-duced sets that were neither very robust nor very reliable. They required a high level of maintenance and highly skilled operators. Coastal Command units were poorly equipped to provide either, and personnel seldom knew enough about the equipment to be able to get the best out of it. Joubert scored an important success by reducing these deficiencies. What he could not do much about was the fact that the radar equipment had been added to airplanes designed much earlier, and had to be located in the planes as space allowed. This led to some very inconvenient arrangements. Nonetheless, it was an aircraft suffering from poor radar placement, an Armstrong Whitley of 502 Squadron, RAF Coastal Command, which detected a surfaced German U-boat in the Bay of Biscay at a range of five miles on November 30, 1941. The attack that followed sank U.206, the only U-boat killed by Bay of Biscay air patrols in 1941.[32] U.206's sinking may be said to mark the real beginning of Coastal Command's interdiction effort over the bay to which the American ASW squadrons were to make their contribution in late 1942 and in 1943.

The Bay of Biscay campaign had one great weakness that would work to prevent significant success before the second half of 1942. The typical U-boat of the period could remain submerged for as long as 19 to 20 hours out of every 24, while making slow forward progress on its electric motors during the submerged period, roughly some 50 to 60 nautical miles. During the other 4 to 5 hours, it could proceed at almost 10 knots on the surface while recharging its batteries. Thus it could cover about 110 miles a day while crossing the bay, and needed to surface only during a small fraction of the time. By surfacing at night, the U-boats rendered themselves invulnerable to air attack. For while the ASV Mark II radar could find a sub, as the plane approached the U-boat, even at low altitude, the boat was lost in the sea return at about a half-mile, too far away for the pilot to see and attack it except under unusual conditions of moonlight. To attack the U-boats, that half-mile visibility gap had to be closed, an achievement credited primarily to Squadron Leader Humphrey de Verde Leigh.

The Leigh Light

Leigh developed a searchlight powerful enough to reveal a submarine on the surface at a half-mile's distance, thus enabling an aircrew to pick it up visually just as the plane's radar lost it. The plane's speed and the surprise of the sudden, blinding light allowed an attack to be pressed home before the U-boat could submerge. This clever idea, which Leigh worked out as early as October 1940, proved to be difficult to develop. Nonetheless, Leigh managed to demonstrate his concept successfully in May 1941 when a Vickers Wellington, equipped with the light manipulated by Leigh himself, picked up a test submarine just as it was supposed to. But Leigh's light also had to compete for priority with another, quite different, and also quite unsatisfactory proposal. At first, Sir Philip Joubert—who had just come to Coastal Command—favored the alternative, but by August 1941 he was convinced that Leigh's light was preferable, and gave it his backing.[33]

By late 1941 all major technical problems were surmounted and the Leigh Light had demonstrated its ability to do the job. Yet not until May of 1942 would Coastal Command have even a half-dozen Wellingtons equipped with Leigh Lights and ASV Mark II radar. This prolonged delay reflected poorly on both the commitment of the RAF to ASW and on the efficiency of the British aviation industry and its ancillary manufacturers. Joubert had wished to wait on committing his Leigh-Light Wellingtons to action over the bay until he had enough of them to make a major impact, for he feared that the Germans would adapt quickly to the threat posed to their submarines at night. But he came to fear even more delaying too long, lest the Germans develop a counter to the metric radar that the planes needed in order to get within a half-mile of the U-boats. Accordingly, he initiated operations in the summer of 1942. Even his handful of searchlight planes produced dramatic results. In June and July, they made eleven sightings and six attacks on U-boats crossing the Bay of Biscay.[34]

Above all, the Leigh-Light Wellingtons produced a decided overreaction on the part of the German U-boats' commander, Admiral Doenitz. Not for the last time Doenitz failed to examine the new threat to his boats dispassionately, but rather proceeded to change his tactics without, it appears, thinking through the consequences. On July 16, 1942, he ordered his submarines to reverse their tactics of submerging by day and running surfaced at night. This decision produced a large increase in the number of U-boats that would be potential targets for daylight attacks. As Coastal Command's 19 Group, which operated over the bay, had a great many more planes suitable for day ASW operations than it had searchlight-equipped Wellingtons, Doenitz's decision significantly increased his U-boats' vulnerability to attack. The figures quickly demonstrated this. Where there had been fourteen U-boat sightings in June and sixteen in July in the bay, the numbers for August and September were thirty-four and thirty-seven. Numbers of U-boats sunk in the bay campaign remained undramatic, four between early June and the end of September. Still, this compared favorably to none in the previous five months.[35]

Metox

Toward the end of September 1942 the blow Joubert had feared finally fell. A sharp decline in sightings made clear that the U-boats could at last detect the metric radar of the Coastal Command aircraft. The detection device, named *Metox* after its manufacturer, could pick up radar emissions at roughly twice the range at which the radar could detect the presence of a submarine.[36] Admiral Doenitz could now order his U-boats to return to the surface at night, confident that they would know of the presence of an approaching ASW aircraft before the plane was aware of the presence of any submarines. The fact that there were only two night sightings in the bay in September, and only one in October, was proof of *Metox*'s effectiveness. The day searchers were equally frustrated, for now subs were no longer crossing the bay on the surface in daylight. The need after September 1942 was for centimeter radar, which *Metox* could not detect, in Coastal Command planes. As these would be slow in coming, the assistance of American ASW aircraft equipped with the centimeter radar was pressed vigorously by the British.

The Luftwaffe

Another complication in the Bay of Biscay campaign emerged in September 1942. After the German invasion of Russia in June 1941, the Luftwaffe had been largely inactive in the west. The German Air Force's leadership showed, on the whole, little interest in aiding the war at sea. But Admiral Doenitz's persistent pleas for help in the face of the onslaught against his U-boats in the late summer of 1942, while only 200 or 300 miles from the coast of German-occupied France, did produce tangible assistance. About thirty JU 88 twin-engine fighters were assigned to operate in support of the U-boats.[37]

The JU 88 carried a formidable armament of 20mm cannon and 7.9mm machine guns, and had a reasonably good range, allowing it to operate well out over the bay. Its appearance was distinctly unwelcome to Coastal Command, whose aircraft were not very swift or maneuverable, burdened as they were with ASW equipment. With only modest defensive firepower, typically operating alone, the British planes were sitting ducks if found by a pack of roving JU 88s. The best defense lay in avoidance, detecting the approaching JU 88s by radar and using the frequent heavy clouds over the bay for cover. It was yet another reason for the British to seek American assistance in the form of the four-engine Liberators with their relatively good defensive armament.

How to Attack: The Fruits of Operational Research

The first imperative in the ASW war had been to deter U-boats attacking surface ships, which the simple presence of an aircraft was often sufficient to accomplish. But direct attack on the submarines themselves was bound increasingly to be viewed as a measure of the success of aircraft in the anti-submarine war. The substitution of an air-dropped depth charge for the use-less 100-pound antisubmarine bomb had demanded reconsideration of how to attack a U-boat. The Mark VIII 250-pound depth charge had emerged in 1941 as the weapon of choice, and its lethality was improved by substituting Torpex for TNT as its explosive charge. (The 250-pound, Torpex-filled depth charge was designated the Mark XI.) One of these exploding within 20 feet of a submarine's pressure hull was likely to sink the sub.[38] What was troubling was that even with this weapon, the percentage of attacked subs that were sunk remained very low. Coastal Command assessed the rate of U-boats attacked which were sunk at 1 percent in the first 22 months of the war,

September 1939–June 1941. In the next 18 months, July 1941–December 1942, the rate came up to a respectable 5 percent, but Coastal Command had hoped for much better results.[39]

Even when depth charges appeared to have fallen close enough to a visible submarine to destroy it, the sub often emerged from the froth and foam that followed the explosion still clearly afloat. What was the problem? At first, when a U-boat was spotted from the air it was attacked, regardless of how quickly it submerged. Depth charges were set to explode at between 100 and 150 feet, the average depth a sub could reach if it began its dive at the average distance at which it was likely to have detected an approaching aircraft. The problem was in this average figure, which masked great differences of circumstances. The chance of sinking a sub that had reached 100 to 150 feet was almost nil, as it had left the surface sufficiently early that extraordinary accuracy or luck was required to put a depth charge within 20 feet of its hull. But an easy target—one caught while still fully surfaced—could also survive attack, since the charges were set to explode too deep, far enough from the sub's hull that it did not fracture. Operational Research scientists working at Coastal Command identified the problem and recommended a significant change in tactics.

The Operational Research Section (ORS) noted that over 40 percent of U-boats were attacked while still visible or submerged less than 15 seconds. These were the only reasonable targets to attack, as only they gave an adequate aiming point. It followed that the depth settings on the charges should be adjusted for the depth for this vulnerable 40 percent of U-boats. The ideal setting would be about 25 feet, able to rupture the hull of a surfaced sub, or of one submerged less than 15 seconds if it fell near enough. This revealed a new problem. The shallowest setting possible on existing hydrostatic pistols was 50 feet. After all, the pistols had originally been designed for depth charges rolled off surface ships. If they exploded at too shallow a depth, the attacking vessel would itself sustain damage. So, in the short term, the 50-foot setting had to be accepted as better than nothing, while work proceeded on design and manufacture of a 25-foot setting.[40]

This analysis also led Coastal Command to refine its tactical instructions to concentrate on attacking only those targets that offered a reasonable chance of damaging or sinking a U-boat, and for which the shallow depth charge setting was appropriate. It also greatly increased chances of sinking a U-boat if a considerable number of depth charges were dropped in a single stick, with a specified distance between them. The tactical instruction in effect for attacks on U-boats when the American squadrons arrived in Britain had been issued by Coastal Command in July 1942.[41] This clearly specified that the policy of the command was to "concentrate efforts on sinking those U-Boats which are still on or near the surface." While the normal attack weapon was to be the Torpex-filled Mark XI 250-pound depth charge, as long at it remained in short supply the older Mark VIII would remain in use, although with a modified nose and tail designed to slow its sink rate.[42]

The standard number of depth charges released in an attack was to be six, spaced at 36 feet, which would give a lethal area to the attack of roughly 20 feet at greatest width and 220 feet in length.[43] This was about as short as one could go and allow for the typical range error likely to occur in trying to maneuver a plane flying at 150 MPH or more across a moving submarine, after the plane had rapidly descended to about 50 feet off the water. Further, in aiming the plane and releasing the weapons, pilot and bombardier had to compensate for the forward motion of the sub and for the trajectory of the depth charges as they moved first through the air and then through the water, at a different rate of velocity in each medium. The 36-foot spacing ascribed a very limited lethal area to the depth charges, and suggests a lack of confidence in the test data. However, as confidence improved, the spacing would be extended to 60 feet, which still left no gaps in the lethal area (allowing for an average U-boat pressure hull diameter of about 20 feet) while extending the length of the lethal area to 340 feet. This allowed a pilot considerable latitude to compensate for range error, which experience indicated was very much needed.[44]

Coastal Command doctrine also prescribed that the route of attack should be the shortest, even if this meant the angle of attack was difficult. Better a poor angle of attack than to allow a submarine time to submerge. Depth charges should be released at 50 feet, both to guard against their breaking up on hitting the water and to improve aim. Depth charges released from 50 feet were estimated to take about one to two seconds to cross the 50 feet of air, two to three seconds to reach a depth of about 25 feet in the water, and three to five seconds to detonate. In that time, their forward movement was calculated to be about 40 feet from the point of release. The speed of a U-boat in the process of crash diving was about 10 feet per second. If the submarine managed to submerge entirely, the forward end of its conning tower left a swirl on the surface. The tower (which was always taken as the center of the target for attack purposes) would have advanced 150 feet beyond the apex of that swirl in 15 seconds, the longest period of submergence that allowed for an accurate attack.[45] The plane had to estimate this progress on the part of the U-boat in calculating when to release the depth charges. This is what made attacks on U-boats something of an art. (There was as yet no reliable low-level bombsight, although a fair amount of energy had been expended on trying to design one.) It also is why constant practice was the best way to improve accuracy of attacks.

By late 1942 the use of cameras to document attacks had come into use, and was of great benefit in improving assessments and in convincing crews of the extent of their range and line errors. These errors were almost always underestimated, particularly the range error, as distance was foreshortened for observers in a rapidly moving plane in the process of losing altitude. Data compiled by March 1943 from earlier attacks which could be adequately documented by photographs suggested a normal range error of 150 to 180 feet and an average line error of about 60 to 90 feet.[46] It was almost always easier for a crew to calculate accurately for line than for range. Coastal Command aircrews, supported by their squadron commanders, insisted that the average errors for line and range in their attacks were on the order of 30 and 60 feet respectively. They thus required convincing proof that the true figures were more on the order of three times greater than their own visual estimates.[47]

Desired Aircraft Characteristics

The desirability of dropping a stick of at least six depth charges in an initial attack, with some remaining for a follow-up attack on a damaged U-boat, or to attack a second submarine, placed a premium on the employment of large aircraft. These planes had the added advantage of long range. Effective patrol ranges were always closer to one-third than one-half of maximum one-way range. Of aircraft in Coastal Command's inventory, the Hudson had a useful 500-mile patrol range, while the Whitley and Wellington could spend about two hours patrolling at this distance from home. The big Sunderland flying boats, always in short supply, could put in two hours some 600 miles out. The remarkable Catalina flying boat could do the same at more than 800 miles. However, this aircraft lacked a large weapons capacity, and flew so slowly that it had difficulty reaching a U-boat before the boat saw it and submerged.

The big, four-engine, land-based aircraft, the British Lancaster and Halifax and the American Fortress and Liberator, had the greatest potential as ASW planes. These four-engine aircraft also brought with them improved safety and ability to absorb punishment, whether from a sub's antiaircraft (AA) guns or enemy aircraft. Their larger crews allowed better rotation of watches and improved the likelihood of sighting a U-boat. However, the RAF jealously guarded its Lancasters and Halifaxes for strategic bombing missions; only a few of the latter would be allocated to Coastal Command. The Fortress was considered to lack an adequate range and payload combination. The American-built Liberator was thus the RAF's most desired ASW aircraft. It was able, in its long-range (LR) form, to patrol two hours at 800 miles, and the very long range (VLR) model could do the same at 1,000 miles, although this usually meant reducing the number of depth charges carried from ten or twelve to six or eight.[48] By late 1942, then, Coastal Command's desires in aircraft and equipment were relatively clear: more Liberators with centimeter radar. This is why the arrival in the United Kingdom of the 1st and 2nd Antisubmarine Squadrons of the USAAF was so welcome.

American ASW: The Beginning Efforts

The American aircraft were available in part because the need for ASW planes operating over American coastal waters had decreased, a change from less than a year earlier, when the first U-boats arrived to operate in those waters. In January 1942 the USN was woefully unprepared to cope with the German submarines, and for months thereafter failed to deal effectively with the U-boat threat to American shipping.[49] In the crisis, the Navy turned to the USAAF for help. Congressional legislation, dating back to 1920, had provided that land-based aircraft be controlled by the U.S. Army and sea-based aircraft by the U.S. Navy. In 1935 the Navy had accepted the terms of *Joint Action of the Army and Navy,* which gave it responsibility for all inshore and offshore patrol to protect shipping and defend the coastal frontier.[50] This patrol was responsible for providing the aircraft needed for the service's proper performance. The Navy seems not to have considered that its patrol aircraft would need to fulfill anything more than a reconnaissance role, much as the Royal Navy had at first expected from RAF Coastal Command. Notably, the British experience of 1939–41 did not seem to produce a major revision of American thinking on this subject. Thus when war came to America's shores in early

1942, the Navy had only a few squadrons of Catalinas in the Atlantic.[51] A large part of the burden of aerial ASW along the American coast fell on the USAAF, which thus gained a mission it had not foreseen. Not surprisingly, performance was at a minimal level.[52] The authors of the history of the AAFAC put the matter succinctly: "Hunting submarines is a highly specialized business."[53] As this became clear, the Army set about improving its ASW capabilities. In May 1942 the Operations Division of the Army instructed the USAAF to establish an organization to develop antisubmarine weapons, tactics, and techniques. This would lead eventually to the creation of a separate antisubmarine command within the USAAF. The U.S. Army Air Forces Antisubmarine Command (AAFAC) was activated on October 15, 1942, as the USAAF's antisubmarine organization, but it was, perhaps, not entirely a welcome development for that service branch.[54]

The Navy came finally to accept that coastal convoys were necessary to control shipping losses, and these were instituted over the months of May–July 1942. The beneficial effects were immediate.[55] Monthly sinkings along the eastern coast of the United States had reached twenty-three in April; the start of convoys in May dropped the number of sinkings to five in that month. While thirteen ships were sunk in June, the number fell to three in July, and then to zero for the remainder of the year.[56] Few U-boats visited American coastal waters after August 1942 because the results achieved were a poor return on the long times such voyages involved. Consequently, by the end of August, both the Army and Navy had substantial ASW air forces with very few U-boats to attack. In the Eastern Sea Frontier, stretching along the eastern shore of the United States, the USAAF had by the end of July 141 planes, and the USN 178 planes and seven blimps.[57] The Gulf and Caribbean sea frontiers had comparable air forces in the months that followed.

For the Navy, this was entirely satisfactory. Once that organization had embraced the doctrine of the primacy of the "safe and timely arrival of convoys," long the core of the Royal Navy's ASW doctrine, the safe passage of the merchant vessels was sufficient. Its mission was being accomplished. This view, however, was not shared by the USAAF, for which the offensive mission of attacking and destroying U-boats was dominant. With a surplus of aircraft to requirements in the Western Hemisphere, the USAAF was certain to look for ways and means to employ its ASW forces in carrying the battle to the German submarines. It was this search that would send the 1st and 2nd Antisubmarine Squadrons across the Atlantic at year's end.

2

The 480th Antisubmarine Group in the United Kingdom

Transatlantic Crossing

In late November 1942 the 1st Antisubmarine Squadron, USAAF, was ordered to England, followed early in the new year by the 2nd Antisubmarine Squadron. Both these units had begun life as bombardment squadrons, being officially redesignated antisubmarine squadrons only on November 23, 1942, although they were already operating in that capacity. The 1st Squadron had been activated as a provisional, heavy squadron as early as October 27. Its aircrews were drawn from the 20th, 49th, and 96th Bombardment Squadrons of the 2nd Bombardment Group. These units had been operating in an antisubmarine role since Pearl Harbor. Lt. Col. Jack Roberts, the executive officer of the 2nd Bomb Group, was chosen the first commanding officer (CO) of the new antisubmarine squadron and given the privilege of selecting the personnel.[1] The 2nd Antisubmarine Squadron had been activated on November 15, its aircrews drawn from bomb squadrons of the 2nd Bomb Group and also from the 121st Observation Squadron. Commanding officer of the 2nd Squadron was Maj. Wilkie A. Rambo.[2]

In general, the crews tended to be quite experienced, and the command pilots rather senior in rank. Of the original nine airplane commanders in the

1st Squadron, two were majors and the other seven captains. Many of the squadron personnel were career military men, but there was a good mixture of more recent volunteers, whose numbers would grow. Not all were enthusiastic to be flying in an antisubmarine outfit. One of the 1st Squadron's initial copilots recorded:

> Probably the damn'dest duty a pilot can be assigned to in time of war is that of an instructor. Next would be assignment to a tow-target outfit. Coastal Command, or anti-submarine patrol comes next and it's not much better as far as any young pilot is concerned. It's a good job for middle-aged complacent old pudgies with growing waist lines, but it's a bore for anyone with blood in their veins.[3]

In November 1942 the two squadrons consisted of twenty-one B-24D Liberators, nine in the 1st Squadron and twelve in the 2nd. Their transatlantic crossing was a sharp reminder of the difficulties of that passage well into World War II. Things got off to a transparently easy start. Three aircraft of the 1st Antisubmarine Squadron lifted off from Gander, Newfoundland, early on November 6, and arrived at the RAF field at Benbecula, in the Hebrides Islands north of Scotland, after flying times of eight to nine hours. This swift passage was made largely at altitudes between 12,000 and 16,000 feet. The outside temperature at 15,000 feet for most of the crossing was about 10 degrees above zero, but heaters in the forward part of the plane kept the pilots' and navigator's areas warm. This was not the case farther back in the planes.[4] On November 10, two of the original three aircraft arrived at the RAF station, St. Eval, Cornwall, which would become their operational home until early March of 1943. The third plane, delayed for some maintenance, reached St. Eval two days later.

This promising start was not sustained. The next flight from Gander, of six aircraft, had a tragic outcome. After waiting in Maine and again at Gander because of the weather, six Liberators left on November 23 for the United Kingdom. Two planes managed to get across, but three were forced to turn back to Gander. The sixth plane was never heard from again, and presumably went down somewhere in the North Atlantic. The two aircraft that were successful in crossing were forced to 22,000 feet and were still unable to break clear of clouds, icing conditions, and severe turbulence. Colonel Roberts reported that one of the pilots described the flying conditions as the worst "he has ever encountered. At times it required the combined effort of both pilot and co-pilot to right the plane. The crew chief, in the rear, was of the opinion that the tail would break off."[5] Temperature was again a problem; Bill Pomeroy, who was a second lieutenant in Capt. Kenneth L. Lueke's crew at the time of the November 23 crossing, was succinct: "We all froze."[6] This plane made its initial landing in Europe at an RAF field in Northern Ireland. Captain Lueke was unfortunate enough to get stuck in the winter mud there, and not until November 26 was the plane able to fly on to Benbecula in the Hebrides to join Capt. Douglas C. Northrop and his crew. On November 27 these two crews joined the initial contingent at St. Eval.[7]

Navigator in one of the planes that turned back was Lt. Samuel B. McGowan. He recalled that the forecast proved to be badly off the mark, and that icing conditions were extremely serious. He managed only one celestial fix because of the weather, and when his plane reached the North American coast after turning back, its landfall was "far up the coast of Labrador," the result of much stronger winds than predicted.[8] After another wait at Gander, and evidently in consequence of the lost aircraft, it was decided that the remaining planes would be sent to England by the southern route. This was no less daunting a task, as the record of McGowan's plane reveals. Having originally left Langley Field, Virginia, piloted by Capt. Arthur J. Kush, for Gander via Presque Isle, Maine, the plane was one of those that turned back on November 23. It again left Gander on December 5, but now bound for Morrison Field, Florida. It got as far as Langley Field, again via Presque Isle, Maine, where loss of oil from the number 1 engine and a nonfunctioning de-icing boot led to a stopover at Langley for repairs. These were quickly effected and the plane was on its way again on December 6, reaching Morrison Field where it remained for its 100-hour maintenance check.

On December 11 the Liberator departed Morrison Field and the continental United States, arriving at Trinidad the same day, from whence it flew on to Belem, and then Natal, Brazil, reaching the latter on the thirteenth. The next day it left the South American coast for Ascension Island, and then flew on to Accra in Africa. From Accra it proceeded to Bathurst, Gambia, and finally to Marrakech, Morocco, which it reached on December 22. On landing there it was ascertained that a nose-wheel tire had blown on departing Bathurst, and that the nearest spare tire was at Morrison Field, back in Florida. It was January before the spare tire reached Marrakech, and the plane at last left Africa on January 5, 1943, for St. Eval, where it arrived on January 7 via Gibraltar. It was the last of the eight surviving aircraft of the 1st Antisubmarine Squadron to reach Cornwall, exactly two months to the day after it had departed Langley Field for the United Kingdom via Gander. The actual flying time involved was 93 hours, 25 minutes.[9]

The 2nd Antisubmarine Squadron also flew by the southern route, which posed its own danger. All twelve aircraft left Langley Field, Virginia, between December 10 and 24, 1942. However, one of the squadron's planes, piloted by 2nd Lt. Jack S. Enochs, was never heard from again after departing Trinidad. The first of the 2nd Squadron's planes to reach St. Eval did so on January 2, 1943, the remaining ten following over several weeks' time. The 2nd Squadron's advance air echelon of forty-five officers and enlisted men had departed Langley Field in C-54s 10 days before the first combat crew left. This group was forced to remain at Accra almost a month in its insalubrious climate, waiting for air transportation to move them onward, and they arrived at St. Eval only on January 6 and 7, 1943. Consequently, the "advance" air echelon beat the squadron's ground echelon, which left Langley Field almost a month later and traveled by sea, to St. Eval by barely a week.[10]

Unlike the aircrews, the ground echelons had an uneventful crossing. The day after Christmas, 1942, they departed Langley Field with rifles and full field equipment, evidently ready for the most primitive operating conditions. These conditions manifested themselves on arrival at Fort Dix, New Jersey, where they had ample opportunity to practice marching and a week of "rigid and extensive training." The ground echelons escaped gratefully from Fort Dix on the evening of January 5, traveling to Jersey City by rail, whence they transferred to ferryboats that took them up the Hudson to where the RMS *Queen Elizabeth* was in the process of loading some 14,000 American military personnel. The giant liner slipped away from New York harbor in the night and was on the high seas when the sun rose the next day. The Atlantic crossing was "pleasant and uneventful and the sea unusually calm." Arriving in the Clyde estuary on the evening of January 12, the ground echelons were transferred by rail to St. Eval. Theirs had been a much easier passage than that of the aircrews.[11]

The 1st Antisubmarine Squadron flew its first operational mission from England on November 16, 1942 (Capt. Isaac J. Haviland, pilot), just nine days after its arrival in the United Kingdom. But operations developed very slowly, as aircraft trickled in and the requirements of training and maintenance became more evident. The change in initial operating theater for the two antisubmarine squadrons and the fact that they were not attached to an American parent organization in the theater made for difficulties. Lt. Col. James H. Rothrock and his crew of the 1st Squadron, flying out by the southern route, arrived at St. Eval only on Christmas Eve. They had been "passed from station to station in Africa because nobody knew where to order them. By chance, at Gibraltar, they encountered an VIII Air Force Officer who informed them of the whereabouts of the squadron."[12]

It was from this newly arrived crew that Roberts learned that another one of his aircraft (Kush and McGowan's) was stranded at Marrakech, waiting for a nose-wheel tire and tube, and yet another of his aircraft was "known to have landed at Accra," but of its present location he knew nothing. Not until January 16, 1943, would the 2nd Antisubmarine Squadron fly its first mission.[13] As late as January 15 the two American squadrons had a total of only thirteen aircraft between them at St. Eval, just one over the establishment for one full squadron. Roberts reported at that time that four more aircraft of the squadrons were "known to be somewhere in Africa enroute to this Station," a full two months after he had arrived at St. Eval—and a painful commentary on how considerable a handicap the Atlantic crossing had imposed on his resources.[14]

Finding a Home in the United Kingdom: RAF Station, St. Eval

The 1st and 2nd Antisubmarine Squadrons had originally expected to fly to the United Kingdom, there to familiarize themselves with the current state of airborne ASW in the eastern Atlantic, and then move on to operate from North Africa, covering the eastern terminal area of convoys from the United States and United Kingdom, which were supplying Allied operations in northwest Africa following the TORCH landings of early November 1942. When they arrived in England at the RAF Coastal Command station at St. Eval, on the north coast of the Cornish peninsula, the leading units of the 1st Antisubmarine Squadron discovered that no one knew what the squadron was to do. Its CO, Colonel Roberts, contacted Maj. Gen. Ira C. Eaker, Commanding General, U.S. Eighth Air Force, and it was decided that the squadron should be attached to VIII Bomber Command for supply and administration, but that it would remain at St. Eval under the operational control of RAF Coastal Command.[15]

As the American aircraft lacked an adequate maintenance base, their own ground echelon still crossing the Atlantic by ship, VIII Bomber Command assigned some sixty-six mechanics, ordnance men, armament specialists, and guards to the units.[16] These arrived at St. Eval on November 17. This arrangement had its problems. Roberts reported that the VIII Bomber Command men arrived without pay cards, adequate clothing, or equipment. "A surprisingly large number of them are excellent men," Roberts noted, so the command evidently did not take the opportunity to unload its duds on him. However, they came from seven different squadrons, and had to work into an effective unit without benefit of having separate American messing facilities at St. Eval. As the Yanks took a dim view of what passed for food in the RAF messes, morale was not improved.[17] Roberts also testified to the simple difficulty of reaching VIII Bomber Command by telephone—"two days were spent in fruitless effort," and later, "telephone service to these points [is] difficult and sometimes impossible." It is not clear whether this was a locational problem or just the English phone system.[18] As late as December 27, 1942, Roberts was writing to AAFAC to complain that aircrews from the United States were still arriving without any winter clothing, and he noted, "This is obviously in error."[19] Presumably, the origin of this problem was that the two American squadrons were originally intended to operate from French Morocco, and notification of their change of station had not yet reached all the parties concerned.

As the Americans had to share the British messing facilities, here was potential for international friction, and General Eaker had stressed to Roberts that he expected the American colonel to maintain "cordial relations with the British."[20] This Roberts found easy to do. The station commander at St. Eval was Group Capt. W. L. Dawson, RAF. Roberts described him as a "splendid officer, capable, efficient, and particularly apt at dealing diplomatically with a foreign unit." This did not of itself solve the messing problem. Roberts noted, "Due to the standard of living provided by the RAF for its airmen the meals are poor compared to U.S. Army meals."[21] Another American officer was even more dismayed; he reported that in general the quarters available were poor, "and the mess was unbelievably bad." His comments on the prevailing diet indicated his dismay: "The mess seemed to be a continuous diet of cabbage. Brussel sprouts was considered a rare treat and once we were given cauliflower with a cream sauce for dessert!"[22] Accepting the limited variety of food available in wartime Britain was perhaps the hardest adjustment the USAAF squadron personnel had to make to their new home, if it may be said that they ever accepted it. It was a happy event when at the beginning of February the American unit was able to open its own messing facilities. The group diarist recorded that "everyone looked forward to this event and everyone was well pleased to eat some real American chow."[23]

Most of the housing for officers in the American units had to be provided off the RAF station, often at a considerable distance, creating problems in maintaining efficiency, group cohesion, and discipline. The units lacked convenient access to USAAF supply depots and finance offices. Even postal services and other communications were inadequate at first.[24] The arrangements did have their positive side. Samuel McGowan was one of the officers living at the Trevelgue Guest House, a resort hotel in Newquay. He remembered the English tea and biscuits if the Americans happened to be at the inn at 3 P.M., and that except when scheduled for early morning missions, the officers were awakened by "a very pleasant English maid who always had a pot of tea. . . . We had outstanding relations with the English civilians." He recalled morale was excellent then.[25] The history of the 1st Antisubmarine Squadron also noted that "the presence of a large number of WAAFs [Women's Auxiliary Air Force] on the post added to the pleasant memories of St. Eval. Morale was very good."[26] The ubiquity of WAAFs on the RAF station was a "striking revelation" to Roberts, who noted that they were widely employed "on duties which it is thought only a man can do in the U.S." In addition to such traditional roles as clerks, stenographers, telephone operators, and cooks, the WAAFs also drove trucks and worked as mechanics, "gas station operators," and as communications encoders and decoders. All of this, Roberts observed, freed "many males for combat duty."[27]

The RAF station, St. Eval, was located on the site of a small hamlet, some five miles northeast of Newquay, Cornwall, and about a mile inland from the northern coast of the Cornish peninsula. It was decided in 1937 to level the small village of St. Eval for the establishment of a standard RAF expansion scheme station, designed to accommodate two general reconnaissance squadrons, that is, some thirty-two to forty aircraft. Work was started in 1938, and by the arrival of war in 1939 four hangars were under construction. The station's first tenants, a squadron of Ansons, arrived in October 1939, although most of the construction around the airfield was unfinished. Throughout the war, construction on the station tended to lag behind the demands of the occupants. The size of GR aircraft grew dramatically during the war, from the small twin-engine Anson to the substantial four-engine Liberator and Halifax, which increased the space and facilities required for each aircraft. One hangar was destroyed in a German air raid and never rebuilt, and two of the other three were damaged severely, but eventually restored. The officers' and sergeants' messes were also virtually destroyed in air raids, but repaired. The need for repairs and rebuilding made it difficult to complete expansion construction. In late 1942 the airfield was stretched to its limits to accommodate the demand on its facilities.[28]

Operating Difficulties, Winter 1942/1943

Operating from St. Eval in the winter of 1942/43 posed many problems. The field was already saturated with RAF units. In addition to two small units, a few Spitfires of 543 Photo Reconnaissance Unit (part) and some varied aircraft of 1404 Meteorological Flight, St. Eval was home to 502 Squadron of Coastal Command, which was at the time making the transition from the elderly twin-engine Whitley to the newer four-engine Halifax aircraft. But the largest unit present on the station was a part of Bomber Command's No. 10 Operational Training Unit (OTU), whose most advanced crews were flying antisubmarine patrols in obsolescent Whitleys to acquire operating experience before transferring into frontline bomber units.[29]

All these units made for considerable congestion on the RAF Station. By mid-January, as aircraft of the 2nd Antisubmarine Squadron began to arrive in numbers, Colonel Roberts was of the opinion that both American squadrons could be accommodated only if an RAF squadron were moved elsewhere. While he had expected this to occur, "its failure to be effected has resulted in considerable confusion upon the arrival of both [U.S. squadrons'] ground echelons," retarding the process of getting the 2nd Antisubmarine Squadron up and running.[30] However, the removal of one British unit was taken in hand in late January to reduce the overcrowding at St. Eval. British airfields in the southwest got good marks for normally having at least one 6,000-foot runway, a comforting thought for a Liberator outfit, but Roberts did note that "no great effort is made to level an [airfield] prior to laying the runways." Roberts had been agitating to get hardstands built for his aircraft, but had to report no progress achieved by early January 1943.[31]

By January 7 fourteen American Liberators were on the station, and their number thereafter fluctuated up and down by one or two aircraft, as planes were lost and replacements arrived. The high was sixteen on January 29, but when the squadrons prepared to depart for North Africa in early March, their strength was again fourteen aircraft.[32] As there was no hangar space available for the B-24s, all maintenance had to be done outside during the limited day-light hours in the raw weather of an English winter along the windswept coast of Cornwall. The long North European winters restricted maintenance work to between 0830 and 1730, Roberts reported. The inability to perform normal service routines on aircraft after dark also impinged on the unit's operating tempo. As Roberts noted: "Airplanes returning from a mission at or after dark, requiring only two hours of maintenance which would normally be performed during the night, must now be declared non-operational for the following day."[33] As the unit in late December 1942 still lacked sufficient aircrews to sustain anything more than a very modest operating tempo, it is unlikely that this added difficulty impinged seriously on the aircraft sortie rate.

Not too surprisingly, the American units were plagued with a high percent-age of personnel who became ill with colds and associated congestion. The American flight surgeon had no dispensary, and at first no medicines, and was also serving as recreation officer and mail censor, due to the shortage of staff officers. He appears to have fully earned his pay. The American squadron offices were set up in a lean-to adjacent to the hangar destroyed by bomb-ing. Roberts judged the accommodations not spacious but adequate.[34] Nor were personnel levels generous. Even with the men provided by VIII Bomber Command, Colonel Roberts noted in early December that he was working with half the normal personnel strength established for his unit. However, he was also short nearly half a normal squadron's aircraft.[35] Despite all problems, the American fliers were anxious to get on with their mission.

The 1st Antisubmarine Group (Provisional)

As the 1st Antisubmarine Squadron was still only a provisional unit, Colonel Roberts had at first only limited control over the American personnel.

> The problem of operating a squadron, without powers of promotion and de-motion, and without authority to revise combat crews, is becoming more dif-ficult daily. At present a recalcitrant Staff Sergeant, who has also proven to be an unsatisfactory member of a combat crew, can neither be disrated nor re-placed on the crew.[36]

Roberts closed his letter to General Larson of AAFAC emphasizing "that the present status of the squadron is undesirable and that it will be absolutely unsatisfactory in months to come." However, authorization was quickly forthcoming to put both squadrons on a permanent basis, and Roberts acknowledged his appreciation to General Larson.[37]

This was not, however, the case with the group organization that Roberts decided to impose on the two squadrons, once the bulk of both units had arrived at St. Eval. On January 15, 1943, on Roberts's initiative, the two squadrons were organized into a single unit, the 1st Antisubmarine Group (Provisional), under his command, working as a detached unit of the 25th Antisubmarine Wing of the AAF Antisubmarine Command.[38] This organization would undergo two further changes of name, becoming the 2037th Wing (Provisional) on March 1, 1943, and finally the 480th Group (Separate) (Special) on June 21, 1943. It will be uniformly described by its final name in this account. Roberts and his executive officer, Lt. Col. James H. Rothrock, then operated a small group headquarters, including five additional officers and five enlisted men.[39] As well as acting as executive officer of the group, Rothrock headed the Operations Department (A-3) with Maj. Carlos J. Cochrane and Capt. Ralph A. Reeve working directly under him. Administration (A-1), notably abbreviated in the case of the group, was the responsibility of 1st Lt. James P. Mahoney, while Capt. Swayne Latham was responsible for Intelligence (A-2). Supply and Engineering (A-4) was the domain of Maj. Wilkie A. Rambo.[40]

With the establishment of the group headquarters, there was also some shifting of crews and aircraft between the two squadrons, in order to balance the two more equally in numbers and in the seniority and experience of personnel. Capt. Alfred J. Hanlon Jr. was named to command the 1st Antisubmarine Squadron, while Major Rambo was transferred from command of 2nd Squadron to the group staff, and Capt. Isaac J. Haviland transferred from the 1st Squadron to become CO of the 2nd Squadron.[41]

On January 21, 1943, Brig. Gen. Westside T. Larson, the commanding general of USAAF Antisubmarine Command, flew in from the United States to inspect the group's progress at St. Eval, where he met with Brig. Gen. Newton Longfellow, head of VIII Bomber Command, so that the two general officers could assess the group's condition and plan for its future. Larson stayed until the twenty-fourth, when he left on a week's tour of the United Kingdom. On February 6 he was back at St. Eval, now joined by Air Chief Marshal Sir Philip Joubert, AOC-in-C, RAF Coastal Command.[42] General Larson's inspection tour closed the gap in communications between the parent organization in the United States and the squadrons deployed in the

United Kingdom. Joubert, who had a long-standing interest in radar development, returned on the ninth of February to inspect the American group's SCR-517 10-cm radar equipment and maintenance procedures. On February 28 Maj. Gen. Ira C. Eaker visited the group, along with General Longfellow.[43]

After something of a famine, the group thus had a feast of attention from senior commanders in late January to late February. Sir Philip Joubert told Roberts realistically that he doubted the Americans would be fully settled in and operating at their best before March 1943. Joubert was not all that far off the mark in his estimate. It is a compliment to the efficiency and dedication of the Americans that they managed to shave about a month off his estimate.

Navigational Considerations

Before the American squadrons could hope to operate effectively from the United Kingdom, they needed to master the particular problems posed by navigation in the congested and dangerous airspace of the coastal region of Western Europe, an operational theater of war. British control methods, navigational aids, and communication procedures all had to be learned. Even small errors of navigation on long flights could produce the dangerous results of ending up over German-occupied Europe or wandering into the Atlantic beyond reach of airfields before one's fuel supply ran out. Roberts reported that he found British air-ground radio communications and direction-finding (D/F) "far superior" to what he had experienced in the United States.[44] The American fliers were especially impressed with the ability to ask for their own aircraft's position. The British D/F system was so efficient that within 10 to 15 minutes they would be given an evaluated position, indicating the reliability of the D/F "fix." An A evaluation indicated that the fix was accurate to within 5 miles; a B fix was accurate within 15 to 20 miles; and a C position to within 30 miles. Along with the aircraft's position, the crew would receive instructions on how to home on the nearest open airfield, if they so requested.[45]

Weather fronts move in rapidly from the Atlantic during the North European winter, frequently requiring missions to be terminated early and for planes to be diverted to alternate airfields. The ability to do this accurately was vital to the safe operation of the aircraft. Although the American units had experienced personnel, the adjustment to flying from English bases was not an entirely easy transition. The most notable demonstration of how difficult it could be came on December 20, 1942, when a plane of the 1st Squadron, piloted by Capt. Bertram C. Martin, lifted off the runway at St. Eval at 0415 for a patrol out into the Atlantic. While the plane was in the air, a shift of wind direction brought a solid low overcast over the British Isles. After 11 hours in the air, the plane's dead-reckoning navigation was evidently thrown out badly by the wind shift. The heavy weather prevented celestial fixes, and it was clear to the crew that they were well and truly lost. Using radar, they established a distinct headland below them, which later reconstruction of the plane's course suggested was probably along the southwest coast of County Kerry, in Eire, which was a neutral country.

The plane, flying under the overcast at 150 feet, evidently proceeded up the coast of Ireland to the vicinity of the Shannon estuary, where the crew made out on the ground people "not dressed like English," and concluded they were over occupied France. The plane then made a course west-northwest, aiming for England, which was in fact to the east. After making its way out to sea again, the plane turned back east to make a landfall. That appears to have been the northwestern coast of Ireland. The plane had now been airborne well over 12 hours. Flying due east, at an altitude of about 500 feet, through solid murk (and across a part of Northern Ireland that contained land above 500 feet), the aircraft finally established communication with an airfield, and managed to set down at Jurby, Isle of Man, in the middle of the Irish Sea, at 1715. Jurby is about 150 miles north of St. Eval. The plane had been in the air for 13 hours, and had about 40 to 50 gallons of gas left in its tanks when it landed.[46] It was a sober crew that returned to St. Eval on December 22. Captain Martin attributed his eventual safe landing to his radar operator, who "prevented him from running into [the] cliffs of Ireland and yet enabled him to follow the Irish coast at a reasonable distance."[47]

Operational Aircraft Losses

In retrospect, Captain Martin and his crew seem to have been favored by fortune on this occasion; not all crews were as lucky. An aircraft of the 1st Squadron vanished while on patrol on January 6, 1943. The Liberator, piloted by Capt. Lawrence W. Lolley, with a full crew aboard, was on a routine daylight patrol, and the plane was simply never heard from again. While it was the crew's first operational patrol in the European Theater of Operations (ETO), they had received a thorough orientation, and the patrol route did not take the plane near any known area of enemy aircraft operations. Without any evidence, speculation concerning the cause of the loss seems inappropriate.[48]

Colonel Roberts had felt moved to lay out several essentials in preparing AAFAC crews for operations in the ETO which reflect the importance he attached to navigational matters in light of early experience in England. He stressed that no replacement crews for the squadrons should be sent over until each crew had completed "at least one fourteen-hour mission, entirely over water and without reference to visual navigation check points." At least five hours of this flight should be at night, using dead reckoning navigation only. "This introduces the problem common in this theater, of reading drift at night during unfavorable weather conditions." He urged that "navigators should be thoroughly impressed with the necessity for extremely accurate navigation under extremely difficult conditions." He also stressed the importance of efficient radio operation as "essential for the safe return of crews from missions in bad weather."[49]

Almost prophetically, Roberts went on to note that radio operators "should be thoroughly proficient in setting accurate frequencies," and in D/F procedure.[50] Failures in these areas would figure prominently in the loss of another American aircraft. On January 22, 1943, aircraft S of the 2nd Squadron (S/2) (2nd Lt. George O. Broussard, pilot) was returning from a patrol when bad weather settled in over southwest England.[51] Approaching the coast of England, the plane requested that it be assisted by the 19 Group controller, who was asked to give it homing directions according to established procedures to enable the plane to find its airfield. Unfortunately, this request was made on the wrong radio frequency, and the group controller declined to respond. Although the local controller at St. Eval then attempted to do so, he was too late, as the plane, flying through the pea soup, slammed into the shoreline cliffs about two miles east of Hartland Point, 40 miles up the coast from Newquay, killing the entire crew. The plane hit the cliffside about 50 feet below its crest.[52]

In the judgment of the American unit, this loss was quite unnecessary, and could have been avoided either by the pilot, who had adequate fuel, remaining off the coast until he was able to get ground assistance, or "if he was going on instruments, to proceed to do so at a safe altitude," or by "the exercise of better judgment by the officer in charge of the . . . 19 Group radio station." With some feeling, the loss report observed: "The aircraft was obviously in difficulty, consequently it is believed that the 19 Group Station should not have quibbled about a technicality." The report also noted that "strong verbal representation has been made to the AOC, 19 Group [that it was essential] that in an emergency all possible assistance will not be withheld because of a technicality."[53]

On February 8, 1943, came another aircraft loss. As with the first loss, there was no sign as to the cause. A plane of the 1st Squadron, piloted by 1st Lt. David E. Sands, was on a routine antisubmarine patrol. His experienced crew had completed five training and five operational flights before their loss. The weather was reasonably good for the time of year, and no radio transmission was received from the plane.[54] No information subsequently has come to light concerning this or Captain Lolley's loss. Aircraft crashes at sea, after a very short time, usually leave no visible traces. Causes for aircraft losses over deep water thus cannot be deciphered from their remains.

Accidents could be just as deadly on the ground as in the air. On January 10, 1943, Capt. Bertram C. Martin had taxied his plane out for takeoff on an operational mission, and was waiting several hundred feet back from the runway, to allow an RAF Whitley of No. 10 OTU to take off. This unit, as noted above, belonged to RAF Bomber Command, and was on loan to Coastal Command to enable more complete surveillance of the Bay of Biscay. Normally, a Bomber Command aircrew would fly three to six antisubmarine patrols, picking up some flying and navigational experience, before being assigned to a regular bomber squadron. This morning, the Whitley never got airborne, swerving off the runway and careening head-on into the waiting Liberator. Both aircraft had full military loads, and flames erupted immediately on impact. All members of the Whitley's crew died in the crash.[55]

The bombardier and navigator in Martin's plane were killed instantly upon the collision, as most of the rest of the crew scrambled frantically to evacuate before the inevitable explosions of the depth charges aboard the aircraft destroyed it completely. Martin's radio operator, T. Sgt. James R. Lowry, was so badly burned that he died within 24 hours, while Martin himself re-entered the plane, evidently to try to rescue the bombardier or navigator. His burns were also fatal within 24 hours. He was later awarded a posthumous Distinguished Flying Cross (DFC) for his action. After several minutes, the twelve 250-pound depth charges in the Liberator exploded. One observer noted: "I dove for cover behind a truck to avoid being hit from large debris blown every direction. The headless, legless torso of one of the British crew landed a few feet from me. Very unpleasant ending."[56]

The copilot and five others survived, but several were too badly burned to return to active duty in an operational theater. Bill Pomeroy, who had been in the same aviation cadet class with Martin's copilot, 2nd Lt. Walter A. Krozel, visited the burned aviator in the Royal Cornwall Infirmary, Truro. For Pomeroy, it was "the most difficult and disturbing thing to affect me in the United Kingdom. . . . I had difficulty recognizing Walter and he sensed it. He spoke up, however, and after a quick greeting he said what was most on his mind: 'Bill, will my wife still love me now that I look like this?'" Pomeroy recalled that he said everything he could think of to ease Krozel's worries and "stressed that his appearance would come back, that he was still on the road to recovery."[57] Krozel would return to the United States for further treatment and recovery. Six men of the 1st Squadron were later awarded the Soldier's Medal for "displaying heroism beyond the call of duty" in connection with the crash and rescue efforts.[58]

Colonel Roberts was unhappy about sharing the airfield with the Bomber Command OTU and its inexperienced crews. He reported that the "tracks of the Whitley clearly showed that it went in a straight line towards the B-24D once it had left the runway. The pilot apparently 'froze' at the controls inasmuch as he had ample time to stop, turn to either side, or ground loop, had he chosen to do so." As the Whitley pilot died in the collision, we do not know why he was unable to avoid the Liberator, and in the emotion of the event Roberts may have been overly severe in his comments. He was certainly correct, however, in observing the inexperience of the OTU aircrews. Only two days earlier, there had been a close call when an OTU Whitley in taking off managed to clear a parked B-24D by no more than 25 feet.[59]

Aircraft and Weapons

A matter of confidence and satisfaction to Roberts was the reliability and performance of the B-24D Liberators that equipped his group. The B-24s, on arrival at St. Eval, had their bomb-bay fuel tanks (which had given them their extra range for the transatlantic crossing) removed so that they could carry ten to twelve depth charges of British design on their patrols over the Bay of Biscay, an area that did not require the extreme ranges of planes operating in support of convoys in the mid-Atlantic.[60]

The standard British depth charge in use by the time the Americans reached England was the Mark XI, containing 250 pounds of Torpex. It had a concave nose to slow its descent through the water in order to allow its hydrostatic fuse to function effectively to detonate at about a 25-foot depth, which was by late 1942 the normal depth setting for air-dropped ASW weapons. However, until well into 1943, there were chronic problems with depth charges exploding below their set depth.[61] A fair amount of instruction was required in the loading of British-type depth charges, and adjustments were made to the B-24's bomb racks and release mechanism to accommodate them. This remained something of a problem throughout the time the squadrons were in the United Kingdom. While the B-24D proved to be a robust and dependable antisubmarine aircraft, a full load of depth charges shifted aft the aircraft's center of gravity, which already had a bias in this direction, and required some modifications to restore safe handling characteristics.[62] Colonel Roberts reported in early December that "three planes have dragged their tails upon landing putting them out of commission for a week for smoothing of skin and replacement of rivets."[63]

The B-24D operating as an ASW aircraft normally carried a crew of ten: pilot and copilot, bombardier and navigator, engineer and assistant engineer, radio operator and assistant radio operator, radar operator, and tail gunner, who was the only man with an exclusive gunnery job. The first four were usually, although not always, commissioned officers, and the rest of the crew normally were sergeants. The navigator or bombardier manned the nose guns as necessary, the engineer the top turret, and the assistant radio operator and the assistant engineer the two waist-gun positions.[64] As much as possible crews were kept intact and "a strong effort is being made to have crews fly their assigned plane only."[65]

Radar

While the two American squadrons alone in Coastal Command possessed the prized centimetric radar, in their case the American SCR-517C set, it was very new and prone to difficulties. Further, a supply of spare parts was lost somewhere en route to Europe. The new radar had been installed just prior to departure, and the radar operators lacked experience calibrating and operating the equipment, as did mechanics in maintaining it. There were also simply too few mechanics who knew how to repair and maintain the sophisticated equipment.[66] Colonel Roberts felt acutely the need for a specialist radar officer, but was fortunate in gaining valuable assistance with the equipment from Walter Pree, of Western Electric, who was in the United Kingdom "on another project but was devoting about fifty percent of his time to checking and improving our radar maintenance and operation."[67] On January 16, 1943, VIII Bomber Command assigned a radar officer to the antisubmarine group, as efforts to secure one from Antisubmarine Command had met with no response.[68]

At first, the centimetric radar was not allowed to be used when flying within 200 miles of the coast of France, a regulation imposed by the RAF for security reasons. This was soon relaxed to when flying within 100 miles of France, as long as the aircraft was flying beneath 1,000 feet in the 100- to 200-mile zone. This Roberts deemed "a great help because it enables planes to use radar throughout the entire mission, [and] to check the functioning of the equipment on coast and island targets when departing on and returning from missions."[69]

Difficulties with the new equipment were troublesome enough that Colonel Roberts requested that his aircraft be taken off operational missions from December 14 to 19, during which time the American planes operated over the Irish Sea, flying training missions specifically devoted to mastering the SCR-517 equipment and gaining confidence in it. Roberts believed that both efficiency and morale benefited from this effort.[70] The primary cause of the radar failing to work up to its theoretical capability became a contentious issue. The group submitted two reports on the subject based largely on its experience in the United Kingdom. The first was the work of the young radar officer borrowed from VIII Bomber Command. He found that 55 percent of failures in the equipment were due to improper maintenance.[71]

This report produced a vehement reaction within the group, with "exception taken by experienced enlisted and civilian ASV mechanics." This led Roberts to ask H. V. Childs, a civilian employee of Western Electric, manufacturer of the SCR-517, to undertake a second study and report.[72] Childs's report used a different standard of assessment, was calculated over a longer period of time, and produced the following figures:

Number of hours flown using the radar   1909.4
Number of hours of satisfactory performance   1197.8
Percent of time equipment performed satisfactorily   62.7[73]

In Childs's assessment, 42 percent of the occurrences of unsatisfactory performance could be attributed to electrical equipment failures, and a generous 33 percent to "undetermined" cause. Servicing of the equipment accounted for only 5 percent, in his analysis. The prime culprit in the high percentage of electrical problems he identified as defective vacuum tubes (65 percent of all electrical faults).[74]

Whatever the merits of this dispute, Roberts did clearly address a significant limitation of the SCR-517 equipment from the operational standpoint, that it used a Range Azimuth screen (A-scope) rather than a Plan Position Indicator (PPI) screen. As Roberts noted, the A-scope's most significant operational limitation was that the operator often found it difficult "to form in his mind a picture of the target's location in relationship to the airplane." Further, physical formations were so distorted by the way the A-scope presented them that the equipment was "almost useless for navigational purposes, other than obtaining range and bearing on a coast line." By contrast, the PPI screen presented "a perfect map of the terrain directly below . . . when flying over coastlines, land, rivers and hills."[75] While this was rather optimistic, it was indisputable that the PPI form of presentation greatly assisted the operator in correctly assessing what he was seeing.

It is possible to sum up the state of the American unit's equipment for operations from the United Kingdom. The B-24D was a plane that gave little trouble and generally inspired confidence in its crews. While the American planes alone possessed the prized 10-cm SCR-517 radar equipment, which the Germans could not detect, that radar equipment proved to be very hard to keep operating efficiently throughout the time the two American squadrons were at St. Eval. The British Mark XI depth charges were among the best ASW weapons available at that stage in the war. There were, however, some problems in matching the British weapons to the American bomb-bay equipment. This would prove a source of difficulty during anti-U-boat operations. Antisubmarine operations, of course, were the raison d'être for the group and its presence in England. How well planes, radar, and depth charges performed was ultimately in the hands of the men who used them.

3

480th Group Operations from the United Kingdom

Operating under RAF Coastal Command

In Coastal Command, operational flights for LR aircraft, such as the Liberators, lasted about ten to eleven hours, while USAAF Antisubmarine Command policy normally limited flights to about six hours, on the theory that crew fatigue decreased operational effectiveness on longer missions. Here Colonel Roberts and the Coastal Command leadership reached something of a standoff. Roberts initially supported the American practice, arguing that the longer flights were "both unproductive and uneconomical."[1] But he early on agreed to eight-hour flights, and then slowly accepted that flights of ten or more hours would have to become the rule for the two American squadrons.

By February 1943 ten-hour flights were becoming the norm. The need in the Bay of Biscay, as indeed was even more the case in Atlantic convoy-escort missions, was for LR aircraft. This was the primary attraction of the Liberator to the British. They already had sufficient aircraft to provide good coverage out to about 600 miles from shore on a regular basis, with some patrolling as far out as 800 miles. Predictably, the U-boats moved their activities further out, and thus the need was for adequate coverage beyond 600 and especially beyond 800 miles. The LR version of the Liberator, which the 1st and 2nd Antisubmarine Squadrons flew, could manage 800 miles comfortably, and even 1,000 miles with reduced load.[2] The consequence of providing coverage that far out to sea was longer duration of missions. There was no escaping the logic, which Roberts came to accept.

In view of the debate over the length of missions, the question naturally arises of how crew fatigue affected operational efficiency. At the end of 1943, the Operational Research Section (ORS) of Coastal Command produced two studies based on squadron experience earlier in the year which throw some light on the subject. One report examined operational performance as an index of fatigue of aircrews.[3] The ORS unit had analyzed the data by dividing all antisubmarine patrols into four quarters. As the typical flight would use much or even all of the first and fourth quarters transiting between base and patrol area, the frequency of subs detected in these two quarters was expected to be low. But if the fourth quarter rate was notably lower than that in the first quarter, the effects of fatigue would be evident. The same principle applied to the second and third quarters, except that these would be flown largely in the patrol area and a higher frequency of U-boats detected could be expected. Again, the question was, would the third quarter rate of detection decline from that of the second quarter? The study found no statistically significant variation between the frequency of U-boat sightings in the first and fourth quarters, or between those in the second and third quarters of aircraft patrols. In short, the ORS concluded, "there is no evidence that any reduction in the efficiency of lookouts occurs," and that "as far as they go the figures give no evidence of any increased fatigue."

The ORS also measured whether there was any falloff in the efficiency of the actual attacks on submarines as a result of length of flight. This was done by looking at the Admiralty assessments of air attacks on U-boats, to see if accuracy of attacks fell off over time of flight. The conclusion was that "there is no alteration in the efficiency of the attack even when the crew have been airborne for 6 to 11 hours." It did note that "there is a slight increase in the percentage of unsuccessful attacks after 8 hours." The reason for the general resistance to a decrease in efficiency of attacks the ORS attributed to the fact that "the pilot and other members of the crew have been carrying out a skilled job and may well be suffering from fatigue, but these effects can be overcome for the short period required to carry out the attack." The general pattern of the evidence, then, was that there was little discernible decline in search efficiency as a result of long missions. But this was not necessarily good news. As the ORS report concluded: "The sighting of U-boats is . . . a mental occupation with boredom the principal governing factor." What happened was that "the individual members of the crew adapt themselves to the general monotony of their visual task by keeping their general efficiency at some small fraction of the maximum possible." It was not that efficiency of lookout was uniformly high; rather, it was uniformly low, which produced no significant variation of data in the quarters compared. The report concluded that "measures taken to combat boredom and fatigue of lookouts and of the crew in general are valuable not so much for overcoming these ill effects towards the end of a long patrol but because they raise the general efficiency throughout the patrol."

The second ORS report was less significant, but did produce some interesting observations. It was undertaken to discover how U-boats were sighted from the air, and how the efficiency of lookout for submarines could be improved.[4] The report found that the cockpit was the "principal position from which sightings are made. The nose or front lookout position is the next in importance." It also discovered that the frequency of U-boat sightings fell off rapidly toward the beam, suggesting a preoccupation with the view ahead. Overall, it suggested that the efficiency of lookout could be improved generally by efforts to fight boredom and fatigue. The ORS recommended that the feeding of crews during a sortie should be kept at a high standard "as an essential item in the general fighting efficiency of an aircrew. Frequent and tasty meals should be the aim of all feeding arrangements." Anecdotal evidence from squadrons equipped with the Sunderland flying boat, which had both a large crew and a built-in galley, gives support to the ORS analysis.[5] The Coastal Command unit also advised that lookout watches should be changed every hour, and even every half-hour if possible, in order to break the monotony involved in this task.[6]

The two reports in tandem make clear that if long missions were necessary, and they were, then the business of searching for U-boats had to approached in an analytic manner, and efforts made to raise overall effectiveness. Although they did not directly address the issue of aircraft size, the evidence of the reports also suggests that larger aircraft, such as the Liberator, possessed clear advantages in this respect, beyond the obvious capacity for long flights. A larger plane accommodated a larger crew, which in turn made alternating lookouts to break monotony and relieve fatigue a feasible procedure. The larger aircraft also had space to feed crews on long missions, as well as meet the crews' other natural requirements.[7]

In practice, many of the recommendations in the reports were incorporated into standard operating procedures. In addressing visual lookouts, the standard RAF Coastal Command manual noted that it was "a fact that large numbers of U/Boats come within visual range of aircraft and pass unseen." The recommendations regarding duration and rotation of watches in the ORS reports were adopted. A particular problem that arose in the Bay of Biscay was also addressed by Coastal Command. Its operating procedures provided that a special sky lookout should be established in areas where enemy aircraft might be operating, "otherwise the whole crew may find themselves looking for enemy aircraft to the detriment of the A/U [anti-U-boat] lookout."[8] In the summer and autumn of 1943 this would become a pressing concern, but this was not yet the case in the winter of 1942–43 when the 480th Group was operating over the bay.

For its part, the USAAF Antisubmarine Command remained unrepentant in its advocacy of short-duration search missions. This remained true even after General Larson visited Britain and had opportunity to discuss the matter with Coastal Command authorities. The Antisubmarine Command's standard operational manual was prescribing short search missions as late as July 1943. Indeed, AAFAC held that "missions over five (5) hours duration are increasingly unproductive due to fatigue" and recommended that aircraft controllers should not normally assign longer missions if it could be avoided.[9]

Operational Tempo

An unavoidable consequence of missions that lasted 10 or 11 hours was a reduced operational tempo for the group. As Colonel Roberts noted to General Eaker: "In the beginning it was planned that each combat crew would fly an operational mission every third day. This schedule has been interrupted because of the physical inability of crews to repeatedly recuperate from 10–14 hour missions within two days time."[10] By December 26, 1942, the American antisubmarine units at St. Eval had been flying operational missions for a period of some 40 days. They had managed in that time only thirty-two missions of a total 257:25 hours.[11]

The primary reasons for this low operational tempo were:

1. The need to acclimate arriving aircrews to RAF operational procedures and operating conditions in the ETO;

2. The extra duties imposed on flying personnel as a result of an inadequate number of American ground personnel available;

3. The small number of aircraft and crews available and the fatigue longer flights imposed on them;

4. The limitations imposed on aircraft maintenance by the inability to work at night; and

5. The winter weather in the ETO.[12]

On special occasions, preparatory to a predetermined period of saturation flying over a given area where U-boats were expected to be present in numbers, crews would reduce their operating tempo. This enabled them to be adequately rested for a short, intensive period of frequent patrols, and the group's mechanics would have sufficient time to raise the average number of aircraft available for operations. The duration of missions increased, with the February monthly average for the group 9.48 hours per mission and the March average 11.6 hours.

A point Roberts did win in his dealings with RAF Coastal Command concerned a proposal to use his planes "to seek and attack enemy surface craft with high explosive bombs." He felt that "the deliberate exposure of this equipment and these trained crews, when not necessary, to attack by a preponderance of enemy fighters or to anti-aircraft fire at low altitudes, is considered to be inconsistent with the nature of the mission."[13] He was, of course, entirely right. By the end of December, Air Chief Marshal Joubert had accepted Roberts's argument "that the use of B-24D planes with SCR-517-C radar for shipping strikes would be uneconomical and unwise."[14] One can see how 19 Group of Coastal Command would be tempted to use the powerful Liberators for such a task, given the unsuitability of their own LR types for this mission. But the British did not press the issue in the face of Roberts's opposition, and a potentially serious conflict was avoided. The proposal to use the Liberators with their centimeter radar on such missions reads strangely when one considers that the British had been representing to the Americans the critical need for such well-equipped aircraft for the antisubmarine mission. Either priorities were not laid out clearly to lower levels of command in the RAF, or the need was much less critical than the British maintained.

Operational control of the American squadrons by RAF Coastal Command could have been sticky; however, it worked well enough in practice, thanks to sound judgment and common sense on the part of the British and Americans concerned. The American group operated under the RAF station commander at St. Eval, who received his orders from the headquarters of 19 Group, one of the four that made up the operational side of Coastal Command. (The RAF groups corresponded to the wings that made up USAAF Antisubmarine Command.) As noted above, it was initially intended that the normal operational cycle over the bay would be for a three-day rotation. A crew would fly a tactical mission on day 1 of its cycle, have the next day off, and on the third day fly training missions, working on such matters as accuracy of attacks, radar and radio training, transitioning to command pilot for copilots, and familiarization with alternate landing fields. Then the cycle would repeat. However, something like a four-day cycle quickly became the norm. Operating under Coastal Command, the American squadrons followed RAF procedure of assigning each plane a letter, hence the expressions "C for Charlie" or "V for Victor" to identify individual aircraft. The group continued this practice in North Africa. Crews assigned to planes received similar letter designations, although in practice they often flew planes other than their own.

The usual mission assignment procedure was for each squadron to inform the RAF station operations office at St. Eval of the number of aircraft it would have available for operations on the following day. This was passed on, along with the availability of aircraft in the British squadrons on the station to 19 Group headquarters, which would send back to St. Eval mission assignments for the next day. The local controller then assigned takeoff times and patrol routes. Crews reported for mission briefings two hours before takeoff time. In the case of early morning takeoffs, crew members were picked up three hours before estimated time of takeoff, and fed at the air station prior to briefing and departure. All crew members were required to be present for the briefing, and the pilot was responsible for verifying that his radioman was familiar with all the signals for the day. After the briefing, the crew picked up from the station's flight kitchen a lunch to eat while on the flight.[15] The American antisubmarine group commander retained the final decision on all mission assignments, as well as on all questions of diversion or recall of missions. American aircraft controllers were trained by the British at St. Eval, and they then worked directly with the British controllers, with each American having full control over his aircraft.

December Attacks on U-boats

It was not until the very end of 1942 that the American antisubmarine crews were rewarded with U-boat sightings. The earliest came on December 29.[16] Aircraft E/1st Squadron (E/1) was flying a patrol that day in typical winter weather, 10/10 cloud cover with its base at 100 feet, although visibility below the cloud base was reasonably good at six to eight miles. In position 52.12°N/24.00°W, what appeared to be a bow wave was sighted one to two miles away. At about the same moment, the radar operator reported a contact in the same position. As the plane closed the contact, a submarine's conning tower was seen to be emerging, as the U-boat was surfacing. However, as the plane approached, the U-boat proceeded to submerge, and the B-24 pilot, Capt. Douglas Northrop, was unable to reach the U-boat's position until some 20 to 25 seconds after it submerged. Twelve British Mark XI 250-pound Torpex depth charges set to explode at shallow depth and spaced 25 feet apart were released from an altitude of 150 feet as the plane crossed the U-boat's estimated track about 200–300 feet ahead of the apex of the swirl created by the conning tower as it went under.[17] No results from the attack were observed, other than the customary brown scum the depth charges always left.

Analysis of the attack indicated that the conning tower of the sub would have been about 280 feet beyond the apex of its swirl when the depth charges detonated. If the crew's estimate that the charges fell 200 to 300 feet ahead of the swirl was correct, then there was a reasonable chance that a straddle of the sub had been achieved. The difficulty was that the top of the pressure hull of a submerging sub would have reached a depth of about 54 feet, or just beyond lethal radius of a Mark XI depth charge exploding at 25 feet. Without photographs, little more could be said, other than that there was no sign that the U-boat had been affected by the attack.[18] Given the tendency for most antisubmarine aircrews to have underestimated range and line errors when their reports could be compared to photos, the actual distance of the depth charges from their intended target was perhaps greater than assumed as the basis for the staff analysis. It seems certain the U-boat lived to fight another day. The experience of Captain Northrop and his crew was more typical than not. U-boats were normally fleeting targets of opportunity, which gave aircraft crews precious little time to get in a good attack.

A more promising attack on a U-boat occurred on December 31, 1942, when A/1, piloted by Lt. Walter E. Thorne, was on patrol in 51.20°N/

20.58°W with fairly heavy broken cloud at 1,000 feet and visibility about five miles.[19] Radar indicated a possible U-boat eight miles distant bearing 30 degrees to starboard. Turning toward it, Thorne gradually lost altitude, and the U-boat was sighted visually about 4½ miles ahead, still fully surfaced. As the aircraft began its attack run, the submarine crash-dived. Flying at 200 MPH at 175 feet above the water, the Liberator released a stick of nine depth charges spaced at 16 feet and set to explode at 25 feet. These appeared to straddle the hull just behind the conning tower. Although this would seem to have been a lethal attack, if observed data were accurate, there followed only a minor disturbance such as one would expect from a diving submarine, and nothing more. Unfortunately the photographs of the attack were useless because the camera's mirror, essential to get the correct angle to show the attack as the plane pulled away and gained height, had fogged over. In the absence of adequate evidence, an assessment of likely damage to the U-boat was the best that could be made. Given the described position of the depth charges, the lack of physical evidence of damage to the U-boat suggests that the crew's estimates of distance were inaccurate and that the assessment was perhaps overly optimistic.[20]

Operation GONDOLA, February 6–15, 1943

RAF Coastal Command believed that the U-boat's technical limitations made it possible to interdict the passage of submarines across the Bay of Biscay with a high degree of certainty. It was known that in every 24 hours a U-boat had to remain on the surface for roughly 4 in order to charge its batteries for submerged operation. With a policy of maximum submergence, a submarine could progress about 110 to 120 miles in those 24 hours. By adequately covering a search area of sufficient width, say 130 to 140 miles, with patrolling aircraft, it was theoretically possible to catch on the surface every submarine crossing the interdicted zone at least once in its passage.

Crucial to the success of this approach was achieving and sustaining an adequate density of aircraft operating both day and night. The theory was put to the test in Operation GONDOLA of February 6–15, 1943. During these 10 days ASW aircraft were to fly set patrols over the designated areas (Inner and Outer Gondola) so as to bring every U-boat under potential attack at least once. In practice, success was limited. Aircraft and equipment problems limited the density achieved and the number of U-boats sighted. Total flying hours over Inner Gondola were 1,182 for the 10 days, and 1,078 over Outer Gondola.[21] Of all the Allied aircraft operating in Gondola, only the two American squadrons were equipped with centimetric radar. The LR American B-24D Liberators operated only in Outer Gondola, along with British LR aircraft.

While forty U-boats entered Inner Gondola and thirty-eight Outer Gondola in this 10-day period, there were fourteen submarine sightings and six attacks in Outer Gondola, and only four sightings and one attack in the inner area.[22] The better record in Outer Gondola, although there were slightly fewer U-boats present, and slightly fewer patrol hours flown, appears to have been the result of the U-boats not anticipating they would meet many Allied air patrols so far out in the Bay of Biscay. Of the enemy contacts in the outer area, all but one were by the two American squadrons, which accounted for a majority of all U-boat sightings in the GONDOLA operation. Of the seven attacks made within the Gondola areas in this period, four were by the Americans, including the only one that sunk a U-boat. In the month of February 1943, RAF Coastal Command achieved twenty-nine sightings and thirteen attacks on U-boats in the Bay of Biscay; fifteen and five of these, respectively, were by the two USAAF squadrons.[23]

The first American attack on a U-boat since December came on February 6, the first day of the GONDOLA operation. Aircraft E/1, piloted by 1st Lt. David E. Sands, was flying a patrol in 48.12°N/17.35°W at an altitude of 4,200 feet through broken clouds which had their base at 3,500 feet.[24] Visibility was 10 miles, with some haze. A U-boat was sighted at about 2½ miles, bearing 10 degrees to port. There was no radar contact, as that equipment had not been working satisfactorily throughout the flight. The plane executed an S-turn while losing altitude and actually made the attack from the U-boat's starboard quarter at an angle of about 30 degrees to the submarine's course. The U-boat was still fully surfaced at the time of attack, and thus highly vulnerable to damage from the stick of six depth charges, spaced 38 feet apart and set to explode at 25 feet. The B-24 released these from 700 to 800 feet as it crossed over the U-boat aft of its conning tower. The rear gunner observed the stick to just overshoot the target, with the first of the six depth charges falling close to the port quarter of the submarine, somewhat forward of its stern. However, only two of the six depth charges exploded, numbers 3 and 6 of the stick. With a 38-foot spacing, this put the closer of the two, number 3, well outside lethal range. The height of the plane when the depth charges were released is notable. Recommended altitude for release was not higher than 200 feet, both to improve accuracy in the attack and to avoid the risk of the depth charges breaking up or malfunctioning when they hit the water.

Sands circled and delivered a second attack on the U-boat, which was by now quite awake to its danger and submerging. As the plane passed over the submarine at a height of 200 to 250 feet, the crew attempted to drop six more depth charges. Only two charges actually fell, however, the other four hanging up. The two that did fall were good for line and distance, but neither exploded. The assessment was never in doubt: "An exceedingly well executed attack which was completely nullified by failure in armament and release."[25] This marked the beginning of a problem the American planes would have dropping the British Mark XI depth charges, which required some adjustments to the planes' release equipment. As these hangups did not always occur, it is clear that careful attention to this matter produced successful results, which were not achieved in this case. However, it was highly unusual for the Mark XI depth charge not to explode. One might speculate that the altitude of release, 700 to 800 feet, on the first pass was a factor in only two of the six depth charges in that stick functioning. However, the second pass was low enough to reduce the likelihood of this occurring, and again the depth charges failed to explode. This in turn suggests inadequate attention to depth-charge fusing. (This aircraft also had a malfunctioning radar set; the pattern is disturbing.) Lacking a report on the causes of the problems, it is only possible to note the disappointing result of a promising attack.

The second American attack on a U-boat during GONDOLA came on February 9.[26] Plane B/1 (1st Lt. Emmett O. Hutto, pilot, and 2nd Lt. John E. Dale, copilot) was on antisubmarine patrol in 48.10°N/20.35°W. Dale was in the pilot's seat, a normal procedure in preparing a copilot for command of his own aircraft. The plane was flying at 2,200 feet, just below solid cloud cover, with visibility some five miles over a very rough sea, when the bombardier and navigator both saw a U-boat about 3½ miles ahead and 20 degrees to port of the Liberator's course. The U-boat was seen to dive just as it was sighted. B/1 delivered an attack at an altitude of 150 feet while traveling 200 MPH. Six depth charges, spaced at 30 feet, were released as the plane crossed the U-boat's track about 75 to 100 feet ahead of the swirl left by its conning tower. The crew estimated this was five to eight seconds after the submarine had submerged. The tail gunner estimated that the depth charges had straddled the probable course of the U-boat. He disagreed with his pilot and copilot on the character of the patch left on the water, which by his description appeared to be the characteristic brownish-red scum of exploded depth charges. Pilot and copilot thought the patch was an oil slick and not depth-charge residue.

Unfortunately, the photographs of the attack showing the depth charges exploding did not reveal any visible mark, such as the conning tower's swirl, which would allow location of the depth charges. Given the extreme roughness of the water, this was not surprising. The 1st Squadron commander observed in his comments on this attack that it was not possible to reconcile all the evidence provided by the crew. In addition to the disagreement about the surface evidence, there was a problem of time. If the U-boat was indeed 3½ miles away from the plane when sighted, and promptly dived, as reported, it was not possible for the B-24 to cover that distance in the five to eight seconds after submergence estimated by the crew. In fact, with a ground speed of 200 MPH it would have required about a minute to reach the point of submergence, or long after a successful attack could be hoped for. He concluded that "D.C.'s probably fell too far short for an effective attack."[27] The Admiralty assessor, however, thought that the plane was closer to the U-boat when it dived than the crew recognized or made clear to the squadron commander, and that B/1 was probably only 500 yards from the U-boat at the time it submerged. If this were so, then, he wrote, "this may have been a well executed attack." He also assessed the slick shown in photographs to be oil, as the pilot and copilot had stated, and not depth-charge scum. Therefore he concluded that it was possible that the submarine had been damaged. If, on the other hand, the squadron commander's opinion of the time elapsed between submergence and stick release was right, then the stick missed astern.[28]

This case nicely illustrates the difficulties attached to assessing attacks on U-boats with anything approaching certainty, except when there was convincing evidence of serious damage or a sinking. More often than not, there was too little evidence to allow certitude in the analysis of the attack, a matter quite frustrating to ASW aircraft crews, who maintained they had to bring back the U-boat commander's underwear to get the attention of the assessors. Postwar comparison of German with Allied records indicates that the assessors were seldom far off in their conclusions, however disappointing this was to the aviators.

The next American attack during Operation GONDOLA also came on February 9, in position 47.43°N/17.53°W with rough seas running beneath broken overcast at 2,000 to 2,500 feet and a 40 MPH wind blowing. U/2 was patrolling under the overcast at 1,500 feet when the pilot, Capt. Lawrence E. Jarnagin, sighted a wake about 4 miles ahead and to starboard. At the same time, the copilot, Capt. Gerald L. Mosier, made out the conning tower of a submarine. The U-boat appeared to be diving when it was spotted; it had probably spotted the aircraft at about the same time it was seen. As the plane approached, a radar contact was made at 3 miles, but lost at 2½ miles. It is not clear if this was because the U-boat's return was swallowed up in the sea return from the rough seas running, or if it disappeared because the U-boat had submerged. The B-24's pilot had some trouble discerning the U-boat's course because the high seas broke up its wake. An attack across what was thought to be the U-boat's course was delivered 40 seconds after it had submerged. Not surprisingly, no evidence of damage was forthcoming. Given the time elapsed between submergence and depth charge release, as timed by the aircraft's crew, the attack had almost no chance of success and Coastal Command tactical instructions strongly discouraged releasing depth charges in such circumstances. The 2nd Squadron commander, Maj. Isaac Haviland, ascribed the action of the crew to the fact that it was the pilot's first sighting and attack.[29]

In an unusual aftermath to this attack, over 2½ hours later, U/2 was still on patrol when Captain Mosier sighted a periscope and its feather about 4 miles ahead and 45 degrees to starboard, in 47.21°N/20.08°W. The plane turned to close, and when about 2 to 2½ miles away, the periscope dipped and did not reappear. Nonetheless, about 30 to 35 seconds later, the plane crossed what was estimated to be the U-boat's course at an altitude of 50 feet and endeavored to release four depth charges. However, the depth charges failed to drop. After waiting about 15 minutes in the area, the plane set out for home because of fuel considerations. No assessment was attempted on this incident.[30]

Both Captain Jarnagin and Captain Mosier were experienced and competent aviators; their efficiency is adequately indicated by the fact that they would successively command the 2nd Antisubmarine Squadron following Major Haviland's return to the United States. However, even good aviators can have a bad day, and February 9 appears to have been theirs. The first attack was simply made too late on what was at best a poor target indicator in a rough sea. The difficulty Captain Jarnagin had making out the wake of the

U-boat is sufficient commentary on this point. The second attempted attack was likely on a nonsubmarine. Spotting a periscope at four miles is too difficult an achievement to be easily accepted. This is particularly the case in a rough, broken sea running that throws up lots of whitecaps and spray. The fatigue of a long mission too easily converts an oceanic phenomenon into a periscope. Not surprisingly, there are few verified sightings of periscopes among the great amount of sighting materials amassed during World War II, especially at four miles in a very rough sea.

February 10, 1943, marked the peak of activity during Operation GONDOLA. For the Americans, it produced two attacks on U-boats with sharply contrasting results. P/2, piloted by Lt. John E. Kraybill, was flying in 47.25°N/14.50°W on the morning of the tenth in weather that saw a decline in wind velocity and sea roughness from the ninth, but cloud was solid with its base at 1,200 feet and scattered showers reduced visibility, which at best was about four miles. At 0830 the crew saw a submarine two miles ahead and to starboard. Kraybill promptly attacked, and passed over the U-boat at 100 feet while it was still fully surfaced. However, all depth charges hung up. P/2 circled around and attacked again, and again succeeded in passing over the sub while it was still vulnerable on the surface. But again the depth charges failed to release. Kraybill attempted yet a third attack, but by now the U-boat had submerged. This was the only occasion during the 480th Group's time at St. Eval that a U-boat chose to fight back, firing on the B-24 during the first two passes. Machine-gun fire from the Liberator silenced the U-boat both times, although no casualties appear to have been inflicted. The Admiralty assessor adequately summed up the situation: "A well executed attack entirely ruined through failure of armament."[31] The assessor also took note of the U-boat's flak. Presciently, he observed that antiaircraft fire from the U-boats "must be reckoned as a growing habit." This would certainly prove true in the summer of 1943. The Americans were commended for pressing in and silencing the submarine's fire.

U.519 Sunk

About an hour after P/2's disappointing experience, T/2 (1st Lt. William L. Sanford, pilot) made a sighting while patrolling in Outer Gondola, some 800 miles west of the U-boat base at St. Nazaire. Four days earlier, Sanford and his crew had been flying in aircraft N/2, as their own plane was not available, and had suffered the frustration of carrying out two passes over a U-boat while their depth charges hung up.[32] After that experience, the crew was anxious not to miss another chance. On February 10, while flying at 300 feet at the base of solid low cloud in 47.05°N/18.34°W, the left waist gunner spotted a U-boat four miles away to port. Radar contact had been attained by the operator, T. Sgt. Fred A. Pribble, at about the same time. Because of the amount of sea clutter being thrown up on his scope by the choppy sea, he had hesitated to report it until the visual sighting came.[33]

The U-boat apparently detected the aircraft at about the same moment it was seen, for as the B-24 approached to attack, the sub submerged abruptly, with about 40 feet of its stern protruding at about 20 degrees from the water. However, something seems to have gone wrong with the U-boat while in the process of diving, and Lieutenant Sanford was able to make a good attack. T/2's bombardier, Capt. Ralph E. Jones, had no difficulty releasing his depth charges, and six were dropped while the plane was moving at 200 MPH some 200 feet above the water. However, the entire stick overshot, with the first (and closest) depth charge exploding about 30 feet to starboard of the U-boat's hull, too far to inflict lethal damage.

The U-boat, however, came up on an even keel, with conning tower again clearly visible and its deck awash. This allowed Sanford a second run a full two minutes after the first attack, when Jones released three more depth charges, which the tail gunner observed bracket the submarine. As the spacing of the stick was estimated at 19 feet, two of these charges should have been lethal, if the tail gunner's observation was accurate. The U-boat now began slowly to settle while the aircraft delivered yet a third attack. A final three depth charges were released, detonating an estimated 200 feet ahead of the now disappeared submarine. As the U-boat appears not to have had any way on, it seems likely these did no damage. A large dome-shaped bubble appeared where the U-boat had gone down, and then nothing, although the plane remained in the vicinity for another 30 minutes.

Photos taken by a hand-held camera were too poor to be able to determine how close to the boat the charges exploded. While they suggested that the depth charges from the second attack all fell on one side of the U-boat, the tail gunner was firm in his conviction that there had been a straddle. As he did not hesitate to say that the first stick overshot the U-boat, his testimony seems reliable. The large bubble observed by the aircrew was consistent with a phenomenon observed a bit later in the war, as the acoustic homing torpedo came into use. This weapon was normally dropped just as a U-boat dived. It caught up with the boat and ruptured its hull just below the surface, causing a massive release of air from inside the boat, which produced a large dome-like bubble on the surface of the water, and then nothing.

The initial Admiralty assessment given was a *B* for a U-boat probably sunk. Somewhat later this was revised to definitely sunk. The victim of "Tidewater Tillie," as T/2 was known to her crew, was U.519, a Type IXC U-boat. She had sailed from Lorient on her second war patrol on January 30 and was estimated to be in the position where Sanford's attack occurred on February 10. The following day, Admiral Doenitz's staff noted the failure of the submarine to report, and concluded: "Her loss must be presumed." All fifty of her crew, including her CO, Kapitaenleutnant Eppen, were lost with the boat.[34]

Although Operation GONDOLA continued until February 15, the two actions on the tenth were the last by planes of the American group during that operation. The group's score in GONDOLA, one U-boat sunk in five attacks (including the case of the failed release of depth charges), may strike the innocent reader as a modest accomplishment. So it should be noted that this gave a 20 percent kill rate at a time when the average of attacks on U-boats converted into sinkings was closer to 5 percent. Sinking a submarine was a difficult task, as the above descriptions should make clear.

After GONDOLA

There were only two further attacks on submarines by the USAAF planes after the conclusion of GONDOLA. One of these produced definite results. On February 20, 1943, C/1 (1st Lt. Wayne S. Johnson, pilot) was on a Biscay patrol in 40.30°N/21.00°W, flying at 1,600 feet through broken clouds which extended down to 800 feet.[35] The navigator, Lt. Bernard E. Benson, in the plane's nose, noticed a U-boat about three miles ahead. Lieutenant Johnson immediately dived to attack, emerging from the broken cloud cover about a mile from the submarine, which still did not notice the rapidly approaching aircraft. Six depth charges were dropped from 200 feet, set for a 36-foot spacing and with an observed spacing of 32 to 33 feet. These were seen to straddle the hull just ahead of the bow. The sub quickly disappeared, leaving a bluish oil slick about 400 feet long on the water. Although the plane employed baiting tactics, no further sign of the submarine was seen.[36]

Photographs of the attack taken with a hand-held camera by T. Sgt. James T. Hickie, the radar operator, while lying on the catwalk above the bomb bay showed only the depth charges leaving the plane, and not their points of entry into the water relative to the submarine. The attack was assessed by the Admiralty as probably causing significant damage. The assessor was correct. The subject of C/1's attack was U.211, a Type VIIC U-boat, which reported to base that she had been attacked and heavily damaged at the time and place of Lieutenant Johnson's action. The submarine had sailed from Brest on February 13 on its third war patrol. The damage from Johnson's attack had seriously reduced its diving capacity, presumably crushing its forward diving tank, critical to the U-boat being able to submerge promptly. It was forced to return to port for repairs. On February 25, U.211 limped into Brest for a long stay before it became seaworthy again. The boat was eventually lost with all hands, fifty-four, east of the Azores in November 1943, to attack from a British aircraft.[37]

The last attack by the Americans while flying from St. Eval came on March 2. E/1 (Capt. Kenneth L. Lueke, pilot) was flying a patrol at 1,700 feet below solid cloud with its base at about 2,000 feet.[38] In position 47.10°N/21.23°W a U-boat was sighted off to port about 2½ miles ahead. As Captain Lueke closed to attack, the submarine began to crash-dive. Twelve seconds after the boat had submerged, the plane crossed its path at an altitude of only 70 feet, releasing eight depth charges set for shallow detonation and spaced at 36 feet. The crew estimated the charges dropped about 200 feet ahead of the apex of the U-boat's swirl. Only the typical depth charge scum was observed on the water afterward. Photographs taken with a hand-held camera by the starboard waist gunner suggested that the stick had fallen more than 200 feet, and perhaps as much as 300 feet, ahead of the swirl. The assessor rightly called this a "well executed attack," most probably a near miss ahead of the submerged submarine. Had the U-boat been less alert it would have been in severe difficulties. Even a prompt attack, skillfully carried out, was not enough to catch those submarines maintaining good aircraft lookouts.

For aircraft crews who flew long hours without sighting a U-boat, the opportunity to attack one was the compensation for much toil, fatigue, and boredom. The crews of the two USAAF squadrons, nine of whom attempted attacks on U-boats between December 1942 and March 1943, must have found the results disappointing. In seventeen passes over targets, depth charges failed to drop or malfunctioned on eight occasions, or nearly half of all passes. This was bound to reduce drastically chances for success. Radar was as disappointing as depth-charge release mechanisms. Only once was a U-boat detected by radar, and on one other occasion the presence of a U-boat was confirmed by the radar. One can only guess at the opportunities missed because of poor radar performance, but the number was likely significant. Problems in the maintenance and use of equipment thus seriously hampered the accomplishment of the squadrons while operating from the United Kingdom.

Of the attacks carried out by the American crews, that on February 6 by Lieutenant Sands was doomed to failure, with passes made from too high an altitude and the weapons malfunctioning. Captain Jarnagin's attack on February 9 was simply too late. Perhaps the most frustrating of all was Lieutenant Kraybill's attempted attack on February 10 when depth charges failed to release on three consecutive passes, all of which had a good target available. Sanford's kill on February 10 had an element of good fortune attached to it. The depth charges likely fell beyond lethal range on the first pass. If the U-boat had got under as efficiently as most of its sisters did, the opportunity for a lethal attack on the second pass might not have occurred. On the other hand, some good attacks produced disappointing results. Those of Lieutenants Dale and Hutto on February 9 and Captain Lueke on March 2 could not have missed by much doing critical, perhaps fatal, damage.

On balance, the best that can be said is that the performance of the Americans showed both how difficult it was to kill a U-boat, and how important to give meticulous attention to equipment and to practicing attacks in preparation for that fleeting opportunity when the main chance occurs. For many crews, such a chance came only once in a tour of duty, if at all. The two squadrons would be fortunate in that respect. They would get a remarkable second inning in July 1943, when they were flying from North Africa. And when that opportunity came, they were much better prepared to take maximum advantage than during operations from St. Eval.

4

Transition
From St. Eval to Port Lyautey

Hunting a Blockade Runner

While most of the group's work was in seeking out U-boats, occasionally they were put on special assignments. In late February 1943, British intelligence indicated that a German blockade runner would be trying to slip across the Bay of Biscay to reach a German-occupied port, and a heavy schedule of flying was laid on to find it. The blockade runner was the *Hohenfriedberg*, ex-prize (Norwegian) tanker *Herborg* (7,892 GRT), which had departed Yokohama on November 11, 1942, for the long and dangerous voyage through the Allied blockade. British intelligence intercepts gave a good idea of when the ship would be approaching the Bay of Biscay. The Americans at St. Eval were tasked to fly a series of patrols to the extreme limit of their range, in order to try to find the blockade runner far enough out at sea so that a British warship could have time to close and sink the German vessel before it came under air and U-boat protection in the bay approaches.[1]

It was still pitch black when C/1, piloted by 1st Lt. Wayne S. Johnson, lifted off from St. Eval at 0342 on February 26. The night was sufficiently clear that the plane's navigator, Lt. Bernard E. Benson, was able to get three star fixes before the arrival of daylight, some 4½ hours after takeoff. Accordingly, the plane was in a good position to achieve an intercept, if intelligence on the ship's movement was sufficiently accurate.[2]

The crews had been briefed to look for a tanker, painted grey, and of about 8,000 GRT. At 0947, this was just what C/1 sighted in position 41.25°N/21.25°W, almost due west of Oporto, Portugal, and about 1,000 miles distant from St. Eval. As instructed, the aircraft shadowed the tanker, got off a message identifying it, and thereafter provided radio homing, so that the tanker's progress could be followed. The nearest British warship patrolling in the area, the cruiser HMS *Sussex*, was some 200 miles away, and would require considerable time to close the German ship. Because of this, the crew of C/1 could not remain to see the fruits of their labor. At 1200 the Liberator was at its prudent limit of endurance (PLE), and had to depart for home. By the time the Americans landed, however, the German blockade runner had been sunk. At 1800, HMS *Sussex* found the ship and destroyed it by gunfire. C/1 did not land until 1832, after a flight just 10 minutes short of 15 hours. It was one of the longest operational missions the group aircraft ever made, and was rewarded with success. Both Johnson and Benson received British DFCs for their performance.[3]

The same operation, however, brought tragedy to the squadron. The 480th Group had sent out several planes in the search for the blockade runner. One of these aircraft, piloted by Lt. Charles A. Tomlinson, transmitted a message received in garbled form to the effect that it was being attacked by enemy aircraft. The plane was never heard from again. Its position at the time of its radio transmission was about 75 miles from Brest. Possibly it was detected by German radar there, but more likely it simply had the bad luck to run into one of the intermittent Luftwaffe sweeps along the Biscay coastal zone.[4] Tomlinson's encounter was in fact the last occasion when a plane of the 480th Group ran into enemy aircraft near the coast of France. In all, there were only four engagements with the enemy, and one with "friendly" aircraft. Encounters with enemy aircraft are tabulated in Table 4.1.

The 480th Group had little contact with enemy aircraft at this time as compared to its later experience off Cape Finisterre when operating from North Africa, or that of the 479th Group when it operated over the bay in the summer of 1943. The first encounter came on December 3, 1942, while aircraft E/1 (Capt. Kenneth L. Lueke, pilot) was making its first operational patrol. The plane was west-southwest of Fastnet Rock when the crew noticed a twin-engine aircraft approaching from the front and right of the B-24,

Table 4.1. 480th Group Aerial Combats, December 1942–February 1943

Date	Aircraft	Pilot	Remarks
12/3/42	E/1	K. L. Lueke	One JU 88; no damage
1/26/43	C/1	W. S. Johnson	One JU 88, 7 min. action, no damage
1/29/43	C/1	W. S. Johnson	Two JU 88s, damage to B-24 and one JU 88
2/13/43	A/1[a]	W. S. Johnson	The "enemy aircraft" were likely "friendlies"
2/26/43	G/1	C. A. Tomlinson	B-24 apparently shot down by enemy air craft, no survivors

[a]Crew C/1

Sources: Extracted from 1st Antisubmarine Squadron records, 480th Group records; Bernard E. Benson to author, January 8, 1992.

flying a few hundred feet above the American plane. As it passed the Liberator and banked away, its German markings became visible. At that point, to quote copilot Bill Pomeroy, "we poured the coal to our pregnant egg crate" as the German circled around and drew up alongside the B-24, just beyond machine-gun range. As the JU 88 seemed more interested in observing than attacking the big American plane, Pomeroy speculated that the German's interest may have been in the nose blister that housed the B-24's SCR-517 radar scanner. After a while, the JU 88 turned in toward the B-24 and passed over the Liberator without firing, while the American gunners tried without success to hit it. In all, the encounter had lasted 26 minutes.[5]

Crew C of the 1st Antisubmarine Squadron, piloted by 1st Lt. Wayne S. Johnson, seemed particularly prone to encountering enemy aircraft, and even some not-so-friendly Allied aircraft. The "Jonah" in the crew may have been Bill Pomeroy, who had moved from copilot in crew E to that slot in "C for Charlie" when Colonel Roberts reorganized the squadrons in mid-January. At 0835 on January 26, 1943, C/1 lifted off the runway at St. Eval into a rare January day over the bay which the crew's navigator, Bernard E. Benson, was moved to describe as "beautiful."[6] The B-24 flew just above the few clouds that lay at 3,000 feet over a placid Biscay. At about 1010 Benson sighted an aircraft at 4,000 feet about 15 miles away. The aircraft immediately closed to look over the B-24. The American crew recognized it as a JU 88. The German aircraft moved into position ahead of the port bow of the B-24 about a thousand feet above the American aircraft, at which angle the German pilot had the sun at his back. However, as he turned to attack he "overshot the sun a little," so that the American gunners had a good view of him as he made his attack. At roughly 1,000 yards, the JU 88 opened fire, which was soon returned by the left nose gun, upper turret, and left waist gun of the B-24. At the same time, Lieutenant Johnson turned his plane toward the JU 88, shortening the German's attack angle and time for firing. When the German opened fire, "flame was spouting out of his nose. Tracers were passing over our Liberator." The JU 88 itself passed under the Liberator, and did not renew the attack. He appeared to be smoking as he pulled away. The American crew claimed to have damaged the JU 88 while sustaining no damage to their own aircraft. "C for Charlie" then completed its patrol.[7] It had been a mild introduction to aerial combat for the American crew, and the experience was helpful, for on their very next patrol the Americans again encountered enemy aircraft.

The second encounter, on January 29, was more serious than the first. C/1 had departed St. Eval at 0816 to fly a long leg down across the Bay of Biscay. About 90 miles north of the coast of Spain it turned west, flying parallel to the Spanish coast. The B-24 was well along this leg of its patrol by 1330, west-northwest of Cape Finisterre, and approaching 45.00°N/12.00°W, where it would turn northeast toward home.[8] Just then the top turret gunner noticed two JU 88s about a half-mile distant, and flying only a few hundred feet off the water, about 1,000 feet below the American plane. Perhaps fortunately, there was much more cloud, 8/10 stratocumulus with its base at 2,500 feet, than had been the case three days earlier. Copilot Bill Pomeroy recorded almost constant rain and poor visibility on the flight. Although FW 200s could occasionally be found this far out in the bay, it was unusual for the twin-engine JU 88s to be operating so far to the west. Perhaps low fuel prompted them to put in a quick attack, which would have been required in any case, as Lieutenant Johnson prudently headed for the ample cloud cover about 1,200 feet above him.

The two German aircraft climbed quickly and attacked from about 200 feet above the B-24, coming in one behind the other from the starboard bow quarter. As the first JU 88 closed to a range of 800 yards, the bombardier on the right nose gun, the upper turret gunner, and then the right waist gunner opened fire on him. Bernard Benson in the nose compartment observed that "the lead plane passed under us and did not fire as he could not get his nose into position."[9] As Bill Pomeroy saw it from the cockpit, "The German jockeyed his plane about and though he appeared in fairly good position his guns did not fire and he passed beneath us."[10]

It appears Lieutenant Johnson had turned into his attacker, and the first German, concerned to get in a quick attack, was unable to compensate adequately. However, the second JU 88, following along behind his partner, had ample time to adjust for his attack. Further, as the American crew was occupied with the first JU 88, they had almost no time to line up their guns on the second German as he pressed home his attack. "We turned in on him finally," Bill Pomeroy recorded, "but he was in good position and gave us a long burst with everything he had. His nose was covered with the grey smoke of his guns and the flashes were slightly visible."[11] The JU 88 was able to hit the B-24 with two 20mm shells and a large number of machine-gun bullets with little in the way of return fire. Happily for the Americans, most of the hits were on the fuselage of the B-24 just aft of the waist gunners' positions and ahead of the tailplane and rear gunner. Thus no crew members were hit in the attack, nor vital damage inflicted on the Liberator.

The second JU 88 got off without the American gunners ever getting a good shot at him as he passed above the waist gunners at the end of his firing run. The top turret had a firing jam and was unable to fire on the German. By this time Lieutenant Johnson had reached some broken clouds, and he started weaving in and out of these. During this period one JU 88 was again briefly sighted through an opening in the clouds, but that "was the last we saw of the enemy." This is hardly surprising, as the JU 88s could have had little time to waste if they were going to get back to their base with any fuel in their tanks. C/1 proceeded to complete the final leg of its patrol, landing at St. Eval at 1620. Once on the ground, the crew could inspect the JU 88s' handiwork, which amounted to over 100 holes in the fuselage, wing, and one of the vertical fins of the B-24. Most dramatic were the 20mm holes, which were impressively large. The left waist gunner had picked up some shrapnel holes in his flight jacket, but was unwounded, as was the rest of the crew. The Americans claimed to have damaged the first JU 88.[12]

Bill Pomeroy considered that "we were just plain lucky to get out with our necks. Top turret and tail turret each had one gun out of commission. Nose gunner lacked ammunition." He also recorded unhappily that "the right waist gunner was looking out the left waist gunner's window to see where the 1st JU went when the 2nd one came in."[13] In other words, there was still a certain innocence among the Americans about operating in a theater of war.

This crew was destined to have yet a third encounter with unfriendly aircraft, under distinctly unsettling circumstances. On February 13, now flying aircraft A/1, Lieutenant Johnson and his crew left St. Eval at 0506 on an anti-submarine patrol.[14] The American aircraft was barely an hour into its flight, and had just reached 49.10°N/08.20°W, about 80 miles southwest of the Scillies, when the radar operator notified the pilot that there were two aircraft very near them. A few minutes later the radar man reported that one plane was 90 degrees to the right of the Liberator, at about a half-mile, and the other plane 90 degrees to the B-24's left at a quarter-mile. As it was still dark at 6 A.M. in 49°N latitude in mid-February, their positions made clear that they had radar, and that they were positioning themselves for successive crossover attacks on the American Liberator.

Even as the radar operator passed the word, "red tracers started streaking through the night towards us and crossing under our plane." The two attacking aircraft had A/1's position correct, but were slightly off for altitude. Lieutenant Johnson dived at once to bring the B-24 down to just off the waves, whose reflection would make it more difficult for the nightfighters' radar to identify the Liberator. The B-24's bombardier, in the nose of the aircraft, told Johnson to pull the plane up a bit, as the whitecaps of the waves were threatening to throw up spray onto the plane's nose glass, so low had the B-24 descended. At this altitude, the Liberator's radar operator lost the two attacking aircraft, but they also seem to have lost the American plane. "We then turned around and headed back to St. Eval," Lieutenant Benson, the navigator, recorded, "as we were all a little jittery by then."[15] It had indeed been an unnerving sort of attack to undergo, especially in an area where no attack was expected.

At St. Eval, where it touched down at 0710, the plane was inspected and found to be undamaged. The American gunners had never fired their guns, as "we couldn't see anything to shoot at." This was probably a good thing, as it would likely only have helped the nightfighters improve the accuracy of their attacks on the B-24. The attackers were alleged to be British, and later yet, Polish.[16] A third attack within three weeks, and under such conditions, was bound to be unsettling to the American crew, as death came as easily from friendly fire as from the hostile variety. However, the crew was airborne later the same day to fly a somewhat abbreviated seven-hour antisubmarine patrol.[17]

The 480th Group thus had only four known engagements with enemy aircraft, and one with "friendlies," in the course of the 218 operational missions flown from Great Britain. One American Liberator was known lost to enemy air attack during the group's stay in the United Kingdom. This was a fairly typical experience over the Bay of Biscay for this period of the war, and would come to seem downright peaceful compared to the more intensive Luftwaffe activity of the summer and autumn of 1943. As antisubmarine aircraft flew individual patrols, airborne help was seldom available, and a crash landing into the cold waters of the bay was not a pleasant prospect. During this period the risk of such a fate was not too serious. The greatest danger was from encounters with multiple enemy aircraft, which were hard for a single plane to defend against, especially as the Germans were usually JU 88s, faster and quicker in maneuver than the Liberator. In such situations, seeking cloud cover was usually the best course of action, and the coastal area of northwest Europe normally had a good supply of that commodity.

Achievement

The operations of the 480th Antisubmarine Group in the United Kingdom are shown in tabular form in Table 4.2. On average, one sighting was made for every 98.3 hours of operational flying time, and one attack for every 245.75 hours. The difference between the twenty sightings achieved and the eight attacks was usually the consequence of U-boats submerging so quickly that by the time the aircraft could reach an attacking position to release depth

Table 4.2. 480th Group Operations from the United Kingdom

Month	Missions	Hours flown	U-boats Sighted	U-boats Attacked
November 1942	9	78	0	0
December 1942	30	231	2	2
January 1943	58	490	1	0
February 1943	111	1,052	15	5
March 1943[a]	10	116	2	1
	218	1,967	20	8

[a]March 1–5 only

Note: Fractions of hours greater than 30 minutes have been rounded up, and fewer have been rounded down.

Source: "History of AAFAC," 104.

charges such an attack would have been futile. On perhaps too many occasions, there was no "attack" (which required the discharge of a weapon) because depth charges failed to release.

One disappointment was the SCR-517 10-cm radar, which never performed up to expectations in the ETO. Notably, only two of the eight attacks on U-boats occurred as the result of an initial or near-simultaneous radar detection. It was on one of those two occasions, however, that U.519 was sunk, and on the other occasion a U-boat was damaged. While it is not possible to say that the radar gave the attacker a decisive advantage of surprise, at least it helped make possible successful attacks.

Also disappointing was the difficulty in getting the B-24's release mechanism to operate reliably. The AAFAC history attributes this to an incompatibility with the British depth charge. As the group had difficulties releasing depth charges later on, when operating from North Africa and using American depth charges, this argument is not entirely convincing. Assessed results of the eight attacks executed were: one U-boat probably sunk (later confirmed as sunk), one damaged so severely it was forced to abort its patrol and return to port for repairs, and one damaged; two cases of no likely damage; and three cases of insufficient evidence upon which to base an assessment.[18]

Only one of the U-boats attacked in this period attempted to fight back. However, the American aircraft always had to face a threat from German planes operating over the Bay of Biscay, and engagements occurred on several occasions. One of the group's Liberators was lost to enemy aircraft. As already noted, two other aircraft failed to return from operational missions, but there is no evidence regarding how they were lost. Two more aircraft had been lost on the transatlantic flight, and a further two were lost in crashes. From a group whose original equipment had totaled twenty-one aircraft, the loss of seven planes was a 33 percent attrition. That only one of these was known to have been lost to enemy action suggests the very real hazards that characterized flying in the World War II era. The human toll was sixty-five men lost.

Assessment

It had taken a long time to reach a size and proficiency that allowed the group to make a significant contribution to the antisubmarine air effort. The verdict of the author of "The RAF in the Maritime War" on the two American squadrons is not overly flattering, stating that they "were not trained up to the standard necessary for Bay operations. Their navigation was sketchy, they were not trained in night flying, and the SCR.517 radar was not at maximum efficiency."[19] Certainly the squadrons' early performance could justify this description, and it was only very late in the day that the radar problems were surmounted. Yet by February 1943 the performance of the Americans in the bay compared favorably with anything the RAF could achieve there.

In February all units operating under Coastal Command over the U-boat transit area in the Bay of Biscay achieved twenty-nine sightings and thirteen attacks. Those units operating in daylight (as were the two American squadrons) flew 5,270 hours, and achieved twenty-five sightings and eleven attacks. The USAAF aircraft accounted for 20 percent of the daylight flying time (1,052 hours), but no less than 60 percent of all daylight sightings (15 of 25) and 45 percent of all daylight attacks (5 of 11).[20] By any criterion, this was an impressive showing, and the group's achievement was significantly larger than the limited number of aircraft would justify. Despite all shortcomings, the value of the squadrons to Coastal Command's effort was very real, and the expression by the British of "keen regret" at losing them to the Moroccan Sea Frontier (MSF) at a time when they were beginning to achieve their full potential was, we cannot doubt, entirely sincere.[21]

In early March 1943 the group was transferred to Port Lyautey, French Morocco, in the MSF. This had been the two squadrons' original destination before they were detained to work up their efficiency and assist Coastal Command in the Bay of Biscay. Before departure for North Africa, all aircraft in the group underwent repainting, the upper surfaces RAF Mediterranean blue and the lower surfaces white. Other modifications were also undertaken at this time. Planes had their nose guns raised to improve the angle of fire. In most cases, an RAF F-24 mirror camera had already been installed in each aircraft to record the success of depth-charge attacks.[22]

ASW: The State of the Art, March–July 1943

The transfer of the 480th Group to North Africa removed from RAF Coastal Command's order of battle the only aircraft equipped with centimeter radar. This gap was quickly filled by the Leigh-Light Wellingtons of 172 Squadron, which began to operate over the Bay of Biscay with the British ASV Mark III in early March 1943. The ASV Mark III, although similar to the U.S. SCR-517 equipment, was significantly less efficient, evidently because of poor design of the equipment itself, whose production had been hurried. Nonetheless, it shared one great advantage with the SCR-517: the German U-boats' *Metox* receiver could not detect the 10-cm wavelength. This restored to the Leigh-Light Wellingtons the ability to deliver, without warning, nighttime attacks on surfaced U-boats.[23]

The Germans quickly became aware of the situation when a Leigh-Light Wellington attacked a surfaced U-boat in early March. The submarine not only survived the attack but managed to shoot down the Wellington. The U-boat commander promptly informed Admiral Doenitz that he had undergone a night attack without his *Metox* receiver detecting radar emissions before the event. Doenitz drew the correct conclusion, that the Allies had an airborne radar his subs could not detect, and which left them naked to night attack. Unfortunately for the German submariners, there were serious problems in producing a receiver that would detect 10-cm wavelength transmissions, so for a considerable time they would continue to have no warning against night attacks. The Allied ability to outpace the Germans in scientific development and technological adaptation worked to tilt the scales in the battle of aircraft against U-boats.[24]

The Bay of Biscay Campaign Continues

The British, for their part, were anxious to capitalize on their advantage, which they knew would be temporary. Sooner or later, and the British feared it would be sooner, the Germans would get an effective receiver to sea. It was vital for Coastal Command to make the most of its temporary lead in technology before it vanished, as had happened with the metric radar in the autumn of 1942. The theory that supported Coastal Command's efforts in the bay in 1943 was the technique pioneered in Operation GONDOLA in February, the idea of "the unclimbable fence," that is, to lay on air patrols in sufficient density over a designated area of the bay so that statistically every U-boat should be sighted at least once as it crossed through that zone. The calculations were not too difficult, as it was known that the zone needed only to be wider than the distance a U-boat could travel across the bay when observing a policy of maximum submergence. The difficulty was that the fence always had gaps and holes in it. Both human observers and radar equipment would fail to function up to the assumed averages. Bad weather and mechanical difficulties that shortened or grounded scheduled flights also opened holes in the fence. Despite these known weaknesses, the British were convinced that the effort was worth making.

GONDOLA was only the first of the planned high-density operations over the Bay of Biscay. In March and April of 1943, 19 Group of Coastal Command made a renewed effort in a pair of operations known as ENCLOSE and ENCLOSE II. The February operation had been limited by the fact that only the dozen or so aircraft of the 480th Group available had centimetric radar, and the Americans were trained to fly only in daylight. For the two ENCLOSE operations, thirty-two planes were available with ASV Mark III, and these could operate at night.[25] Much better results could then be hoped for. However, results were disappointing. These are summarized in Table 4.3.

The message that the Coastal Command leadership drew from these efforts was that yet greater efforts were needed to produce the results desired. So in late April a further high-density flying effort was laid on, Operation DERANGE. While the results in U-boats actually destroyed remained less than hoped for, the increased aerial activity had its effect on Admiral Doenitz, who had already shown himself susceptible to this sort of pressure. As he had

Table 4.3. High-Density Operations in the Bay of Biscay, Early 1943

	GONDOLA (February 6–15)	ENCLOSE (March 20–28)	ENCLOSE II (April 6–13)
U-boats present	40	41	25
Sightings	18	26	11
Attacks	7	15	4
Sinkings	1	1	1
Sightings as percentage of U-boats present	45%	63%	44%
Attacks as percentage of sightings	39%	58%	36%
Sinkings as percentage of attacks	14%	7%	25%

Note: The U-boats lost were U.519 (February 10), U.665 (March 22), and U.376 (April 10).
Source: A. Price, *Aircraft versus Submarine,* 120, with additional data by author.

when the Leigh-Light Wellingtons first appeared over the bay in the summer of 1942, he again ordered his U-boats in late April of 1943 to remain submerged at night when crossing the bay. During daylight, they were to surface only long enough to recharge their batteries. As Coastal Command always had more aircraft able to operate by day than by night, Admiral Doenitz had improved the odds of one of his subs being spotted while crossing the bay. On the other hand, the U-boat at least had a sporting chance of spotting the approaching plane and getting below before the latter could attack. Both sides thus girded themselves for a renewed struggle in the Biscay transit area.

May 1943

May 1943 proved to be the critical month in the Battle of the Atlantic. It was in this month that the strength of the surface and air protection for the main transatlantic convoys at last became so formidable that the U-boats stood little chance of fighting their way through to the merchant ships. This was demonstrated convincingly by the brutal losses the U-boat force suffered in that month, while Allied shipping losses declined from the preceding months. Both the RAF and USAAF looked upon convoy escort, however, as essentially defensive in character. Accordingly, in May 19 Group of Coastal Command did not relax its effort to carry the battle to the German submarines in the bay transit area. In the first week of May the RAF group achieved more success than ever before. U-boats were sighted in the transit area on seventy-one occasions, and attacks followed in forty-three cases. The results were three U-boats sunk and three sufficiently damaged that they had to abort their war patrols and return to their bases for repairs.[26]

It was also a notable indicator for the future that on seventeen occasions, when the U-boats involved would have had trouble submerging before coming under attack, they chose to stay on the surface and fight it out with their flak. This development was welcomed at Coastal Command headquarters. Any added losses in aircraft as a result of such tactics was more than compensated by the improved chances of making a lethal attack on a U-boat. For all of May, six of the record forty-one U-boats lost in that month were sunk in the Bay of Biscay. Primary losses had come in the Atlantic convoy zone. On May 24, recognizing that his submarines were being overwhelmed by the forces deployed against them, Admiral Doenitz called off his "wolfpack" operations against the well-defended North Atlantic convoys and summoned the bulk of his U-boats home to their ports to regroup for a renewed effort, aided by improved weapons and electronic sensors. As an interim measure, he would scatter his forces in hopes of spreading the Allied ASW forces.

Acutely sensitive to the need to preserve morale in his battered forces, Doenitz decided on May 29 that one way to achieve improved confidence in his men was to sail his U-boats in groups across the bay, and for these packs deliberately to accept battle with Coastal Command aircraft. Initial results of this tactic were encouraging. As the ASW aircraft normally patrolled alone, this meant one plane was confronted with the combined AA fire of several U-boats. To attack one of them brought the plane under fire from the others, which did not have to worry about direct attack themselves.

But in mid-June, the German admiral had second thoughts; after all, the task of his subs was to sink ships, not to shoot down airplanes. Thus he modified his orders. The U-boats would continue to sail in groups, and to surface by day, but they were not deliberately to seek battle. Their surfaced hours were limited to the minimum four or so in every twenty-four necessary to recharge batteries, and if they could submerge before coming under attack they were to do so.[27] Between the group tactic and the maximum submergence policy, the U-boats had a much less hazardous June than May had been.

RAF Coastal Command Tactical Policy

While Admiral Doenitz was changing his tactics, his British adversaries were refining their attack doctrine. By mid-1943 considerable data on earlier attacks on U-boats had been collected and analyzed, and conclusions drawn. In particular, the use of cameras to document attacks had permitted a degree of certainty in analysis previously hard to achieve. This was of great benefit in improving assessments and in convincing crews of the extent of their range and line errors.[28]

In mid-June of 1943 Coastal Command was able to issue updated tactical instructions for its aircrews incorporating its accumulated experience.[29] The importance of rotating both visual lookouts and radar operators in order to maintain the efficiency of the search for U-boats was stressed. The latter, in particular, were to stand watches of not more than 45 minutes, and be relieved for not less than an hour before returning to the radar scope. In effect, this required no fewer than three members of each aircrew trained in the use of the radar equipment, and all but dictated use of four-engine planes with crews of eight to eleven men.

The weapon of choice continued to be the Mark XI 250-pound Torpex depth charge, considered lethal within 19 feet of a submarine's pressure hull. It was normally set to explode at a depth of 25 feet. The preferred release height was 50 feet, although it could be safely dropped from higher. In addition to this depth charge, the RAF introduced in 1943 a depth bomb of 600 pounds weight, set to explode at a depth of 35 feet. This weapon had a lethal radius of 28 feet. It was released from as high as 5,000 feet, and a special bombsight was used for it. Only the two Halifax squadrons of Coastal Command were ever equipped with this weapon, but they did have some success with it.

A controversial aspect of the revised Coastal Command instructions regarded the spacing for the Mark XI depth charges. This was prescribed in mid-June to be set at 100 feet between charges dropped by eye. As this would open up nonlethal gaps in a stick of depth charges, it met resistance at the squadron level, and crews required some persuasion to accept it. What analysis of past attacks showed, however, was that there was a somewhat greater probability of an entire stick falling short or over the target than the probability of a U-boat's pressure hull, about 20 feet across at the widest point, coming entirely within one of the gaps in a stick with a 100-foot spacing. This was especially the case if the line of attack was at less than 60 degrees to the U-boat's track. The tactical instructions did relent on this issue to the degree of allowing a 60-foot spacing for sticks of six depth charges dropped with the aid of a low-level bombsight, but not for sticks of fewer than six.

Tactical instructions stressed once again the importance of attacking a submarine by the most direct line of approach. It was now recommended, however, that the attack should be as near along the line of the U-boat's track as possible. This worked to reduce the negative effect of the 100-foot spacing, while experience had shown that pilots had an easier time lining up to make an attack when it was nearly parallel to the course the U-boat was following. Given the low probability of dropping depth charges accurately when a U-boat had been submerged a half-minute or more, the release of depth charges in such cases was discouraged. With the 600-pound depth bomb and its greater lethal radius, attacks as late as 40 seconds following submergence were allowed.

The new tactical instructions accommodated the emerging U-boat tactic of fighting back on the surface. In such cases, considerable discretion was allowed the aircraft commander on whether and how to attack. It noted, however, that "he must remember that the primary reason for his existence is . . . to kill U/Boats. . . . It is no coincidence that recently by far the larger proportion of certain or probable kills have been U/Boats which stayed on the surface and fought back."[30] Attacks from directly ahead on surfaced U-boats intent on fighting back was recommended, as the submarine commander had difficulty bringing his flak to bear on a plane attacking from this angle. The U-boat commander was, however, likely to turn away from the attacking plane, thus allowing his guns to bear. Fortunately for the aircrews, a turning U-boat made a poor gun platform.

Evolving American ASW Doctrine

The Americans were no less active than the British in applying the techniques of operations analysis to the increasing amount of data available for such examination. In late July of 1943, the AAFAC promulgated the conclusions it had drawn in the form of a set of standard operating procedures.[31] These showed both similarities and differences in comparison to Coastal Command practice. Realistically, the American guide noted that chances to attack U-boats will always be rare, and that crews performed valuable service simply by their presence over the water, which forced the U-boats to submerge, thus significantly degrading their operational efficiency. It also stressed that attacks on U-boats submerged more than 15 seconds were generally futile, a more realistic attitude than Coastal Command's rather optimistic standard, which considered that attacks as late as 30 seconds (or even 40 seconds in the case of the 600-pound bomb) were worthwhile. However, AAFAC was less hard-headed about patrol length and rotation of lookouts. It adhered to the policy that "missions over five (5) hours duration are increasingly unproductive" in the face of evidence to the contrary. And while it stated that radar watches over 30 minutes in duration (as opposed to Coastal Command's limit of 45 minutes) reduced operator efficiency, it provided no guidelines on how to organize and rotate a radar watch.

American ASW weapons appeared at first glance to be more numerous than the British, with no fewer than seven marks of depth charge described. But in fact these all derived from two weapons.[32] First in use had been the Mark 17 325-pound, TNT-filled depth charge, which had a lethal radius of about 17 feet. The Americans, rather behind the British, were just in the process of adopting Torpex as a filling for this charge in mid-1943, which increased its weight to 350 pounds and its lethal radius to 21 feet. Variants of the Mark 17 were the Mark 41 (TNT-filled) and the Mark 44 and Mark 47 (Torpex-filled). The Marks 17 and 44 had rounded noses, the Marks 41 and 47 flat noses. The other main weapon was a 650-pound depth charge, designated the Mark 29. Improved variants were the Mark 37 and Mark 38. All used TNT and had a lethal diameter of 25 feet.[33]

American attack doctrine, like the British, prescribed attacking by the most direct route. But it differed sharply on the subject of stick spacing, where an interval of 50 feet was standard for the 325/350-pound depth charges, and 70 feet was normal for the 650-pound weapons. This ensured no gaps between lethal radii in a stick, but it also shortened the length of the stick, thus placing a premium on the accuracy of the attack. One British aviator who agreed with the Americans in preferring a shorter stick without gaps was Squadron Leader Terence Bulloch, Coastal Command's most successful antisubmarine aviator. During 1942 he had become convinced of the virtue of the closely spaced stick; indeed, he even used a 25-foot spacing with the 250-pound depth charges.[34] Bulloch, however, was an extraordinarily gifted aviator, and he trained his crew to his own meticulous operational standard. Consequently, his attacks were more accurate than the average pilot achieved.

By late August 1943, Coastal Command showed signs of retreating from its emphasis on the 100-foot stick spacing. It still prescribed that interval for an attack where fewer than six depth charges were released by eye. Non-Leigh-Light equipped aircraft operating at night were also to use the 100-foot stick spacing, as were Leigh-Light aircraft dropping a stick of fewer than six depth charges. Otherwise, it was abandoned. When six or more depth charges were released by eye, a spacing of 60 feet was now described as ideal. When the new Mark III low-level bombsight was employed, the spacing varied from 70 feet for a stick of four, to 50 feet for a stick of six, to only 45 feet for a stick of eight.[35]

While the widespread equipment of aircraft with the low-level bombsight and growing familiarity and facility in using it were the ostensible reasons for the retreat from the 100-foot spacing, one suspects this was the fig leaf that covered Coastal Command headquarters' tactical withdrawal in the face of opposition in the operating squadrons. In any case, by the time the August instructions were promulgated, the hostilities in the Bay of Biscay had passed their highest point of intensity. Such a high number of engagements would not come again to the bay area until June 1944 when the U-boats made one last effort to impede the Normandy landings.

The Battle of the Bay Peaks

Admiral Doenitz's initial sailings of his U-boats in groups across the bay at the end of May had alerted Coastal Command to the need to adjust tactics to cope with the development. Accordingly, a planned flying routine was worked out whereby three times a day a force of seven planes flew along parallel tracks through the designated high-intensity search zone. On sighting a pack of U-boats, a plane on one of these parallel sweeps contacted its headquarters, which could then direct some or all of the other aircraft engaged on the sweep to concentrate on the surfaced group of U-boats.[36] Not until the last half of July, however, did these altered tactics begin to produce the remarkable spectacle of air-sea battles involving two or three U-boats and on occasion a half-dozen or more aircraft. One such action on July 30, 1943, saw three U-boats sunk by a combined air and surface ship assault that included seven planes from five different RAF, RAAF, and USAAF squadrons.[37]

Losses of this sort were bound to stimulate Admiral Doenitz to rethink his tactics. As early as July 18, U-boat commanders at sea had criticized the group tactics. However, Doenitz persisted on the basis of reports indicating that in the first 20 days of July, only three boats had been lost from groups, which constituted 75 percent of the U-boats crossing the bay, while four boats had been sunk from the 25 percent crossing the bay alone. The mass combats of late July and early August were decisive. On August 2, all U-boats that had sailed the previous day were recalled to their bases, groups in transit were disbanded, and inbound U-boats instructed to hug the coast of Spain. U-boats henceforth were to proceed alone, surfacing only at night, and keeping as close as possible to Spanish territorial waters, where the land reflection would make radar detection somewhat more difficult, while at the same time the planes had to worry about violating neutral Spanish air space.[38]

The constant changes of tactics by their leader, at times at heavy cost to the U-boats, could hardly have inspired the German submariners to invest overwhelming confidence in Admiral Doenitz's leadership. Nonetheless, in early August, after several false tries, he had finally got it right. The policy of maximum avoidance of Allied air patrols over the bay was the correct one, as it had always been. The German admiral's follies of the May–July period in the Bay of Biscay were at an end. At what cost is shown in Table 4.4.

Table 4.4. U-boat Losses in the Bay of Biscay Transit Zone

| | U-boats | | Days to sink |
Time period	Sunk	Damaged	one U-boat
7/1/42–4/26/43 (300 days)	8	16	37.5
4/27–8/2/43 (97 days)	26	17	3.7
8/3/43–5/28/44 (300 days)	11	9	27.0

Source: Price, *Aircraft versus Submarine*, 165.

The Luftwaffe Appears

Ever since the trend of increasing losses in the Bay of Biscay had become evident to U-boat headquarters in early 1943, Admiral Doenitz, now commander-in-chief of the entire German Navy, had renewed his efforts to get the Luftwaffe to play a more active role here. The critical losses in May finally produced an increased allocation of JU 88s to the bay area. The JU 88s, however, followed a policy of flying in packs of about six aircraft, so as to be able to concentrate their firepower to destroy the large, four-engine Allied ASW aircraft, which might survive the attacks of one or two German planes. The result of this policy was to limit the Luftwaffe to two or three daily sweeps by the JU 88s. The result of the pack activity could be impressive, as on June 1, 1943, when the twenty-three JU 88s massed to operate that day claimed the destruction of four British aircraft, including two Wellingtons and an unfortunate Dakota that had turned up in the wrong place at the wrong time. From June until the late autumn of 1943, the presence of the JU 88s made life significantly more dangerous for the Allied ASW fliers.[39] What it did not do was lessen the Allied aerial interdiction of the Bay of Biscay transit zone.

5

The 480th Antisubmarine Group in North Africa

A Move in the Wrong Direction

As the crisis of the Battle of the Atlantic was building in the spring of 1943, and as the culmination of the struggle to interdict the flow of U-boats across the Bay of Biscay transit zone moved toward its peak of intensity in the summer of 1943, the 480th Antisubmarine Group was fated to be moved away from the center of greatest antisubmarine activity. This was directly contrary to the concept that underlay the organization of the AAFAC, that it would provide a mobile striking force of antisubmarine aircraft that could be concentrated where the hunting for U-boats was best. Ironically, the 480th Group was not only withdrawn from the best arena for offensive ASW operations, but in its new location it would come under the operational command of the USN, which had not yet embraced such an offensive orientation for ASW. The group thus found itself in the situation the AAFAC had been set up to avoid—the tying down of USAAF assets under a naval area command committed to maximum coverage of convoys, the defensive mission the USAAF staff so deplored.

Yet more ironically, the group's movement occurred at American instigation. This was truly shooting oneself in the foot, and reveals the central flaw in the doctrine of offensive ASW as practiced by the USAAF in the World War II era, that the squadrons were not very mobile or able to respond very swiftly to changed conditions. They simply required too large an infrastructure to be picked up and dumped down as the moves on the ASW chessboard might dictate. And it took much too long to decide when and where to move them. If more irony were needed, the most mobile squadrons were usually the USN's amphibious patrol squadrons, which were designed to work, at least initially, from tenders in rather spartan surroundings until an adequate infrastructure could be built up. The Navy was usually better able to support its patrol squadrons under such primitive conditions. Unfortunately, the Navy was also the service most reluctant to employ its patrol aircraft for other than convoy defense, thus negating to some extent the advantage of greater flexibility. For the USAAF group, what appeared initially a happy change of locale, and especially climate, would all too swiftly degenerate into disappointment and frustration.

Port Lyautey, French Morocco

The move from St. Eval, Cornwall, to Craw Field, Port Lyautey, French Morocco, had in a sense always been in the cards. Harry Hopkins had told Prime Minister Churchill that the assignment of the planes to the ETO could only be temporary, and in the aftermath of the Casablanca Conference they were ordered to move to North Africa.[1] It was a principle with the Americans, that while they were willing to be good allies, their own units were not to be absorbed into British organizations on the model of several squadrons from the British dominions, but rather to operate under American organizations, or those that were fully integrated Allied forces with Americans sharing fully in command positions and decisions. This is what happened to the 1st Antisubmarine Group (Provisional), which on the first of March 1943 became the 2037th Antisubmarine Wing (Provisional).

On March 26, 1943, the 480th Antisubmarine Group (as I shall continue to refer to it throughout, although it received its final designation only on June 21) had sixteen aircraft in North Africa with 96 officers and 281 enlisted men in the flight echelon, and 11 officers and 529 enlisted men in the ground echelon. Sixteen aircraft was well short of the group's establishment of twenty-four, and they lacked the range of B-24s being newly modified in the

United States with additional wing tanks, and which were designated as very long range (extended), or VLR(E). By June 23, after three months in North Africa, Lt. Col. Jack Roberts, the group CO, could report he had nineteen of the VLR(E) type in the group, and six more were in transit from the United States.[2] The new aircraft came with olive-drab upper surfaces in contrast to the planes from the United Kingdom, which had RAF Mediterranean-blue upper surfaces. There was also a steady flow of new crews coming out from advanced training at Langley Field, Virginia.

Replacement crews did not have a much easier time with the transatlantic crossing than had the first crews. In March 1943 Capt. Hugh D. Maxwell Jr. and his crew left the United States via the southern route to join the group. Maxwell recalled that "all down the coast of South America we flew through tropical storms and torrential rains. I couldn't believe that the engines would continue to run or the plane to fly in some of them, where it was like being underwater."[3] He also remembered the flight as the first occasion he encountered St. Elmo's fire. "Electricity would roll in balls around on the wings, then move out and form a circle around the propeller tips, reform into balls and roll all around the outside of the airplane. Weird! And scary!"[4]

During the critical cross-Atlantic hop from Natal to Dakar, the plane repeatedly encountered tropical weather fronts that threw off its navigation. When the navigator could finally establish the plane's location, it was far south of the planned course and there was not enough fuel to reach Dakar. Accordingly, Maxwell landed, of necessity, at Freetown, Sierra Leone. After a safe landing on the marginally adequate field there, the American Liberator made its way up the coast to Dakar, from where Maxwell departed with an approved flight plan to land at Marrakech. To his surprise, at the radio checkpoint at Tindouf, located in the desert in far western Algeria, Maxwell was instructed to land. Questioning this instruction, he was informed that there were already over a dozen aircraft sitting in the desert at Tindouf; the weather over the Atlas range was too severe to attempt flying over the mountains to Marrakech. This had been so for three days, yet Dakar was still clearing planes for the flight into Marrakech. During their unexpected and unhappy stay of several days at Tindouf, Maxwell and his crew "almost burned up by day and almost froze to death by night." The facility, only a radio checkpoint (a 50,000-pound Liberator was landed not on a runway but on the hard-packed sand), could furnish the numerous crews stuck there with no more than K-rations. They slept in their planes as there were no beds. When Maxwell was cleared to continue his flight, his destination was unexpectedly changed to Port Lyautey. The reason for this became clear when the B-24 landed at Craw Field, where its crew discovered the 480th Group, which they had thought was in England.[5]

A manageable problem at Craw Field was the continuing shortfall in personnel assigned to the group compared to authorized strength. In May the group reported that while the group headquarters and the two squadrons had a total authorized strength of 164 officers and 778 enlisted men, the actual numbers assigned were 130 and 670, or 79 percent and 86 percent of authorization. However, the bulk of the shortfall was in the group headquarters, at 35 percent of authorization, while the squadrons were at 90 percent (1st) and 92 percent (2nd), respectively. This problem was never entirely eliminated, but by September 30, the 1st Squadron had 339 enlisted men and 66 officers on its roster, including 11 combat crews to man 12 aircraft. This was slightly over authorized numbers of officers and slightly under authorization for enlisted men. In short, the group had an adequate if not generous number of personnel to accomplish its mission.[6] A real problem upon arrival in North Africa was the almost nonexistent recreation facilities at Port Lyautey. This was serious because, unlike England, there were inadequate alternative activities in the towns and cities of Morocco to occupy the interest and energies of the group's personnel. Colonel Roberts thus developed a program of athletics in an effort to keep his men occupied, fit, and in good spirits.[7]

The SCR-517 Radar

A brighter picture was that of radar operation and maintenance. The SCR-517 had proven hard to maintain and calibrate during the group's stay in the United Kingdom. A concerted effort to get the best out of the equipment, and greater experience with its capabilities and shortcomings, allowed for great improvement in North Africa. The 1st Antisubmarine Squadron could point proudly to the 10-week period from June 5 to August 13, which encompassed the most intense period of flying, during which time the squadron completed 207 missions with 1,980 radar operating hours all told, for an efficiency rating of 92.3 percent, and an average of 91.6 percent fully satisfactory performance.[8]

Not only was the equipment functioning more reliably but its performance had also improved in North Africa. Coastal Command's ORS had studied the 10-cm radar's effectiveness and found it only marginally better than the British LR ASV Mark II. At an altitude of 1,500 feet, the SCR-517 radar had been able to detect an aircraft at an average range of about 8 miles, a fishing vessel at about 12 miles, and a convoy at 30 miles. Coastal Command estimated the average range at which the 10-cm radar would detect a U-boat as about 8 miles, compared to the average for the LR ASV Mark II of 7 miles. Under these circumstances, the greatest advantage of the centimetric radar was simply that the Germans could not detect it.[9]

An Antisubmarine Warfare Operational Research Group (ASWORG) study completed in late May 1943 showed improvement in all detection ranges for the SCR-517. The average range for detecting an aircraft had risen to 14 miles, and for fishing vessels to 15 miles. Convoys were detected at an average range of 40 miles. The ASWORG report anticipated a comparable sort of improvement in detecting U-boats. This would project an average range for U-boat detections of about 12 to 14 miles.[10] In fact, actual detections would slightly exceed the upper end of this range. The reasons for the improved performance were described as the drier atmosphere, improved maintenance, and improved operator skill. Accumulated experience with the equipment was important in this regard. The ASWORG report also verified the findings of Coastal Command's ORS regarding altitude. The British operations analysts found little variation in detection ranges with the SCR-517 in the altitude range between 500 and 4,000 feet, where most ASW missions were flown. Accordingly, the choice of best operating altitude within that range could be made independent of radar considerations. On larger targets, notably convoys and land, detection range rose directly with a rise in altitude. The ASWORG investigator got the same results.[11]

The B-24D Liberator: Strengths and Weaknesses

The B-24D itself had proved to be a highly reliable aircraft, well suited to antisubmarine work. By March 1943, however, the group had identified weaknesses and recommended improvements, based on its operational experience.[12] The aircraft lacked adequate firepower in both the lower rear quadrant and from the nose. There was also a lack of adequate working space for both navigator and bombardier in the nose compartment. The bomb-bay racks had proven to be unreliable and hard to maintain in satisfactory working condition. There also remained the problem of the plane's center of gravity, which was just slightly too far aft, and gave the Liberator its characteristic "head's up" attitude in flight, revealed in many photos of the World War II era. More seriously, it made landings tricky if one wished to avoid dragging the after fuselage along the ground. Certainly, close attention to weight distribution was required with this aircraft.

The reaction of the USAAF's staff to the 480th Group's list of aircraft shortcomings was that antisubmarine aircraft operated at a low enough altitude that the tail turret was adequate for rearward defense; the problem of defending the lower rear quadrant was best remedied by going down "onto the deck" when under aerial attack. The problem of the nose was more serious. However, plans were well along to produce a B-24 model with a nose turret, which was eventually accomplished. This would, however, further cramp the already inadequate working area for navigator and bombardier. The cold comfort offered by USAAF headquarters was that "the present crowded conditions must suffice." For the antisubmarine groups, that certainly remained the case. Later models of the B-24, however, had a stretched nose to help deal with the problem. With regard to the bomb release mechanism, an improved design was already in place, which used cams rather than the elaborate "push-pull rods and bell cranks that caused most of the troubles in the old system."[13]

In April, the 480th Group made specific proposals to the AAFAC for modification of the B-24s intended for antisubmarine work. These included moving the radar and radio operators' stations from just behind the pilot and copilot to a position over the rear bomb bay. The earliest Liberator model, the LB-30 (which in fact went to the British), had its radio operator in this position. The goal was to eliminate the crowded situation in the cockpit area. The navigator would then be moved from the nose compartment to behind the pilot. This proposal, however, ran afoul of the critical center-of-gravity problem in the Liberator, as it would have shifted a considerable weight aft in the plane. Consequently, it was held over for further consideration by AAFAC. The 480th Group report also stressed that "the need for longer and longer antisubmarine missions is becoming apparent."[14]

By June 1943, the AAFAC had defined its ideal Liberator, modified so as to provide maximum range and weapons load, improved forward firepower to cope with U-boats fighting back on the surface, improved location of essential equipment, and "maximum comfort and ease of operation of all equipment for crew members."[15] This last was not a luxury, but necessary to efficiency, especially on very long flights. Finally, it would contain "adequate and effective overwater safety equipment." The matter of maximum range had already been taken in hand by the AAFAC, and all of its new Liberators were equipped with auxiliary wing tanks. This produced the VLR(E)-type B-24D mentioned above. A replacement program for the older variety B-24Ds in the 480th Group was underway by June. Installation of a nose turret was still in development, but progressing well. This would eventually deal with the need for improved forward firepower in the face of U-boat flak.

The AAFAC also proposed to give effect to the April recommendations of the 480th Group, shifting navigator, radar operator, and radio operator aft in the plane. The nose turret's weight would partly offset this movement of weight aft, but more had to be done. The AAFAC proposed removing the tail turret and substituting in its place a pair of manually controlled, flexible .50-caliber machine guns. The plane's center of gravity would further be helped by the addition of armor to protect the bombardier's position and frontal armor for the pilot's and copilot's positions. The AAFAC would go out of business before these changes could be incorporated in operational aircraft. More immediately, a galley kit was "now standard equipment" and was being distributed to all antisubmarine units.

With regard to safety, the AAFAC had authorized all antisubmarine planes to carry an additional life raft. A shipwreck kit had also been standardized, "and will be shipped to all organizations within the next few days." There were other marginal improvements in safety equipment. The most serious safety problem, the proclivity of the B-24 to cave in and break up in the area of the bomb-bay doors upon colliding with the water, was beyond adequate remedy short of a major aircraft redesign, which appears never to have been seriously considered by the AAFAC. Finally, the 480th Group's now aged SCR-517 radar, no longer in production, would be gradually replaced with the SCR-717B set, which was of improved efficiency and used the PPI form of presentation. In all, this constituted an impressive upgrade for the B-24D, and showed the responsiveness of the AAFAC to input from operating units. It was only the disbandment of the AAFAC itself that terminated the full improvement program as far as the USAAF was concerned.

Command Problems in the Moroccan Sea Frontier

In the Moroccan Sea Frontier (MSF) the 480th Antisubmarine Group came under the operational control of the USN, specifically Fleet Air Wing (FAW) 15, and was assigned to the Northwest African Coastal Air Force (NACAF) for administration. This was a combined Anglo-American command, with an RAF air marshal as CO and an American general as his deputy. The head of NACAF, Air Vice-Marshal Hugh Lloyd, was commendably prompt in visiting his new American outfit, flying to Craw Field on April 3. How he assessed the unit is perhaps another matter. He had to be flown out on April 4 aboard a Navy Catalina, after the USAAF plane that was to carry him taxied into a hangar and damaged its wing.[16]

Colonel Roberts found the command arrangements in the MSF unsatisfactory, especially with regard to operational control. His unit had developed its ASW experience under the operational control of RAF Coastal Command, and found that the USN operated in significantly different ways from the British organization. Further, Roberts clearly preferred RAF antisubmarine doctrine to that of the Navy.[17]

The superior level of efficiency in radio communications, radio direction-finding, and air-sea rescue facilities that existed in Great Britain in its fifth year of war did not exist in the primitive circumstances of Northwest Africa in mid-1943. Understandably, the 480th personnel were disappointed by this, however unavoidable it was. But the root cause of the disappointment was friction between the two American services. A particularly sore point with Roberts was the Navy's refusal at first to allow the five intelligence officers assigned to the 480th group to perform briefings and postoperations crew interrogations, although they had been performing these duties at St. Eval. Nor was the group allowed to assign its personnel to watch duty in the control room at Craw Field, as they also had at St. Eval.[18]

Colonel Roberts felt that the briefings provided to his crews by Navy officers were so unsatisfactory that he insisted on their being rebriefed by a 480th Group officer before flying a mission. In short, it was not a happy situation. This standoff between the two American services lasted until May 24, when the Navy at last relented, allowing USAAF intelligence officers to stand regular working shifts along with their naval colleagues and to provide intelligence briefings to crews of both services without distinction.[19]

In Roberts's view, the Navy placed too much emphasis on providing air escort for convoys when intelligence reports indicated no U-boats operating in their vicinity, and too little emphasis on flying patrols over areas where intelligence indicated the presence of U-boats. In short, he wished a more "offensive" doctrine than that practiced by the FAW 15. As he wrote in May:

> The unsatisfactory nature of our present status and operations is due . . . to the difference in the fundamental conception of Moroccan Sea Frontier and this Hqtrs [480th Group] as to how best to defeat the submarines, whether offensively (on sweeps and covering threatened convoys) or defensively (covering all U.S. convoys at all times to the exclusion of offensive sweeps and coverages).[20]

In fact, by March 1943 the Navy and the RAF at Gibraltar had succeeded in driving the U-boats far enough from the coast that the majority of the time most convoys could approach the shipping traffic funnel at the Straits of Gibraltar with reasonable immunity from submarine attack. And from about May/June onward, Allied intelligence on U-boat movements was good enough to permit a high degree of confidence in estimates of their reported positions. When the 480th Group arrived in the MSF in March, however, that naval organization was only beginning to respond to the changed situation and to assign aircraft missions accordingly. Roberts, fresh from the Bay of Biscay campaign, which required only a peripheral concern for the safety of convoys, was intolerant of the Navy's attitudes, which had been appropriate enough to the critical period of the TORCH landings and their immediate aftermath in the period November 1942–January 1943, but which were harder to justify in the changed situation. The notoriously poor relations between the two American services in the World War II era probably served as a background to this difference of views and to Roberts's intense dissatisfaction.

Colonel Roberts's preference for RAF to USN operational control led him to propose that all antisubmarine operations in the region be placed under British control at Gibraltar.[21] As the RAF was operating ASW aircraft from both there and for a time also from Agadir, to the south of the Americans at Port Lyautey, the proposal had merit. The British, for their part, viewed the MSF as an anomaly within an area of primary British interest and strategic control. Thus on April 3, 1943, Roberts flew to Gibraltar for a meeting with the British authorities. The meeting's agenda was "to review the antisubmarine organization both surface and air in the Western Approaches to Morocco and Gibraltar to ensure the best arrangements . . . for concerted action against U-boats." This delightfully bland description covered a combined RAF-

USAAF effort to heave the USN out of its control of ASW air operations in the area. Among the meeting's recommendations was that "all aircraft employed in operations over the sea from GIBRALTAR or MOROCCO are under the general operational control of the Air Officer Commanding Gibraltar."[22]

Only two things flawed this happy meeting of minds: the agreement was "subject to covering approval by higher U.S. authority," and no representative of the Commander, MSF, was present.[23] This latter authority was, however, soon heard from. He notified the commander-in-chief of the U.S. Fleet (Cominch), with copies to all concerned, that he did *not* agree with the proposed arrangements, and that his "position has been and will continue to be that the control of the Moroccan Sea Frontier is a U.S. Naval responsibility," and that "its primary mission is the protection of convoys."[24] On this reef the Gibraltar negotiators came to grief. The USN would not agree to any change in existing arrangements, and Colonel Roberts was left to deal as best he could with the naval authorities in the sea frontier.[25]

Roberts continued his efforts to shake free of U.S. naval control. In mid-May he was writing that "I am going to make a supreme bid to get us out from under the close operational control of the USN." In June he was still trying to get his unit transferred out of the MSF.[26] The response to this effort, "which appears to be final, is that the Navy will never consent to let us leave here," he recorded dolefully.[27] By June 1943, however, relations between FAW 15 and the 480th Antisubmarine Group were improving. With the passage of time and the steady inflow of equipment, the efficiency of communications and the quality of services furnished at Craw Field, which was officially a U.S. naval air station, improved, gradually resolving a major area of dissatisfaction from the USAAF's point of view.

By July the MSF was running a sophisticated submarine plot, which was able, using excellent Allied intelligence, to predict the likely location of U-boats 24 hours into the future. This allowed the aviators to plan which areas to cover on the coming day's flights in order to have the best chance of finding a German submarine. This hunting of U-boats in areas of high probability was a very long way from the USN's earlier insistence on close cover of convoys and suggests the degree to which that service was responding to both improved certainty in intelligence reports and the experience of the RAF and USAAF in offensively oriented ASW. The efficiency of this approach is suggested by the fact that between December 5, 1942, and July 15, 1943, over 90 percent of the twenty-two U-boat sightings by aircraft on ASW patrols (as opposed to flying convoy cover) occurred within 80 miles of the MSF's plot of where a U-boat should be. The average error was only 41 miles.[28]

Colonel Roberts still rated air-ground liaison as only "reasonably satisfactory."[29] Nonetheless, he felt able to make a flying trip back to the United States at the end of June to consult with AAFAC about the future of his organization. Departing on June 30, he was back at Craw Field on July 23, having returned via the United Kingdom, where he picked up a group aircraft that had been left at St. Eval for lack of spare parts. This was the last of the group's original and surviving aircraft to reach North Africa, four months after the group's departure from England. But this was the most notable achievement of his trip; with regard to the future he was able to say little.[30]

Operations in the Moroccan Sea Frontier, March–June 1943

By the time the 1st and 2nd Antisubmarine Squadrons arrived at Port Lyautey, the combined efforts of the RAF and USN had steadily pushed the German U-boats out from the coast, so much so that one was rarely sighted within 400 miles of shore. In the March–June period, twelve U-boat sightings were made, most beyond the 400-mile line. As the Navy PBYs worked almost entirely inside this line, with 63 percent of all PBY flying time spent within 200 miles of base, this meant in effect that any attacks on U-boats would be achieved by the USAAF. The Navy aircraft were simply not flying where the U-boats were.[31]

By late May, fifteen B-24s of the 480th Group were operating from Port Lyautey, along with twelve PBYs of the Navy (VP-92 and part of VP-73). There were another six PBYs (part of VP-73) at Agadir. The 480th began flying operational missions from Morocco on March 19, 1943, although the group was plagued at the time with temporary shortages of spare parts and maintenance personnel. Nonetheless, the group usually managed three ASW patrols daily.[32]

As the Liberators could reach out as far as 1,000 nautical miles from their base, their arrival in the theater came as an unpleasant surprise to U-boat commanders operating in the area. Steady improvement in the maintenance and operation of the SCR-517C radar also allowed the group to achieve sightings that might otherwise have never been possible. Of the sightings made initially by radar, the average range of detection was 18 miles, an impressive figure for the time.[33]

Tidewater Tillie Strikes Again

As early as March 22, 1943, T/2 (1st Lt. William L. Sanford, pilot) found and attacked a U-boat. "Tidewater Tillie," which had earlier made an excellent attack when operating from the United Kingdom, did so again. The plane was now camouflaged in RAF Mediterranean shades, with light blue on its upper surfaces and white underneath. While patrolling at 1,200 feet, in and out of broken cloud cover, with the radar not operating, the copilot sighted a broad wake about five miles on the starboard beam, with a fully surfaced U-boat at its apex. Lieutenant Sanford elected to make a beam attack, which would enable him to approach the submarine from out of the sun. Having descended to 200 feet, and at a speed of 200 MPH the plane passed over the U-boat. As it did so the bombardier, Capt. Ralph E. Jones, dropped four U.S.-type 650-pound Mark 37 depth charges spaced at 60 feet. The exploding depth charges enveloped the after portion of the U-boat, which quickly began to settle by the stern, sinking in about one minute. Several survivors managed to escape the doomed boat, and were left clinging to debris in the water, as a large oil slick spread. The attack was assessed as a certain kill. All members of the crew of Tidewater Tillie were awarded DFCs for this action.[34] Capt. G. A. Seitz, USN, commanding FAW 15 at Port Lyautey, allowed that he was "impressed by the apparent efficiency and excellent team work exhibited by the crew."[35]

A Lack of Aggressiveness

While Lieutenant Sanford and the crew of Tidewater Tillie had got the 480th Group off to a good start in their new operating environment, the next incident was distinctly disappointing. On April 7, A/1 (1st Lt. Walter E. Thorne, pilot), while well out into the Atlantic in position 34.35°N/24.56°W, detected a surfaced U-boat.[36] This time the SCR-517 radar functioned flawlessly, giving a clear return on the U-boat at 30 miles distance. The plane closed on the radar indication, and visual sighting occurred at 5 miles. As A/1 approached the U-boat to attack, rather than diving the submarine put up a sharp AA fire. When machine-gun fire from the plane failed to suppress the boat's flak, Thorne chose to abort his approach and to circle the submarine while radioing for assistance.

About a half-hour later, E/1, piloted by 2nd Lt. H. C. Easterling, arrived to aid A/1. The two planes circled the submarine, one occasionally feinting toward the U-boat to attract its attention, while the other endeavored to attack. These efforts were all frustrated by the submarine skipper, who maneuvered his boat though a running series of S-turns and all the while kept up vigorous AA fire. As the planes were at extreme range and rapidly approaching their PLEs, A/1 eventually carried out an attack that dropped six depth charges well ahead of the submarine. The first three charges failed to explode. While the last three did so, they were well off for both line and range. A/1 then flew off, leaving E/1 to make its own attack up-track toward the U-boat, releasing six depth charges. Four of these fell about 600 feet short, and the other two 150 feet ahead of the U-boat, suggesting problems in the release or spacing of the weapons. Both planes returned safely to Craw Field in undamaged condition.

Colonel Roberts was not satisfied with these attacks, and two days later he wrote to the commanders of the 1st and 2nd Antisubmarine Squadrons with regard to the events of April 7.[37] While he "realized that there were some extenuating circumstances which partially explain the failure of this U-boat attack," Roberts noted that the consequence was to leave the U-boat free to continue its efforts to sink Allied shipping. He went on to say that "the only solution and policy for crews of your squadron, will be to execute a low altitude bombing and machine gun attack on any U-boats sighted with all possible aggressiveness." While the timing and character of the attack was the responsibility of the airplane commander, the attack "must be ruthlessly pushed home before contact with the U-boat is lost." The squadron commanders were instructed that "your crews must be so indoctrinated immediately." Colonel Roberts concluded: "They must be made to realize that their country is at war, that they are part of the Army of the United States, and that hesitancy or timidity in the face of the enemy will not be tolerated."

It is not clear to what degree this letter was written for the record, to cover Roberts's evident embarrassment while operating under a USN command, and with his parent organization, AAFAC, apt to query the conduct of the crews in the April 7 incident. Roberts's choice of the words "partially explain" with regard to extenuating circumstances (distance from land, and lack of specific instructions to attack U-boats putting up defensive fire) suggests that he himself did not accept these circumstances as an adequate explanation for the less than heroic performance of the two crews. During the group's operations from the United Kingdom, defensive fire had been encountered only once, and the attack had been carried through vigorously in the face of that fire; presumably Colonel Roberts expected that to be the norm for his group.

Later experience gained in the Bay of Biscay campaign when groups of U-boats with augmented AA guns stayed on the surface to fight it out suggests that a maneuvering U-boat is a poor firing platform, and that successful attacks could be pushed home without unacceptable casualty rates. That experience also indicated that a surfaced U-boat attacked by two Liberators was almost certain to be sunk. The combination of two aircraft able to drop a large number of weapons tilted the law of averages too far against the U-boat. Only one weapon had to fall within lethal range of the boat's pressure hull to make it impossible to submerge and thus a certain victim to continued attack, if that were necessary. Accordingly, Colonel Roberts's dissatisfaction in this instance seems to have been justified.

May Attacks on U-boats

A month would pass before the 480th Group would have another chance to attack a U-boat. The sighting on May 7 was by plane Q/2, with Maj. Douglas Northrop of the group staff as pilot, flying with crew O/2.[38] The plane was flying escort for convoy SL.128, bound for the United Kingdom. Off the coast of Portugal, while flying in position 41.20°N/18.05°W, a waist gunner sighted a surfaced U-boat some four to five miles to starboard. As the plane turned toward it, the submarine crash dived, and was entirely submerged when the attack was made from 100 feet at 230 MPH. Two figures are given in the same official report for the time the U-boat had been submerged before attack: 15–20 seconds and 25–30 seconds. This conflict is of some significance. The plane released four American Mark 37 650-pound depth charges with a shallow depth setting and 60-foot spacing. The stick is described as crossing the assumed track of the sub about 175 feet ahead of the apex of the U-boat's swirl. If the time was 15–20 seconds, the U-boat should have been just inside the lethal radius of at least one of the depth charges. Given the lack of visible results, it seems more likely that the time was closer to 30 seconds, by which time the sub would have been deep enough to have received a severe shaking up and perhaps some internal dislodgement of equipment, but still survive the attack. This seems to have been the view of the Cominch assessor, who rated the attack as causing slight damage to the submarine.

Later the same day, another aircraft of the second squadron (1st Lt. J. H. Darden, pilot), also flying convoy cover, spotted a surfaced U-boat in position 41.00°N/18.50°W.[39] Although an attack was made and four of the Mark 37 depth charges released, the crew estimated the time of release as 25 seconds after the U-boat had vanished, and perhaps a bit longer. Cominch found insufficient evidence of damage.

Just over a week later a good attack that had disappointing results was made on May 15 by aircraft O/2 (1st Lt. Earle A. Powers, pilot).[40] The plane was at 4,500 feet in broken clouds when Lieutenant Powers sighted the wake of a U-boat 10 miles ahead and off to port. He let down at once to begin his approach, but about a minute after sighting, the U-boat began to dive. A good attack was made on the submerging U-boat. The conning tower had been under about 15 seconds, but the stern of the boat could still be seen and a large swirl provided a good marker for the Liberator's bombardier. Four 650-pound depth charges were released, straddling the course of the submarine forward of the swirl. A good set of photos taken by the flight engineer revealed that there had been a straddle, but that the depth charges had probably fallen just too far ahead of the submerging U-boat to be lethal.[41]

Nonetheless, a significant oil slick, about 200 by 80 feet, showed up on the water. Colonel Roberts praised Powers's prompt attack and effective use of cloud cover, and noted in his endorsement that Powers had considerable experience, having participated as a crew member in six earlier attacks on subs. Roberts estimated the result as certain damage and possible destruction of a U-boat. Cominch assessors judged the attack probably caused slight damage, however. The old lesson was repeated here, that an attack had to be very accurate to sink a submarine, and that a very near miss could look promising but prove disappointing.

June Attacks on U-boats

June would produce two attacks on U-boats by 480th Group planes. On June 3, F/1, with a member of the group staff, Maj. Ralph A. Reeve, acting as pilot, was flying at an altitude of 1,200 feet when radar showed a possible submarine 28 miles ahead.[42] There was a solid overcast, haze, and scattered showers falling, which allowed Reeve to make a calculated approach before descending under the overcast to 400 feet to pick up the U-boat visually at 1–2 miles range. The surprised U-boat was still fully surfaced when the Liberator passed over it. The bombardier, however, was able to release only one of the six Mark 47 350-pound Torpex depth charges he intended to drop, and its fall and explosion were not observed by anyone in the plane. While the left waist gunner managed to fire a burst at the sub, the nose gun jammed and was unable to add its fire to the attack, which had been commendably low, at 75 feet off the water. Reeve promptly circled around and made a second attack on the still-surfaced submarine, again at 75 feet and a speed of 200 MPH. This time no depth charges would release, although the bombardier had rechecked his equipment between runs. The plane did fire from its top, waist, and tail positions on the second run. Gunfire was observed from two positions on the U-boat, but did not hit the aircraft.

After the abortive second run, Reeve climbed into the overcast and circled for 10 minutes while the jam in the nose gun and the bomb-bay equipment were again checked. During this time, one depth charge was released to test the equipment; it fell away and exploded as intended. Reeve then made his third attack on the sub, which was about three-quarters of a mile distant when the plane dropped below the overcast at 400 feet. Evidently, the U-boat commander felt that twice was enough, for he pulled the plug and crash-dived as F/1 approached, and the plane passed over the submarine's esti-mated position 15 seconds after the conning tower had vanished. The bom-bardier attempted to release four depth charges by manual trip lever, but only two fell away. The crew estimated that the first exploded about 100 feet short and the second about 40 feet beyond the U-boat's estimated track. Both were thus beyond lethal range. Over a half-hour had been absorbed by the three attacks before the plane departed for home after reaching its PLE.

In his comments, the squadron commander, Major Hanlon, noted cor-rectly that the U-boat "probably escaped undamaged." The mechanical fail-ure, he wrote, "was of a freak nature which was impossible to detect in rou-tine checks of the bombing equipment made by both the bombardier and the ground crew." Colonel Roberts in his comments elaborated on this point: "The rack failure apparently was caused by the bombardier unlocking the racks before the bomb bay doors were fully open, thereby springing and throwing the entire mechanism out of adjustment." The group commander added that later-model Liberators, which the group was then receiving, "incorporate a device which will prevent similar occurrences." The two reviewing officers politely omitted noting that the bombardier evidently didn't know enough about his equipment to understand how it worked. Upon reflection, Colonel Roberts was evidently more disturbed by this failure than his initial reaction, gauged by his comments on the attack report, would indicate. In his June report to the AAFAC, he noted that "depth charges are being unloaded and bomb racks checked prior to all operational missions," a procedure he had put into effect 10 days after the failed attack.[43]

In a personal letter to the chief of staff of the AAFAC, written at the same time as his official monthly report, Roberts commented further:

> The soundness of one policy, which we adhered to strictly in the U.K. but which we lapsed on somewhat here, was that only *assigned* airplane commanders would fly as airplane commanders. This is based upon the assumption that any "ground pilot," no matter how proficient as a pilot is not as capable an airplane commander as a pilot who knows his crew intimately, who flies almost daily, and who is thoroughly familiar with the routine of an attack from constant practice.[44]

Roberts went on to discuss the June 3 attack, and to comment that henceforth any staff pilot, including himself, would fly on an operational mission only as a copilot. He concluded that airplane commanders "will more than ever be held strictly responsible for the training and conduct of their crews. We find that an indifferent and careless crew on the ground is the same in the air." The principle was sound, but not easy to apply. Staff pilots normally flew only because the regular command pilot was unavailable, usually through illness or on temporary leave. In effect, under such circumstances, the regular copilot would presumably become the command pilot for the mission. While this was probably better than using a staff pilot as the airplane commander, as the copilot would know the crew and procedure intimately, it was not foolproof. Major Reeve was hardly responsible for the bombardier's inadequate level of training, and there is no reason to think the results would have been any different had the copilot been the airplane commander that day.

William Sanford, now promoted to captain, was again the pilot on June 19, 1943, flying a convoy escort mission. He was, however, without his regular crew. On June 10, the bulk of Tidewater Tillie's crew had departed for the United States, including the plane's navigator, Capt. John H. Shaw, and bombardier Ralph E. Jones.[45] On the nineteenth, Sanford was flying aircraft R/2 and had the bulk of crew O/2 with him. This crew had been flying with Lt. Earle A. Powers, who had recently returned to the United States himself. For them it was the third attack in five weeks, while for Sanford it was the fourth attack since February.[46] While chance was usually a major factor in ASW work, it also seems to have been the case that certain crews had a knack for finding and attacking whatever submarines were within their reach. Sanford and his original crew had sunk two U-boats in two months, an impressive showing at any time during the war.

A good attack was made on June 19.[47] At 0622, with darkness still limiting visibility to about 1½ miles, while flying at 1,200 feet, the radar operator reported two indications 20 and 22 miles distant from the plane, the nearer about 10 miles behind the convoy which R/2 was protecting. Sanford promptly lost altitude to begin a radar approach on the nearer target, but it disappeared from the scope. After the aircraft climbed again to 1,500 feet, a further indication was registered about 7 miles distant. Again the plane began a radar approach. This time, with the plane flying at 400 feet, a U-boat was seen visually about a mile distant. It immediately opened fire on the Liberator, which returned fire as it approached the submarine. Six Mark 47 350-pound depth charges were released from an altitude of 100 feet, spaced for 60 feet and fused for a 25-foot depth, as the plane crossed its target at a speed of 200 MPH. The tail and left waist gunners reported depth charges 3 and 4 straddling the target, and the U-boat was seen to submerge. A second attack was made along the U-boat's track, guided by a flame float that had been released in the first attack to mark the location, and two more depth charges were released. No photographs were taken, but on oral testimony the attack was initially thought to be a good one. However, Cominch assessed it only as probably causing slight damage.

The First Three Months of U-boat Hunting from North Africa

Between the first operational flight from North Africa on March 19 and Sanford's attack on June 19, just three months had elapsed, during which time the group had made eight attacks on U-boats, resulting in assessments of one U-boat known sunk, three slightly damaged, one possibly damaged, and three occasions when no damage was thought inflicted on the enemy submarine. While this was a respectable showing for the time, examination of the individual attacks reveals some weaknesses in training and technique which the group needed to address. Time was short, for in July there would come to the

480th Group its period of greatest opportunity. In the space of 10 days, running from July 5 through July 14, planes of the group would attempt no fewer than thirteen attacks, and crews would need to be at their peak of performance in order to reap the rewards that this remarkable period of opportunity offered.

6

Climax in July
480th Group Operations off the Iberian Peninsula

The Battle in the Bay of Biscay Approaches

The 480th's Liberators based on Port Lyautey could reach out as far as Cape Finisterre on the northwest tip of the Iberian peninsula, at the entrance to the Bay of Biscay. Thus they could cover an area beyond the limits of most patrols originating in the United Kingdom. In July 1943, Admiral Doenitz was attempting to operate his U-boats west of the Iberian peninsula. The U-boat group *Trutz* had been patrolling in 50°W longitude between the 30°N and 35°N latitude in late June in an effort to interdict convoys from the United States sailing for the Mediterranean. This effort had met with no success, so the U-boats were ordered to move steadily east until they were about 200 miles southwest of the Azores, where they were reorganized into three patrol lines, *Geier* 1 to 3, and were directed at the beginning of July to move steadily east-northeast along three parallel lines, passing just south of the Azores, and arriving eventually just to the west of Cape Finisterre. These three lines were to intercept convoys moving between the United Kingdom and destinations in the Mediterranean or Africa. This movement would bring the U-boats within range of the planes of the 480th Group.

The *Geier* lines were doomed to failure. Allied intelligence was reading Admiral Doenitz's orders to his U-boats as quickly as were the U-boats themselves. Thus it was possible to alert the American group at Craw Field to make a maximum patrol effort over the area the *Geier* boats would have to traverse in the first two weeks of July. As the Allies had changed their convoy codes at the beginning of June, Admiral Doenitz no longer had the reciprocal advantage of knowing where the Allied convoys were likely to be. The U-boats thus had the cards stacked heavily against them. Rather than hunting merchant ships, the German submarines would find themselves the hunted, with the aircraft of the 1st and 2nd Antisubmarine Squadrons as their pursuers. The boats of the *Geier* lines were still 500 miles west of the coast of Portugal and Spain when air attacks began. These became so intense that on July 8 commanding officers were given authorization to return to harbor if the situation proved too difficult. Some would never get home.[1]

Coming to Grips

On July 5, a Liberator piloted by 1st Lt. Carl G. Damann was on patrol in position 38.52°N/18.12°W, roughly due west of Lisbon.[2] While Damann was flying in and out of the cloud base at 1,300 feet, radar detected a submarine indication at 17 to 18 miles range. As the plane homed on the radar indication, the plane's bombardier spotted the U-boat 5 miles away. The U-boat did not attempt to submerge, nor did it fire on the rapidly closing Liberator, which passed over it at 100 feet. However, the B-24's bomb-bay doors failed to open fully, therefore the safety device that prevented release of the depth charges remained engaged, and no weapons were dropped. Nor were any guns fired by the B-24's crew at the U-boat. Damann made a second attempt, crossing over the approximate position of the sub's course some 10 seconds after it had crash-dived. Again, the depth charges failed to release. As a consolation prize, the crew was left with a set of excellent photographs of the fully surfaced U-boat and of the swirl left where it had submerged. The AAFAC Monthly Intelligence Review for July 1943 made the obvious comment on the failure of weapons to release on this and other occasions: "It is clear that the problem arises because of a failure of the mechanical or the human elements involved."[3] Without a report of the subsequent investigation, it is not possible to say which it was in this case.

The next day the aircraft commanded by 2nd Lt. James Q. Adams took up where Damann had left off.[4] Adams was actually flying protective cover for a convoy at the time a U-boat was detected, which rarely happened. Only twice in July did an aircraft flying convoy cover detect a U-boat; all other attacks were during planned antisubmarine patrols. Adams was at 2,500 feet, flying through broken overcast, when the bombardier, T. Sgt. C. E. Franklin, spotted a wake at eight miles. Adams went into a steep dive, leveled out, and approached the U-boat at 100 feet to release his weapons. The submarine had promptly submerged; its conning tower had vanished only eight seconds before the plane roared over its track, and the silhouette of the U-boat just beneath the water was visible to the crew. However, for the second day in a row, no weapons fell on a still highly vulnerable U-boat. Adams made a second run, and this time four Mark 47 depth charges fell away. But only one explosion was observed, at the leading edge of the swirl, or well behind the position the sub would have reached by that time.[5]

The Cominch assessment predictably concluded no damage was done to the submarine. In two days, two aircraft of the 480th Group had made four passes over U-boats, managed to release a total of four depth charges on one of the four passes, and had one explode. As the depth charges were American, the British Mark XI depth charge could not be blamed for the hangups. It was not an encouraging beginning to a period of intense activity when U-boat targets would be more plentiful than they had ever been or would be again.

If things got off to a shaky start on July 5 and 6, the next two attacks, both on July 7, showed considerable improvement. On that date, 1st Lt. T. H. Isley, flying aircraft C/1, was on patrol 250 miles southwest of Lisbon. While flying at 1,500 feet in scattered cloud with unlimited visibility, a radar contact was made at fifteen miles and a fully surfaced U-boat sighted at eight miles.[6] While the aircraft was still four miles away, the U-boat crash-dived. Isley continued his attack, dropping six Mark 47 depth charges from 200 feet 10 seconds after the submarine had disappeared, aiming for roughly 200 feet ahead of the swirl. Following the depth-charge explosions a large black oil bubble was observed. In the photos of the attack the swirl was obscured by the depth-charge explosions so that it was hard to verify the crew's estimate of the distance at which they entered the water, but if it was 200 feet ahead of the swirl, then the U-boat might have been just too deep to suffer a mortal wound. That the submarine did sustain some damage is suggested by the large amount of oil that came to the surface. The size of the slick, some 600 to 700 feet in diameter, would have gone a ways toward emptying the sub's fuel bunkers. Cominch assessed this attack as inflicting probable severe damage to the submarine.

U.951 Sunk

Also on July 7 Liberator K/1, piloted by 1st Lt. Walter S. McDonell, sighted a fully surfaced U-boat in position 37.40°N/15.30°W.[7] Radar reported an indication at the same time the pilot saw the U-boat at a range of seven miles. The sub did not attempt to submerge, but rather maneuvered so as to bring its flak to bear fully on the American plane. As McDonell passed over the sub while flying barely 50 feet off the surface, his bombardier, 2nd Lt. James R. Goolsby, released seven Mark 47 350-pound Torpex depth charges spaced for 60 feet. This attack nearly suffered the fate of that on July 5, for the bomb-bay doors stopped a foot short of fully open, which left the safety still engaged. On this occasion, however, the radar operator immediately used the manual utility handle to crank the doors open the remaining foot. Thus the depth charges fell away and straddled the target, which appeared to break up aft of the conning tower. The plane's top turret and tail gunners had fired vigorously on the sub, as had the nose gunner/navigator until he was wounded by the U-boat's flak.

McDonell did not remain to confirm the damage or make a further attack as a 20mm shell had struck the plane's nose area, wounding the navigator, bombardier, copilot, and assistant radio operator. The B-24's radio compass, its hydraulic system, the copilot's controls, and most of the cockpit engine instruments were knocked out. Lieutenant Goolsby and the assistant radio operator, Sgt. C. R. Alleman, were in relatively good shape, although bleeding from large shrapnel wounds. The navigator, 1st Lt. J. E. Richards, was in worse shape, suffering shock from a chest wound, and unable to assist the pilot in finding his way home. For 3½ hours McDonell navigated on his magnetic compass, which was accurate enough to give him a landfall on the coast of North Africa not too far from Craw Field, where he landed safely. The four injured men all made a good recovery. Photos showed an excellent straddle and the U-boat was initially assessed as probably sunk, and later the loss of U.951, a Type VIIC boat, was confirmed. Built at the Blohm & Voss

Yard in Hamburg, it had been launched in October 1942 and entered operational service in that December. During its brief operational life of seven months it had never succeeded in sinking a ship. This submarine was one of the *Geier* boats, commanded by Oberleutnant Pressel. He was among the forty-six lost; there were no survivors.[8]

U.232 Sunk

On July 8, Q/2, piloted by 1st Lt. James H. Darden with crew S, was flying at 3,000 feet through broken overcast when radar detected a possible U-boat 18 miles ahead and to starboard.[9] Darden took full advantage of the cloud cover and his early radar indication to position his plane so that he would approach the U-boat from out of the sun. Visual contact was made at 8 miles in position 40.37°N/13.41°W, and the aircraft crossed over the submarine at 50 feet, releasing four Mark 37 650-pound depth charges spaced at 60 feet, which were seen to straddle the U-boat ahead of the conning tower. The U-boat showed immediate signs of damage, circling aimlessly as it steadily lost speed and began to settle by the stern.

The submarine put up vigorous AA fire, causing minor damage to the plane's nose. The U-boat was still circling when Darden approached for a second attack. This time the U-boat's fire was more accurate, repeatedly hitting the Liberator on the wing, fuselage, and bomb bay, cutting hydraulic and fuel lines, and damaging radio equipment. The damage to the bomb bay made it impossible to release the remaining depth charges on the second run. The crew succeeded in getting the bomb-bay doors, which had partially closed from flak damage, back open as Darden made a third approach over a now submerged U-boat. Two more depth charges were released and large explosions were seen by the crew. An excellent set of photographs revealed the U-boat to be swiftly sinking, stern first, even before the third run. The crew was lucky, considering the punishment the plane had taken, and only the left waist gunner sustained minor injury from the U-boat's flak. U.232 was later confirmed sunk. Built by Germania Werft in Kiel, this Type VIIC boat had been launched in October 1942 and entered operational service in late November. In less than eight months of service it sank no ships. Its CO, Kapitaenleutnant Ziehm, was lost with his entire crew of forty-six men.[10]

Three Attacks in One Day

The first of three attacks the 480th Group made on U-boats on July 9, the busiest day in the group's history, was made by aircraft X/2, piloted by 1st Lt. Carl G. Damann.[11] Four days earlier, Damann and crew X, flying in plane S, had experienced the frustration of having their depth charges refuse to release during an excellent run over a fully surfaced U-boat, which escaped to fight another day. They would do somewhat better in their own plane. On the ninth, first contact was visual, by the bombardier, who spotted a U-boat at 12 miles while the plane was flying at 4,200 feet in excellent weather. This submarine began to crash-dive during the Liberator's approach. Its conning tower had vanished 17 seconds earlier when the plane crossed its track, dropping four Mark 37 650-pound depth charges spaced at 60 feet. These appeared to straddle the assumed track of the submarine about 200 feet ahead of the conning tower's swirl. Photographs supported these visual observations. The squadron and group commanders thought the U-boat had been seriously damaged in this attack. Cominch, however, assessed it only as probably slightly damaged.

The second attack on July 9 was by a plane of the 1st Squadron (1st Lt. William W. Pomeroy, pilot). Pomeroy had flown for some time as copilot in Wayne Johnson's successful crew before moving up to command his own aircraft. Pomeroy was patrolling at 3,100 feet, with his radar not functioning, when a U-boat was sighted 10 miles ahead and to port by the bombardier.[12] The plane attacked promptly, and the U-boat stayed on the surface and fired on the approaching Liberator. No hits were scored on the B-24, which passed over the submarine at 50 feet. No depth charges were released, however, as the bomb-bay doors refused to open. There appeared to have been a mechanical fault, since the indicator lights in the nose and flight deck of the plane showed that the doors had opened, while the radar operator was able to observe that the doors were still shut and the safety engaged when the bombardier called out "bombs away."

Pomeroy circled about while the radar operator opened the bomb-bay doors manually, and then renewed the attack on the sub. The U-boat commander, however, pulled the plug as the bomber came around to attack again, perhaps because his AA personnel had suffered from the machine-gun fire the B-24 had put down on its first pass. In any case, the conning tower had been under seven seconds when the plane crossed the sub's path. This time six Mark 47 350-pound Torpex depth charges fell away, spaced at 60 feet, entering the water about 100 feet ahead of the swirl. Four explosions were noted by the crew. No evidence of damage to the sub could be seen after the plumes of the depth charges settled, although the plane remained in the area for over a half hour. Cominch assessed no damage likely to the U-boat, although there may have been casualties in the submarine's crew. Problems with the B-24's bomb bays and their release mechanisms continued to be the Achilles' heel of the 480th Group.

The third attack on July 9 was also by a plane of the 1st Squadron (1st Lt. T. E. Kuenning, pilot).[13] The Liberator was flying at 3,200 feet in 3/10 clouds when the bombardier, 2nd Lt. T. N. Gerhart, sighted a U-boat just four miles ahead. As the radar was functioning satisfactorily, and detected the submarine just as the bombardier did, it is possible the U-boat had just surfaced. To be caught at this point was about the worst sort of luck a submarine can experience, since it is blind to its enemies until a watch can be established on its conning tower. Kuenning did not miss his chance. Attacking at once, the plane crossed the U-boat at 50 feet while Lieutenant Gerhart released six depth charges spaced at 60 feet. One was observed to fall short of the U-boat's bow, and the other five over the bow.[14]

Kuenning circled and delivered a second attack, this time almost head-on to the U-boat and parallel to its track. Two more depth charges were released, exploding aft of the conning tower along the port side of the submarine. Crew members observed the U-boat's bow rear up as it slipped backward beneath the surface. Unfortunately, the plane's bomb camera malfunctioned, so the only photographs were from a hand-held camera that did not clearly establish what had happened to the submarine. As the crew's testimony seemed impressive, the squadron and group assessment was optimistic, estimating a likely kill. The final assessment, however, was only for a U-boat seriously damaged. It appears that visual evidence on this occasion was overly enthusiastic and that the U-boat had a lucky escape.

The Last Five Days

Never again would the group make attacks on three U-boats in one day, but sightings remained steady for the next five days, with one attack made every day from July 10 to 14. The attack on July 10 was by aircraft W/2, Capt.

Lawrence E. Jarnagin, pilot, flying with crew Q.[15] The plane was flying at 2,100 feet in good weather and unrestricted visibility. As the sea return was unusually strong, despite an observed wind of only 21 MPH, the radar set was not in use when the copilot spotted a U-boat on the surface six miles away and roughly 90 degrees to starboard. Jarnagin promptly turned toward the sub and began his approach while steadily losing altitude. As the plane reached the release point, the U-boat commander put his helm over sharply to starboard, turning into the attacking plane. The stick of six Mark 47 350-pound depth charges overshot the sub. As the B-24 came about for a second attack, the U-boat submerged. When the plane crossed the assumed track of the U-boat, its conning tower had been under 25 seconds, and the remaining two depth charges, released from 100 feet, fell about 50 feet ahead of the apex of the conning tower's swirl. They would thus have missed astern of the submarine. Although the plane had fired on the U-boat during its first run, there had been no return fire. Rather, the skipper's skillful handling of the boat had thwarted a promising attack. Cominch assessed the attack as no damage likely.

On July 11, Lieutenant McDonell got to make his second attack on a sub in four days. While all his noncommissioned officers were the same as on the seventh, McDonell had a different copilot, navigator, and bombardier flying with him, seldom conducive to operational efficiency. The plane was flying at 3,000 feet through 8/10 cloud cover when radar reported a possible U-boat some 14 miles ahead and to port.[16] Using cloud to cover his approach, McDonell dropped below the cloud base at 1,500 feet to establish visual contact at 5 miles. Seven British Mark XI 250-pound Torpex depth charges spaced at 40 feet were released from an altitude of 100 feet, but all fell short, the last of the stick being about 250 feet from the U-boat's hull. Although the shortfall was unusually bad for a crew of the 480th Group, it does serve to illustrate the case of the RAF Coastal Command ORS staff for using a 100-foot spacing with the Mark XI depth charge. Such a spacing would have added 360 feet to the length of the stick, bringing the U-boat's hull well within lethal range. An exchange of gunfire did some minor damage to the Liberator's tail, and perhaps some superficial damage to the U-boat.

As McDonell brought his plane around for a second attack, the U-boat submerged. Its conning tower had been under at least 30 seconds when the B-24 passed over the submarine's estimated course 300 feet ahead of the swirl's apex and a further three depth charges were released. Cominch assessed this attack as showing insufficient evidence of damage to the U-boat. The reason given for the bad first attack was that the bombardier was inexperienced and flying with the crew for the first time as a last-minute replacement for the regular bombardier who was in the hospital. Given the good opportunity, and the excellent attack McDonell and his crew had made on the seventh, this unavoidable change of personnel may well have saved the U-boat from the fate of its sister in the earlier attack.

U.506 Sunk

On July 12, 1943, aircraft C/1, piloted by 2nd Lt. Ernst Salm, was 200 miles northwest of Lisbon at 5,600 feet flying in solid overcast when a radar contact showed up 23 miles astern of the aircraft.[17] Salm was making his first operational flight as airplane commander; he would get off to a spectacular start. Turning and descending as he was guided by his radar operator, Sgt. Llewellyn A. Williams, Salm emerged from the overcast at an altitude of only 200 feet to see a surfaced U-boat one mile away, just off the starboard bow, in position 42.30°N/16.30°W. It was a nice piece of radar direction and of flying in difficult conditions, which presented the opportunity for an excellent surprise attack. Seven Mark XI 250-pound depth charges were released and straddled the submarine. As Salm turned sharply to make another attack, the U-boat broke in two and sank, leaving about fifteen survivors in the water. The plane then dropped a life raft and smoke flares, and six of the U-boat's crew survived in the life raft to be taken prisoner.

The Cominch assessment this time could be predicted with confidence: U-boat known destroyed. C/1's victim was U.506, a Type IXC U-boat. Its CO, Kapitaenleutnant Erich Wuerdemann, had been awarded the Knight's Cross in March 1943 for his previous successes as a submarine commander. U.506, which sailed on its first war patrol in September 1941, had sunk fourteen vessels in its 22 months of operational life. The submarine had been built by Deutsche Werft in Hamburg, where it had been launched in June 1941. It was outbound as part of Group *Monsun* on its fifth war patrol, bound for the Far East, having departed Lorient on July 6. Of the crew of fifty-four, only six survived the aerial attack, and the CO was among the missing. According to the survivors, the overcast was so thick that they did not see the B-24 until it was a bare 200 yards from them. About a dozen had escaped the boat, but several quickly perished from wounds or exhaustion. The six survivors then drifted in the life raft for two days until located from the air on July 14, and picked up by a British destroyer the next day.

This attack revealed how vulnerable a U-boat was in thick weather to the 10-cm radar, which the Germans could not yet detect. The submarine had no idea of its peril until the Liberator suddenly emerged from the heavy overcast only a few hundred yards away. It also was a fine display of aggressive flying by Salm, who must have reposed great confidence in his altimeter, for he descended from 5,600 feet through solid cloud at well over 200 MPH before he broke through the overcast barely 200 feet off the water.[18]

Final Actions

The attack on July 13 was by an aircraft of the 2nd Squadron, 1st Lt. Henry S. Cantrell, pilot.[19] He had started in the group as a copilot before moving, like Bill Pomeroy, into the left seat to command his own airplane. Cantrell's was the second of the July attacks to occur in the process of flying convoy cover. The plane was flying at 3,600 feet in slight haze, when the radar operator noted an indication 12 miles ahead. Closing the indication, a fully surfaced U-boat was spotted from 2,500 feet while still 9 miles distant. Cantrell was not as lucky in his weather as Salm had been the day before; in the good visibility prevailing the U-boat started a crash dive while the Liberator was still 4 miles away. The American crew reported that the sub appeared to have some trouble getting under, so that the conning tower had disappeared only five seconds before the plane crossed over its track. Four Mark 47 350-pound depth charges, spaced at 60 feet, were released and seen to straddle the sub's track some 50 feet ahead of the apex of the swirl. No results of damage appeared after the plumes of the charges subsided, although the plane remained in the area for another 40 minutes. When the plane reached its PLE, it departed for home.

While the squadron commander viewed this as a promising attack, the assistant group commander thought that the plane should have led the swirl by more than 50 feet. The commander of FAW 15 agreed with the assistant group commander, and also noted that baiting tactics had not been employed by the aircraft following the attack. This may have been because Cantrell judged his fuel supply too low to allow him to execute this maneuver and still have adequate time in hand for an attack and return to base. There is also a problem with the evidence. Unless the U-boat's problem submerging was truly dramatic, the numbers don't fit very well. It normally took no more than 25 to 30 seconds for a U-boat to crash-dive, and it would have required at least a full minute for the Liberator to cross the four miles between it and the submarine when the latter was seen to start his dive. Did it really take 25 seconds longer than usual for the U-boat commander to get his conning tower under? If it did take that long, then in the time between the conning tower vanishing and the depth charges exploding, the U-boat would have moved forward some 90 feet. The depth charges, spaced at 60 feet and set to explode at a depth of 25 feet, should have been within range of the after part of the hull of the sub if all the given times and distances were right. Yet no evidence of damage to the U-boat was seen on the surface. In any case, the Cominch assessor made the only possible assessment of insufficient evidence of damage inflicted.

The last of this intensive series of attacks came on July 14, when 1st Lt. Jordan M. Pennoyer and crew Y were flying in aircraft "V for Victor" in position 40.03°N/17.57°W at an altitude of 2,000 feet in unlimited ceiling and visibility weather. Pennoyer later recalled that the crew had received a special briefing that morning to the effect that headquarters had received from France secret sailing orders for a submarine that would at 1100 that day be located in 40°N/20°W. This briefing was presumably cover for the interception and decryption of Admiral Doenitz's communications with his U-boats. Certainly the intelligence was close to the mark. At 1112 Pennoyer's radar operator, Sgt. Clinton E. Holland, found the submarine somewhat east of its expected position. He then reported an indication at 19 miles ahead and to port.[20]

Visual contact was made at 12 miles from 1,500 feet when the U-boat was still fully surfaced. Pennoyer recalled seeing several German crew members in bathing trunks getting a suntan as the Liberator bore down on them. Nonetheless, the German crew responded promptly to the aerial threat, and as Pennoyer approached to attack, the U-boat opened up an intense AA fire, which finally scored damaging hits on the aircraft just as it reached the target. "V for Victor" sustained damage to the under fuselage, the after bomb bay, and number 1 engine. The hydraulic system was shot out, and the radar scanner in the after fuselage damaged. Despite this, a vigorous attack was delivered from 50 feet, and the bombardier, 2nd Lt. Eugene A. Philbrin, attempted to release six Mark XI 250-pound depth charges spaced at 60 feet. Unfortunately, he had selected the after bomb bay for use, the one that suffered flak damage. Consequently, only one depth charge released and it did not explode.

Pennoyer promptly pulled his damaged aircraft around to attack again, in the process feathering the outer port engine, which was smoking heavily and throwing off a substantial quantity of oil. The second attack was made just 19 seconds after the U-boat's submergence. The submarine in its haste to crash-dive while the plane was circling for a second attack left about five of its crew in the water. Lieutenant Philbrin had switched to the forward bomb rack for this pass, and successfully released six depth charges spaced at 45 feet to compensate for the lower attack speed of the Liberator flying on only three engines.[21] These were seen to straddle the assumed course of the U-boat. The difficulty was with the aiming point, for the crew was confronted with what appeared to be two swirls, about 100 feet apart, and they were uncertain which to use as the target marker. The leading edge of the forward swirl was chosen, and the depth charges were estimated to have fallen from about 75 to 200 feet ahead of it and across the U-boat's presumed course. Oil from the damaged number 1 engine had fouled the fixed camera, so the only photographs were from a hand-held camera, and on its pictures the swirls were obscured by the plane's fuselage.

With one engine out, Pennoyer did not remain over the attack site, and little visible evidence was noted on the surface immediately following subsidence of the depth-charge plumes. Accordingly, it was hard to assess the result of the second attack. The return to base on three engines was relatively uneventful; the problem was landing safely without the primary hydraulic system, which left Pennoyer unable to lower his flaps and with only one application of the emergency brake system available to him. The landing gear had to be cranked down by hand. The young pilot made a careful approach as close to stalling speed as possible, touched down smoothly, and when the nose wheel settled on the runway applied his emergency brakes. The plane stopped before it ran out of runway, but had to be towed from there on as it no longer had brakes. There were no casualties in the crew. Squadron and group evaluators thought some damage to the sub was likely, but the FAW 15 commander was less certain. Cominch assessed the attack as probably causing slight damage to the U-boat. The sub's AA likely saved it at the last minute by damaging the after bomb bay, for everything else looked well set for a lethal attack by the plane.

Evaluation

The thirteen attacks (or twelve attacks and one attempted attack by the AAFAC's reckoning, which omits Damann's on July 5, as no weapon was discharged) in the space of 10 days makes it possible to gain some sort of composite picture of the operational efficiency of the 480th Group at this point in its career. By early July, several of the more notable early crews, such as those of William Sanford and Wayne Johnson, were no longer flying, having been repatriated to the United States or transferred to duties on the group staff. A few former copilots had moved up to command their own aircraft, and a flow of both new crews and replacement personnel had been coming into the group since April. The newer crews were strongly represented in the July attacks, which meant they had no experience of operations from the United Kingdom. A total of eleven different crews participated in the thirteen actions, or roughly half of all operational crews in the group at that time.

The value of the SCR-517 10-cm radar, whose emissions the U-boats still could not detect, was evident in this period of operations. On eight occasions, the initial detection was by radar, at an average range of 15.7 miles, or nearly twice the eight-mile average range on the five occasions when the initial detection was visual. Lieutenant Salm's attack on July 12 which sank U.506, carried out in solid overcast that extended down to roughly 200 feet off the water, was a feat that could only have been accomplished with the help of a reliable and powerful radar (and a trustworthy altimeter). Early radar detection also allowed the pilots to choose the best angle of approach toward their targets before the U-boats were ever aware that they were in danger. Radar was thus a major factor in the group's achievement in this period. Its frequency of use appears to have increased over time. In the eight attacks the group made between March 22 and June 19, initial detection was made by radar on only three occasions, although these averaged an impressive range of 26.7 miles. The five visual sightings in the earlier period averaged six miles.

In all, in the 10 days July 5–14, 1943, the two squadrons made fifteen sightings, which were converted into twelve attacks, with a further attack thwarted by failure of the depth charges to release and of the gunners to fire on the U-boat. Counting only the twelve attacks accepted by the AAFAC, this gives an impressive rate of 80 percent of sightings converted into attacks.

This was better than the 69 percent average (ninety-three sightings converted into sixty-four attacks) for all day ASW aircraft operations over the Bay of Biscay–Cape Finisterre area for the period July 1–August 2, 1943.[22] In eight of the twelve attacks, the U-boat was still on the surface when the initial pass took place, an impressive 67 percent rate. On five of these eight occasions (62 percent), the U-boat chose to fight back, firing on the attacking plane. In the eight attacks in the March–June period the U-boat was on the surface at the time of attack on five occasions (62 percent), and fired on the approaching aircraft four times (50 percent). One plane was slightly damaged in the earlier period.

When there was an exchange of fire in the July actions, the B-24 came off decidedly the better in the contest. The five submarines that fired on their aerial adversaries managed to hit four of the Liberators, in one case inflicting only slight damage to the plane. On the other three occasions, crew members were wounded twice: four men were wounded with various degrees of severity in McDonell's attack of July 7, and one crew member was slightly wounded by shrapnel in Darden's attack on July 8. Only once was an engine badly damaged, and in that case, as in all the others, the sturdy B-24s completed long flights home safely. On the other hand, of the five U-boats that chose to fight it out, two were sunk with heavy loss of life.

An unusual aspect of the attacks in this period is the variety of weapons carried. On three occasions, the weapon was the British Mark XI 250-pound depth charge, twelve of which were carried, and on seven occasions the weapon was the American Mark 47 350-pound depth charge, of which eight were normally carried. In two cases, the weapon was the American Mark 37 650-pound depth charge, of which six were carried. In one case, the records are unclear, but the weapon was probably the American Mark 47, as we know eight were carried on this occasion, which was the normal load for this weapon. With regard to their relative effectiveness, one U-boat was sunk by each of the three weapons employed. However, it is hard to believe that this was an ideal method of operation. Each weapon had its own characteristics, its own ideal release point, and its ideal spacing. While the bombardier had a device, the intervalvometer, to make appropriate adjustments for each weapon's characteristics, the nature of the weapon did affect the character of the attack. If the Kuenning attack of July 9 was made with the Mark 47 depth charge, as seems most likely, then the British Mark XI was not employed until the eleventh, after a period of intense usage of weapons. Was there a shortage of American weapons available at Craw Field? The surviving records don't say.

In assessing the attacks on U-boats by the 480th Group, during the period March–July 1943, the July assessments (including the one abortive attack) were as follows:

A 1 U-boat known sunk (by Salm)
B 2 U-boats probably sunk, both of which were later confirmed
   (McDonell on July 7 and Darden)
D 2 U-boats seriously damaged (by Isley and Kuenning)
E 2 U-boats slightly damaged
F 2 U-boats where there was insufficient evidence of damage
G 4 U-boats not damaged (including Damann's attempt of July 5)

The eight attacks of March–June were assessed:

A 1 U-boat known sunk (by Sanford in "Tidewater Tillie")
E 3 U-boats slightly damaged
F 1 case of insufficient evidence of damage
G 3 U-boats not damaged.[23]

Some picture of the group's efficiency emerges from examining its performance as part of the total daylight ASW aircraft effort in the Bay of Biscay–Cape Finisterre area in the period July 1–August 2, 1943. Planes of the 1st and 2nd Antisubmarine Squadrons flew roughly 400 of the better than 8,000 patrol hours in this area, or 5 percent of all daylight hours. They made twelve of the sixty-four attacks in this period, or 18.75 percent, showing outstanding efficiency at converting flying time and sightings into attacks. They sank three of the eighteen U-boats known destroyed by aircraft, for a slightly less impressive figure of 16.7 percent.[24] To sink three U-boats in twelve attacks, a 25 percent rate, was about average for the antisubmarine war in mid-1943. Different crews revealed rather widely varying degrees of proficiency, and the problem of depth charges not releasing continued to plague the group. On average, however, the group's aviators turned in a respectable performance. It would also appear, by comparison with the March–June operational data, that the efficiency of the group as a whole showed a slight improving trend.

On July 15, 1943, the submarine hunters found no quarry. In fact, they would never have as good hunting again. Between the middle of July and the conclusion of operations in October, no U-boat would be seen by a plane of the 480th Group. Thus the last three and one-half months of the group's eight months of operations in North Africa would be largely unproductive as far as the offensive antisubmarine war was concerned. Whether the group should have been left with so infertile a field to plow for so long seems a reasonable question. The determining factor in this was probably the USAAF's decision in July to go out of the antisubmarine business, and the time required to complete the transition to USN units. Thus the 480th Group was locked into its location at Craw Field until such time as the higher commands could complete the rearrangements put in train as a result of high-level policy decisions.

The flying record of the 480th Group during the first six months in North Africa is tabulated in Table 6.1.

A notable aspect of the 480th Group's arrival in North Africa is the degree to which its Liberators extended the range of operations of ASW aircraft in the Moroccan Sea Frontier. Table 6.2 makes this clear.

During the entire duration of the 480th Group in the MSF, no unthreatened convoy within the sea frontier's waters suffered U-boat attack, yet a great many were provided with air cover, to Colonel Roberts's frustration.[25] This fact gives weight to his contention that his aircraft could have been better used in sweeps in areas of high probability.[26] His contention is also

Table 6.1. Operational Flying Hours from North Africa, March–August 1943

Month	ASW Sweeps	Convoy Cover	Total Operational Hours	Sweeps
March	400	—	400	100%
April	1,122	397	1,519	74%
May	674	733	1,407	48%
June	1,119	541	1,660	67%
(March–June)	3,315	1,671	4,986	66%
July	1,544	624	2,168	71%
August	883	795	1,676	53%
Total	5,742	3,090	8,832	65%[a]

[a]Average percentage.
   Note: This yields the following operational statistics:
   March–June: 8 attacks, or 1 per 623.75 operational hours
   July: 12 attacks, or 1 per 180.67 operational hours
   March–August: 20 attacks, or 1 per 441.6 operational hours
   Source: "History of AAFAC," with additional information and calculations entered by author.

Table 6.2. Total Operational Flying Hours by B-24s and PBYs in the Moroccan Sea
Frontier, November 1942–July 15, 1943

	0–200 miles	200–400 miles	400–600 miles	600–800 miles	800+ miles	Total
November 1942	593	285	53	2	0	933
December	1,164	560	105	5	0	1,834
January 1943	1,380	660	123	4	0	2,183
February	1,352	652	122	4	0	2,130
March	1,558	842	179	5	0	2,584
April	2,558	1,062	384	104	0	4,108
May	1,870	1,468	558	40	0	3,936
June	1,616	1,119	511	101	5	3,352
July[a]	526	597	599	679	17	2,418
Total	12,617	7,245	2,634	944	22	23,462

[a]First 15 days only. The sharp increase in flying hours beyond 600 miles was the result of the 480th Group's Liberators flying to the area off Cape Finisterre, southwest of the Bay of Biscay. Note also how the arrival of the 480th Group in March is followed by increased flying beyond 600 miles.

Source: ASWORG Report of July 22, 1943, in USAFHRC, AAFAC file 424.310C. I have silently corrected some small computational errors in the original calculations.

supported by a statistical study done in July 1943, which demonstrated that patrol hours were most effective when the aircraft searched areas with high probability of a U-boat being present. Table 6.3 shows the results.

In all, between mid-March and the end of July 1943, the AAFAC calculated that the 480th Group made twenty attacks on U-boats, a majority of all such attacks in the MSF. Sixteen of the attacks were made while part of the U-boat was still visible on the surface, perhaps to some degree an indication of the improved technique of the group's aircrews, notably in using cloud cover to make an approach on a U-boat detected earlier by radar. However, the chief reason for so many such attacks was likely the encouragement U-boats received from Admiral Doenitz in this period to stay and fight on the surface.[27]

As intelligence reports showed virtually no U-boats operating in the MSF, in early August planes of the 2nd Antisubmarine Squadron twice made "shuttle-runs" between Port Lyautey and Dunkeswell in Devonshire, England. On the northward flight, coverage would be provided to a convoy. On the return flight to Morocco, an ASW sweep was flown. The flights both ways, however, failed to turn up U-boats.[28] Long hours of tedium were an inescapable part of

Table 6.3. Hours Flown per U-boat Sighting, Excluding Convoy Coverage, in the Moroccan Sea Frontier, November 1942–July 15, 1943

Miles	Total patrol hours per sighting	Total hours per sighting in high-probability areas
0–200	1,540 (5)[a]	327 (4)
200–400	900 (5)	210 (5)
400–600	164 (10)	69 (9)
600–800	95 (6)	45 (6)
Total	540 (26)	195 (24)

[a]Numbers in parentheses are number of U-boats sighted.

Note: Only two of the twenty-six U-boats sighted were not located in high-probability search areas. ASWORG did not perform a similar analysis for convoy protection, "since convoy coverages are defensive and not intended to produce sightings."

Source: ASWORG Report, July 22, 1943, AAFAC file 424.310C, USAFHRC.

ASW operations, and the aircrews of the 480th Group had their full share. But there was ample danger, too, and the 480th Group would have their share of that, largely from encounters with enemy aircraft.

7

Final Innings
The 480th Group's Last Operations

Aerial Combats, July 18–October 7, 1943

It was only after the 480th Group had made its last attack on a U-boat that the Luftwaffe emerged to contest the area with the B-24s. The Liberators' primary opponent was the FW 200 Condor.[1] This plane was the only available Luftwaffe aircraft that possessed the long range necessary for Atlantic operations. The FW 200s were armed with 20mm cannon, as well as 7.9mm machine guns, giving them considerable firepower, but the plane itself was structurally less robust than the Liberator. Pilots of the group reported the B-24 appeared to be about 20 MPH faster than the Condor, and somewhat more maneuverable. The two planes, then, were not ill-matched opponents, although neither had ever been intended to engage in what amounted to dogfights between flying elephants.[2] While the FW 200 was the most common enemy, the planes of the 480th Group also encountered a variety of other German types. All told, during its stay in North Africa, the group's aircraft were credited with having destroyed eight German planes, five of them FW 200s. The price of this was the loss of three B-24s in action with enemy aircraft.[3] Encounters with enemy aircraft by the 480th Antisubmarine Group while operating from North Africa are shown in Table 7.1.

Table 7.1. 480th Group Aerial Combats, July–October 1943

Date	Pilot	Comments
7/18/43	H. D. Maxwell	One FW 200 damaged
7/28/43	E. W. Hyde	One FW 200 destroyed; one member of USAAF crew killed. B-24 had to be abandoned near Craw Field
7/31/43	G. L. Mosier	One FW 200 destroyed
8/13/43	F. W. McKinnon	Action with one FW 200, claimed destroyed
8/17/43	H. D. Maxwell	One FW 200 known destroyed, one known damaged and thought to have crashed; B-24 lost and three crew killed in crash
8/25/43	F. H. Graham	Several JU 88s and other enemy aircraft engaged
8/27/43	L. E. Jarnagin	Several enemy aircraft engaged
8/27/43	T. E. Kuenning	One FW 200 damaged
8/28/43	F. W. McKinnon	B-24 lost, navigator killed in crash
9/10/43	H. McKeown	Three German seaplanes destroyed on surface of the water
9/18/43	L. E. Jarnagin	B-24 and crew of ten lost
10/7/43	G. L. Mosier	Five JU 88s; slight damage to B-24; three JU 88s claimed damaged

Sources: 480th Group and 1st Squadron records, USAFHRC.

July–August Actions

On July 28, while on convoy escort, aircraft E/1, flown by 1st Lt. Elbert W. Hyde, intercepted a FW 200 attempting to attack a convoy straggler. A sharp engagement followed at just above sea level, with the B-24 attacking the FW 200 from astern. Hyde closed to 600 yards and the action continued until the German aircraft crashed into the sea. Hyde's top turret gunner, T. Sgt. James G. Kehoe, was killed instantly late in the action when a 20mm shell smashed into the turret. The B-24's left outboard engine was also shot out by the Condor. The action and German plane's crash into the sea took place before an enthusiastic audience in the convoy, which enjoyed an excellent view of the engagement and the rare pleasure of seeing retribution meted out to an enemy that had often plagued them. Returning to Port Lyautey with one engine out, Hyde arrived at midnight to find the field socked in by fog.

As the sun was setting on July 28, a dense fog bank had rolled in off the Atlantic blanketing the area around Port Lyautey. Maj. Alfred J. Hanlon, the 1st Squadron commander, had been on the coastal road when the fog rolled in, and he returned to Craw Field, anticipating that Hyde might need assistance finding the field and getting down safely. Major Hanlon's concern was justified. When Hyde arrived over Craw Field near midnight, the field was quite invisible to him. The top of the fog bank was only a few hundred feet off the ground, those few hundred feet separating the plane from a safe landing. Major Hanlon, who could hear the engines of Hyde's Liberator, endeavored to coach Hyde into an approach position, hoping that the pilot would be able to pick up the field's boundary and runway lights through the fog. This effort failed; the fog was simply too thick. After several unsuccessful passes over the field, Hyde informed the control tower that his fuel supply was becoming critical. He was then advised to gain altitude and abandon the plane. Accordingly, Hyde climbed to 3,000 feet, set a steady course, and ordered the crew to bail out. All nine surviving crew members parachuted safely, reaching the ground after a memorable flight. Three sustained slight injuries in the parachuting. The wreckage of the plane was located about 25 miles from Craw Field, and Sergeant Kehoe's body recovered for interment. Hyde received a well-merited DFC for his effort, and Sergeant Kehoe was awarded a posthumous DFC.[4]

On July 31 aircraft O/2 (Capt. Gerald L. Mosier, pilot) was on an antisubmarine sweep, flying in heavy clouds, when the radar detected a plane at seven miles, and Mosier altered course toward it. When within a mile, Mosier let down through the clouds, emerging to find an FW 200 about 1,500 yards away. Mosier closed in and followed the Condor at about 600 yards, with nose gun and top turret firing. The B-24 took some damage on wing, fuselage, and starboard rudder. With ammunition running low, Mosier pressed in to point-blank range in an effort to finish off the FW 200, and was rewarded by the Condor bursting into flames. One man was seen to leave the doomed German aircraft before it plunged into the sea after the 11-minute battle. The American crew was uninjured in the engagement, although the starboard rudder of the B-24 was badly damaged and some flight instruments inoperative. Captain Mosier was awarded the DFC for this performance. Gerald L. Mosier was one of those Americans who had joined the RAF early in the war, where he had flown in medium bombers, and transferred to the USAAF after the United States entered the war.[5]

Another single encounter between a B-24 and an FW 200 occurred on August 13, when Capt. Frederick W. McKinnon and his crew tangled with a solitary Condor while flying convoy escort. The FW 200 was persistent in its attempts to get at the convoy, and three times McKinnon closed the German plane, which would then make off into cloud cover. The German's determination was impressive, but also expensive. Eventually, a running combat followed between the wily Condor pilot and McKinnon, at altitudes ranging from about 2,000 feet to near sea level. The B-24's gunners expended no less than 1,790 rounds of .50-caliber ammunition on the pesky German intruder. The FW 200 fired back, but never succeeded in hitting the American plane. Repeated gun jams at inconvenient moments added to McKinnon's frustration in dealing with the big German aircraft. When the FW 200's number 3 engine began to smoke, the German evidently decided it was time to go home. Apparently, he never got there, as a Condor crashed near El Ferrol later that day, which was reported to have been the plane McKinnon had engaged. McKinnon also received the DFC for his performance.[6]

The most spectacular air action for the American antisubmarine squadrons came on August 17, 1943, when Capt. Hugh D. Maxwell Jr. and his crew were providing convoy cover about 300 miles west of Lisbon. After departing Craw Field to meet its convoy, Maxwell's plane received a message that a pair of FW 200s were airborne from their field near Bordeaux and thought en route to intercept Maxwell's convoy. An estimate by the B-24's navigator suggested the big Focke-Wulfs were likely to arrive over the convoy's estimated position about the same time the Liberator got there. Hugh Maxwell later recalled that "I am sure that I and every member of my crew were silently saying a little prayer that they were headed elsewhere."[7]

But the report proved correct. While flying at 1,500 feet in solid overcast, the B-24's radar operator reported first one radar contact at 15 miles, and shortly after another radar contact. Maxwell turned toward the contacts, and as he emerged from the overcast at 1,000 feet two FW 200s could be seen about a mile ahead, just beginning parallel bombing runs on the convoy. The nearer FW 200 broke off its bombing run, opened fire at long range at the rapidly approaching Liberator, and went into a turn to the left. Maxwell closed up onto its tail, and the second Condor came in behind the B-24. The three aircraft then proceeded in line ahead, all firing vigorously. The leading FW 200 descended to just 50 feet off the sea, followed by the B-24 and the second Condor. All three aircraft were taking heavy punishment, and the B-24 had both starboard engines knocked out. Large holes were seen in the wing and fuselage, and the Liberator's right wing was ablaze.

The lead FW 200, however, was in even worse shape, and crashed into the sea. As Maxwell flew over its wreckage, struggling to control his badly damaged aircraft, his top turret gunner was able to join the tail gunner, and also occasionally the right waist gunner, in returning the fire of the second Condor. The plexiglass cover of the B-24's dorsal turret had been shattered and blown away so that the top gunner was exposed to the slipstream as he fired on the second FW 200. The B-24 was now almost out of control, and the crew took up ditching stations. The bombardier was unable to get rid of the depth charges because the hydraulic lines had been cut by enemy fire. The navigator, however, was able to jettison them by using the emergency release and they dropped away barely a minute before ditching.

The right wing of the B-24 hit the water first, throwing the plane into a sideways skid, and it swung through a 180-degree turn. On the second impact, the badly damaged plane broke into three pieces, at the trailing edge of the wing and at the waist windows. The nose section stayed afloat for about a minute and a half, in a nose-down position, but the other two sections sank almost immediately. Maxwell was uncertain if he lost consciousness on impact, but he could recall vividly the shattered window through which he exited the plane. "I momentarily found that I was trapped until I realized my seat belt was still fastened." The copilot also exited through the broken windshield, and the navigator and radio operator through the escape hatch. Two more of the crew escaped through a break in the fuselage near the waist windows, while the tail gunner went out through the top of the tail turret, which had partially broken off. Those from the forward part of the plane were unaware anyone had escaped from the after part of the fuselage. Then Maxwell "heard voices behind the wreckage, and as it sank we saw that three men in [the] rear had survived and had a life raft out." Two life rafts had been released and the seven survivors, all slightly wounded with shrapnel, climbed aboard. Three men were lost in the crash.

Maxwell's crew had not seen the second FW 200 after they crashed, and they thought it too had gone into the water. However, it was observed by the convoy mushing along just above the waves, with its number 3 engine out. Observers in the convoy escorts thought that it crashed, but this was unconfirmed. As the FW 200 disappeared over the horizon, the B-24's survivors were picked up promptly by one of the convoy's escort vessels, which then proceeded to rescue the survivors of the downed Condor. These were four, of whom two were badly burned, and Hugh Maxwell recalled that these two had later died from their burns. The most remarkable aspect of the whole action

Lt. Col. Jack Roberts, the 480th Antisubmarine Group's only commander from its inception to disbandment, awarding decorations to group personnel, Craw Field, Port Lyautey, French Morocco. Roberts was warmly remembered by group members as a strong, effective leader. (Courtesy of Jordan A. Pennoyer.)

Maj. Alfred J. Hanlon, who succeeded Jack Roberts as commanding officer of the 1st Antisubmarine Squadron on January 15, 1943, continuing until its deactivation, passes in front of a B-24D on the ground at Craw Field, Port Lyautey, French Morocco. (Courtesy of Alfred J. Hanlon.)

Maj. Isaac J. "Ike" Haviland, commanding officer of the 2nd Antisubmarine Squadron, January 15–May 29, 1943, relaxes at cards. Haviland returned safely to the United States, but was later lost in the Southwest Pacific Theater. (Courtesy of Bernard E. Benson.)

Capt. Lawrence E. Jarnagin, who succeeded Haviland as commanding officer of the 2nd Antisubmarine Squadron on May 29, 1943. The photo was taken earlier at Bathurst, Gambia. Jarnagin was lost in action on September 18, 1943. (Courtesy of John L. Krebs.)

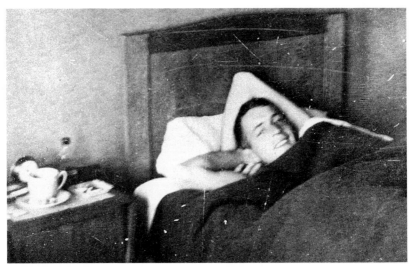

Lt. Wayne S. Johnson, a 1st Antisubmarine Squadron pilot, enjoys his morning cup of tea in the Trevelgue Hotel, Newquay, Cornwall. Cornish hospitality was remembered warmly by 480th Group crews. (Courtesy of Bernard E. Benson.)

RAF Station, St. Eval, Cornwall, England, photographed from the air in the spring of 1943 in unusually good weather. (Courtesy of Bernard E. Benson.)

An aerial view of Craw Field, Port Lyautey, French Morocco, when the Americans were operating from the former French base (c. March–June 1943). A pair of U.S. Navy PBY-5As are visible at upper right. There are two B-24Ds at the lower right, and others to the left of the hanger. (Courtesy of Bernard E. Benson.)

The crew of "C for Charlie," 1st Antisubmarine Squadron, in front of their aircraft at St. Eval. Note USAAF olive drab camouflage. *Top row, left to right:* Wayne S. Johnson, pilot; William W. Pomeroy, copilot; Bernard E. Benson, navigator; Phillip F. Cook, bombardier; James E. Sparks, radio operator; and James T. Hickie Jr., radar operator. In the front row from the left are Thomas A. McGinnis, flight engineer; James P. Corrigan, gunner; Edward E. Layne, gunner (these two were also qualified as assistant radar and radio operators); and William T. Orender Jr., tail gunner. The USAAF normally operated the B-24 as an ASW aircraft with a crew of ten. Usually the first four were commissioned officers, but in this crew the bombardier is a noncommissioned officer. (Courtesy of Bernard E. Benson.)

Bernard E. Benson, navigator of "C for Charlie" of the 1st Antisubmarine Squadron, stands beneath a 20mm shell hole acquired during an action with two JU 88s over the Bay of Biscay on January 29, 1943. (Courtesy of Bernard E. Benson.)

"Tidewater Tillie," 2nd Antisubmarine Squadron, the most accomplished aircraft of the 480th Group, with its most noted crew. *Back row, left to right:* Ralph E. Jones, bombardier; William L. Sanford, pilot; John H. Shaw, navigator; and Harlan L. Jackson, copilot. Second from right in the bottom row is Fred A. Pribble, the radar operator. (Courtesy of John H. Shaw.)

A 479th Antisubmarine Group Liberator crew prior to departure from the United States. This 22nd Antisubmarine Squadron's plane commander and pilot is Wilmer L. Stapel, standing second from left. The roll-up type bomb-bay doors show to good effect. (Courtesy of Wilmer L. Stapel.)

A Whitley of 502 Squadron, RAF, at RAF Station, St. Eval, Cornwall. It was a plane similar to this, belonging to 10 OTU, RAF Bomber Command, and piloted by an inexperienced aviator, which careened into Capt. Bertram Martin's B-24 on January 10, 1943 at St. Eval, with tragic consequences. (Courtesy of Bernard E. Benson.)

A Handley-Page Halifax on the ground at St. Eval, with an American B-24 Liberator behind it. Only two squadrons of RAF Coastal Command were equipped with this fine British aircraft, and one was based for a time at St. Eval. Most Halifaxes went to RAF Bomber Command. The camouflage suggests that this Halifax belonged to Bomber Command and not to Coastal Command. (Courtesy of Ralph E. Jones.)

Servicing the B-24 in the damp Cornish winter could be a daunting chore. Note that the B-24's roll-up bomb-bay doors are open, to allow easy access to the plane's interior. (Courtesy of Bernard E. Benson.)

B-24Ds of the 480th Antisubmarine Group USAAF on the ground at Craw Field, Port Lyautey, French Morocco. Note that the camouflage pattern has light sides to reduce the planes' visibility to submarines. (Courtesy of Jordan A. Pennoyer.)

PBY-5As of Fleet Air Wing 15, USN, on the ground at Craw Field. The building is of French prewar construction. (Courtesy of Jordan A. Pennoyer.)

This photo and the next four show the destruction of U.524 by "Tidewater Tillie" on March 22, 1943. Photos (Courtesy of John H. Shaw.) Here, the U-boat is visible on the **surface.**

U.524 at close range. Note depth charge explosion in the foreground.

Depth charge explosions as "Tidewater Tillie" pulls away from her attack.

U-boat crew members and debris are clearly visible in the water after U.524 has sunk.

Oil slick left by the sunken submarine is clearly visible here, as is the marine marker the B-24 has dropped at the upper right.

A U-boat that lived to fight another day. A 480th Group plane's attack on July 10, 1943, did it no damage. (Courtesy of John L. Krebs.)

HMS *Sportsman* in a Mediterranean port, c. 1943. It would come under attack by a plane of the 480th Antisubmarine Group on September 13, 1943. (Courtesy of the Royal Navy Submarine Museum, Gosport, Hampshire.)

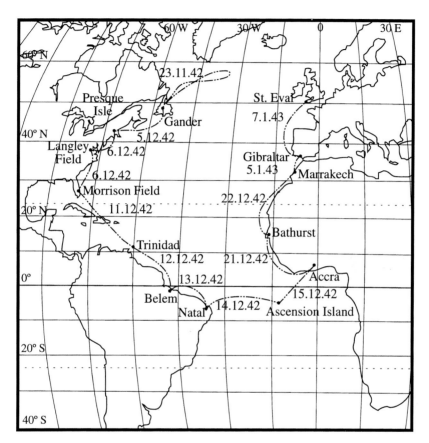

The notional flight path of the 1st Antisubmarine Squadron B-24 of Capt. Arthur J. Kush from Gander, Newfoundland, to St. Eval, Cornwall, England, November 23, 1942–January 7, 1943, including the abortive northern crossing of November 23, 1942.

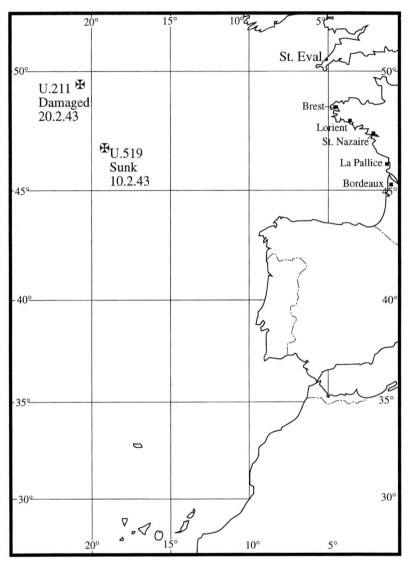

The Eastern Atlantic and the Bay of Biscay, showing locations of U-boats sunk or seriously damaged by the 480th Antisubmarine Group, USAAF, while operating from RAF Station, St. Eval, Cornwall, England. Main U-boat bases on the Bay of Biscay are also shown on the map.

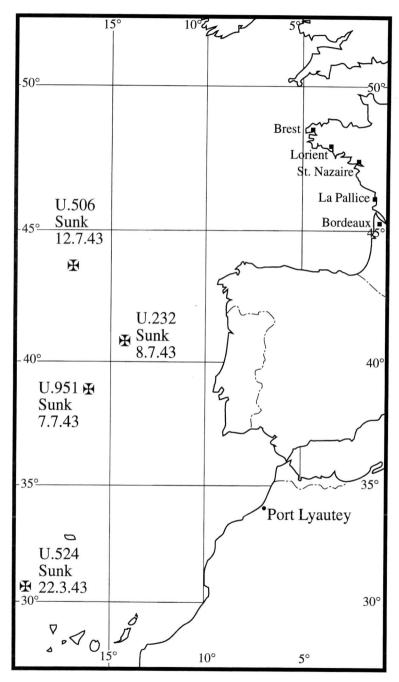

The Eastern Atlantic and Bay of Biscay, showing locations of U-boats sunk by the 480th Antisubmarine Group, USAAF, while operating from Craw Field, Port Lyautey, French Morocco.

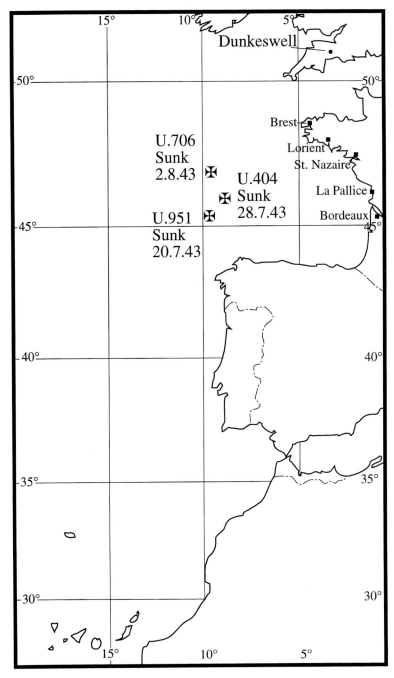

The Eastern Atlantic and the Bay of Biscay, showing locations of U-boats sunk by the 479th Antisubmarine Group, USAAF, while operating from southwest England.

was perhaps the number of survivors from the downed aircraft, considering the violence of the action and the extensive damage to the planes. Further, the Liberator was a notoriously bad plane to have to crash on water. Its high wing and the design of the bomb-bay doors made it all but impossible to put down gently, and the seven survivors were well above the average for Liberator crashes at sea. This high number surely attests to Maxwell's handling of his aircraft and a certain amount of divine partiality in the day's battle. Maxwell was awarded the DFC for the action.[8]

The last week of August saw a sharp series of encounters with enemy aircraft. On August 25, Lt. F. H. Graham and his crew engaged several JU 88s in an indecisive action. Two days later, there were two more actions. In the first, Capt. L. E. Jarnagin briefly exchanged fire with what were thought to be He 111s and Do 217s. As the Americans counted at least thirteen enemy planes, Jarnagin did not linger in the area, but sought cloud cover through which he made a safe retreat. On the second action of that day, Lt. T. E. Kuenning and his crew succeeded in damaging an FW 200.[9] A deadly action came on August 28. That day a message was received from Capt. F. W. McKinnon, who had been in combat earlier in the month, that he was again engaging enemy aircraft. Five minutes later an SOS message followed, and then silence. It was nearly two weeks before the fate of the crew was known. The B-24 had been seriously damaged and McKinnon was forced to make a crash landing at sea off the coast of Portugal. Although the plane crashed with depth charges aboard, and the crew was at considerable risk, McKinnon and two of his crew attempted (unsuccessfully) to rescue the navigator from the plane, for which all three men were subsequently awarded the Silver Star. After several days of drifting, the nine survivors were picked up by fishermen who brought them ashore. McKinnon and five others returned to the group on September 12, only slightly the worse for wear, but three of the crew remained in hospital on that date.[10]

September–October Actions

After the flurry of action in late August, the first half of September was free of encounters with enemy planes. This ended on September 18, when now Maj. Lawrence E. Jarnagin and crew were on patrol. Jarnagin had recently become CO of the 2nd Squadron. The plane reported it was engaging an enemy aircraft and nothing further was heard. The weather on the eighteenth was poor, and even worse on the next three days, which severely hampered search efforts. No trace of the plane or its crew was ever found.[11]

On October 7, Gerald Mosier was again in action, this time against five JU 88s. Mosier had assumed command of the 2nd Antisubmarine Squadron following Jarnigan's loss. While crossing the Bay of Biscay returning to Craw Field from England, the B-24's top turret gunner spotted three JU 88s about two miles away. The B-24's depth charges were promptly jettisoned by emergency release, with some damage to the bomb-bay doors as they dropped away. The initial three JU 88s, joined by an additional pair, took about five minutes to close and set up to attack. The enemy aircraft made eleven firing runs on the Liberator, which always turned into their attacks and returned fire. Although the Junkers closed to 400 yards on several of the passes, their fire was usually high and behind the B-24, which suffered only superficial damage in the action. The engagement lasted 35 minutes, and the American crew estimated they had damaged three of the enemy aircraft, one severely.[12]

This was the last combat by a plane of the 480th Group. While three of the group's Liberators had been destroyed in these actions, only fifteen crew members lost their lives, which would have to be considered fairly light casualties under the circumstances.

Other Aircraft and Crew Losses

An operational loss occurred on July 3, 1943, when one of the planes of the 1st Squadron (1st Lt. Howard W. Fraser, pilot) was last heard from in about 40°N/15°W. Nothing was ever learned of the fate of the ten crew members.[13] Accidents also pushed up casualties in North Africa. The first of these came on May 11, when lieutenants Easterling and Dale, pilot and copilot, crashed on takeoff, killing six of the crew, including Lieutenant Dale.[14] These accidents continued to take a toll well after the chief period of combat for the group had passed. On August 29, plane R/2 (1st Lt. Carl G. Damann, pilot) crashed during a night familiarization flight, killing Damann and the other four crew members who were in the forward part of the plane.[15]

A worse loss followed on September 4 when M/2 crashed. Since Lieutenant Darden was in the hospital, 1st Lt. John E. Kraybill was substituting as pilot with crew S/2. The B-24 took off in the early morning for a planned 14-hour patrol, but the plane was hardly airborne when the port outboard engine erupted in flames. Kraybill notified Craw Field that he wished to make an emergency landing and was immediately cleared to do so. The plane was seen from the ground to be circling to the left, passing over Port Lyautey, and jettisoning its depth charges into the Atlantic Ocean. Still turning to the left, Kraybill passed over the airfield, which tried to contact the plane, but got no reply. The B-24's landing lights were seen to come on while it continued in large circles of about four miles' diameter around the field and city. On his second pass over the field, Kraybill brought the plane down to 700 feet, but appeared to have trouble lining up on a runway. He continued on into yet another wide circle to left, but the plane was then seen to straighten out, waver abruptly, and then plunge directly down into the ground, where it was consumed in flames.

When the fires had burned out, the pilot and copilot were found still in their seats, with the bombardier and navigator directly behind them. The other six members of the crew were found together in the tail section of the plane, aft of the bomb bays, with parachutes on. The investigation team hypothesized that Kraybill had first intended to make an emergency landing, but that after jettisoning the depth charges, he changed his mind and decided to have the crew parachute, and directed the majority of the crew aft preparatory to doing so. The investigators concluded that the movement of the six crew members to the tail area, and the two men in the nose compartment to aft of the flight deck, had shifted the plane's center of gravity aft. The pilot could not then hold the aircraft's nose down and maintain adequate flying speed; the plane stalled less than a thousand feet off the ground and spun in. The team could not explain why the pilot continued to turn to the left, against the dead engine, but this was probably because it gave him the best view of the field as he tried to line up on a runway. He had just leveled out, abandoning his left turns preparatory to having the crew bail out, when the plane crashed.[16]

The thirty men killed in these accidents was twice the number lost to enemy action while the 480th Group was in North Africa.

Ferrying VIPs: An Unpleasant Experience

As early as April 1943 Colonel Roberts had become anxious to begin returning to the United States entire crews who had been overseas since late 1942, and who had seen considerable flying—400 operational hours or more. When the assignment to ferry some VIPs to the United States came up at the beginning of May, it appeared a good opportunity to send a crew home. The group commander was quickly disappointed, however, when it was made clear that this was to be a rush flight that would require using the Liberator at maximum range. This, in turn, meant carrying increased tankage in addition to the VIPs, and left inadequate weight margin to accommodate a full crew as well. Further, as the overwater, nonstop range would be very great, and the VIP very mighty, the flying personnel would have to be selected carefully for their respective skills.

Colonel Roberts selected Maj. Isaac Haviland, the experienced commander of the 2nd Antisubmarine Squadron, to pilot the aircraft, which was the most famous in the group, Tidewater Tillie, deserving of repatriation after her distinguished service overseas. The remainder of the crew of seven came from the 1st Antisubmarine Squadron. Copilot was Capt. Wayne S. Johnson, and the navigator selected to get the plane safely across the Atlantic was Capt. Bernard E. Benson from Johnson's crew. The radio operator was T. Sgt. James E. Sparks.

The chief VIP was Maj. Gen. Walter Bedell Smith, Gen. Dwight D. Eisenhower's chief of staff, who was needed in Washington to represent Eisenhower at an Allied conference. Walter Bedell Smith had a well-deserved reputation for being difficult and demanding. These are traits perhaps necessary in a man who serves as chief of staff to an officer noted for being friendly and accommodating; Smith was undoubtedly a good foil to Eisenhower as well as an able staff officer. This did not, however, make him a congenial person for the 480th Group personnel to deal with, as events would demonstrate.

On May 8, 1943, Tidewater Tillie, suitably modified with additional tanks in the forward bomb bay and a temporary floor and bunks for the VIPs in the after bomb bay, departed Craw Field for Marrakech to pick up General Smith and his party. This accomplished, the plane flew to Dakar and refueled in preparation for the long overwater leg to Waller Field, Trinidad. Dakar to Trinidad was a 2,985-mile flight, which took 21 hours and 17 minutes to complete. The crew's performance was flawless, and the plane put down at Waller Field after a meticulous job of navigation by Benson, who had earlier distinguished himself in finding a German blockade runner for the Royal Navy to destroy.

What had gone so well turned sour at Trinidad. The plane was hardly on the ground before General Smith informed Haviland that they would refuel at once and fly on to Washington via Miami. As the crew had just put in twenty-one hours in the air, following a multihour Marrakech-to-Dakar flight leg, and as Miami was a further eight flying hours from Trinidad, and Washington four more hours beyond Miami, Major Haviland informed Smith that the crew would require eight hours' rest before the flight could proceed. The plane commander observed that while he and the copilot could spell each other, this option was unavailable to the navigator and radio operator, who had to remain awake and alert throughout the flight. General Smith took this badly, and there was a distinct chill in the air when the crew bedded down for some badly needed sleep.

Several of the crew, however, were soon awakened as Tidewater Tillie had to be moved. The aircraft had been refueled, and had to taxi to a revetment as a safety precaution. As darkness had fallen and the crew members were unfamiliar with Waller Field, this turned out to be unfortunate. The taxiing aircraft lost 2½ feet from the left wing when it hit a telephone pole. The accident overtaxed General Smith's patience, not his most highly developed character trait. The enraged general, for whom a new plane now had to be found, ordered the crew of Tidewater Tillie to follow him in their damaged plane all the way to Washington. The crew was not relieved from the ferrying mission until they returned, in a new Liberator, to North Africa. The flight back was, at least, less demanding, by way of Natal to Dakar, which reduced the longest overwater leg to only 10 hours. The crew were back at Craw Field on May 28, following the Washington conference. As one of the flight personnel put it, General Smith's ungracious conduct left "a bad taste" in the mouth.[17]

Detached Service in Support of the Salerno Landings

At the beginning of September 1943, with the invasion of Italy at Salerno rapidly approaching, aircraft of the group departed Port Lyautey and set out for Protville 1, an airfield near Tunis, from where the group could provide coverage for the Allied invasion convoys moving though the Mediterranean toward the landing beaches. Never operating more than a dozen aircraft from their desolate and underdeveloped temporary airfield in northern Tunisia, the group flew patiently day after day from September 4 onward. Their diligent efforts to find and sink German U-boats attempting to attack Allied convoys went unrewarded until September 13.[18]

Just after midnight on September 13, aircraft D/1 lifted off the dusty strip at Protville for another routine patrol southwest of the island of Sardinia. About 0215 that morning the aircraft detected a submarine, but lost it before an attack could be made. Presumably the sub had noticed the approaching aircraft and submerged. However, the aviators' persistence paid off, and at 0345 a submarine was again detected. While flying at 1,000 feet through the moonlit night, the plane's crew spotted the U-boat visually, and the aircraft closed the target at 200 MPH while steadily losing altitude. As it crossed over the sub flying 50 feet off the water, the plane's bombardier dropped a stick of seven depth charges. Several eruptions marked the exploding charges in the water on either side of the U-boat; a perfect straddle had been achieved. Between these erupting gouts of water, where the submarine lay, there was a "large explosion of red flame." The plane circled to renew the attack, but as it passed over the sub a second time, the U-boat appeared dead in the water and sinking rapidly. So no further weapons were released.[19]

When D/1 landed at Protville at 0930 on the morning of September 13, a jubilant crew could claim the group's first kill in the Mediterranean. After nine days of unrewarded effort, this was good news to the antisubmarine group's personnel, who had found the Protville location to be broiling hot by day, bitterly cold at night, and infested night and day with insects.[20] The good news was contagious. Later that day, aircraft Q/2 departed Protville 1 on its patrol near the area of the earlier, successful mission.[21] At just after three in the morning of the fourteenth, Q/2 was also rewarded with a U-boat detection. Indeed, what was revealed to the crew visually in the moonlight was not one, but two fully surfaced submarines. Closing the nearer one rapidly, the American aircraft prepared to drop six depth charges. When almost over the submarine, the pilot recognized something about the silhouette of the surfaced submarine—the conning tower was too large for a German U-boat. He changed direction slightly as the depth charges fell away, and these exploded in the water about 300 feet from the Italian submarine.[22] No harm was done, but it was a disappointed crew that returned to Protville on the morning of September 14. They had not had the good fortune of the earlier crew. Even as Q/2 was landing, however, there was increasing interest being shown in the successful attack of the thirteenth. This had been stimulated by the arrival of His Britannic Majesty's submarine *Sportsman* off Algiers, where from a jury-rigged radio it reported serious damage from an aircraft attack it had sustained at 0351 on the morning of September 13 while operating inside a total bombing restriction area.[23]

Two days earlier, the British submarine was on the closing leg of its patrol, and moving toward the port of Algiers. In the afternoon, the sub sighted a carley float with men in it.[24] As the submarine approached, it found forty-four survivors from the Italian destroyers *Ugolino Vivaldi* and *Antonio Da Noli*. They had been sunk by mines and shore gunfire while passing through the Straits of Bonifacio, between German-occupied Corsica and Sardinia, on September 9. The survivors had been adrift ever since. A submarine is a very small place, and taking aboard the survivors left the British vessel badly overcrowded.[25]

By late on the twelfth, *Sportsman* had entered the Allied total bombing restriction zone, far from German forces, and everyone breathed a bit easier. While running on the surface, at 0215 on the morning of the thirteenth, *Sportsman* detected an approaching aircraft, and unsure of its identity, the submarine's captain promptly submerged. He surfaced 12 minutes later to an empty horizon. However, at about 0350 that morning, the Officer of the Watch (OOW) on the conning tower suddenly noticed a four-engine aircraft only a half-mile away, about 40 feet off the water, and rapidly approaching down-moon. The plane's attitude was unmistakable; it was attacking the submarine. As the OOW ordered the lookouts below, he saw depth charges fall away from the plane as it hurtled past, a few feet over the sub. One charge actually hit the sub, broke up, and gave off a low-level detonation, badly burning the OOW.[26]

As the aircraft was discerned coming about for a second run, the captain submerged at once, despite damage to his vessel. As the plane was seen to have four engines, the submariners were in no doubt as to who had attacked them. The captain set about emergency repairs while he cursed the RAF. When the boat could surface, and damage be assessed, it was found to be extensive to the bridge area, and to the submarine's electrical equipment.[27] As the boat's radio equipment had been damaged, it was not until late on the thirteenth that it was able to transmit a report of the attack, and not until after noon on the fourteenth that it secured alongside the tender HMS *Maidstone* in Algiers harbor, where the Italians could be released from their harrowing trip to safety. Then an investigation could begin into the identity of the submarine's attacker. The culprit was quickly identified, as only the

480th Group was operating four-engine ASW aircraft in the area, and the time of attack matched up perfectly with that of aircraft D/1's attack report. What did *not* match up was the location of the attack.[28]

The investigation quickly brought to light the immediate causes for the attack. The aircraft showed a "large navigational error."[29] There was also disagreement between aircrew and the submarine crew on what was the correct procedure for an Allied submarine to follow at night. The aviators found the first submergence of *Sportsman* at 0215 highly suspicious because they believed that any Allied sub would fire off a recognition flare and remain on the surface. The submarine crew understood this to be the correct procedure for daytime, but not at night.[30] It was a matter of dispute how this misunderstanding came about. The 480th Group's detached service away from its normal base organization was at the core of the difficulty.[31]

The group personnel were happy to return to Craw Field from Protville. The Tunisian field was not only underdeveloped, but overcrowded as well, with a number of British units also operating from it. The temperature on the field reached 134°F on September 7, and while it was a dry heat, it was nonetheless enervating day after day. On September 11 the temperature again went above 130°F. Further, the American unit was hit hard by dysentery at Protville. An awards ceremony at the field had to be called off because many of the Americans were too ill to attend. The last patrol was flown on September 17, and the 480th Group detachment began moving back to the coast of Morocco the same day. No regrets were expressed at departing Tunisia; it had been a disappointing trip.[32]

Group Morale in North Africa: The View from Above

In view of the unhappy experience of the group at Protville, the question of morale is a natural one to ask. However, morale in any group of people is tricky to assess. As a general rule, in military units success breeds high morale, which is hard to sustain in defeat. But boredom and stagnation also have disintegrative effects on military units. Little recognition from higher headquarters is bound to take a toll. The group diary entry for October 1, 1943, reflects something of this problem: "One wonders if the historians will ever know that the Air Corps won the 'Battle of the Atlantic'? Wonder if the

Air Corps will ever know that the 480th Antisubmarine Group played a big part in winning this battle? The 5th Army captured Naples today."[33]

Of course, the Army Air Forces played only a small role in the Battle of the Atlantic, although the 480th Group's work constituted a large part of that limited accomplishment. It is the writer's perspective that is significant here. All military units feel that they are not adequately appreciated, recognized, or rewarded for their achievement. Yet in the case of the 480th Group, the complaint was not ungrounded; the sense of isolation is unmistakable. It comes through sharply in the final sentence, which implicitly contrasts the "forgotten" antisubmarine group, located on the edge of nowhere, with the sort of military action that captures the headlines—taking place over a thousand miles away.

It is possible to get two views on the morale of the 480th Group while it was in North Africa. One perspective derives from Colonel Roberts's letters back to the AAFAC, the other from the anonymous war diarist of the 2nd Antisubmarine Squadron. This individual developed the habit of ending his daily log of operations with a brief summary of how the squadron or at least how *he* felt about matters at the end of the day.[34]

When Colonel Roberts reported to General Larson of the AAFAC in mid-April 1943 on the group's settling in to its new base in North Africa, he noted that the time lag between the arrival of the aircraft and crews and the group's ground echelon, which came by sea and rail, had forced a low operating tempo because aircrew had to be used for a wide variety of base duties. While this had been overcome with the arrival of the ground personnel at the end of March, individual problems remained. "There are . . . personnel, both ground and air, whose work is not satisfactory but yet not unsatisfactory to the point that they can be reclassified." These Roberts proposed to deal with "separately according to the particular situation."[35]

Regarding the unit's morale in general, Roberts stressed the arrival of mail as having "a greater affect on morale than any other factor." He went on to say also that "a need for better discipline became apparent just prior to departure from the ETO." The deterioration in discipline he attributed to crowded conditions and limited recreational facilities at St. Eval, and to "lack of experience and ground training of newly arrived personnel." The prevailing weather and ample space at Craw Field made it possible to institute an ambitious sports program. But Roberts noted that "the adjacent town of Pt. Lyautey has nothing to offer except an excellent Red Cross canteen." More distant towns had better facilities, but transport difficulties made them hard to use.[36]

In his mid-May report to the AAFAC, Roberts was generally satisfied that "morale is good." He noted that causes of the initial improvement in morale, "the novelty of good climate, sunshine, better food, and a new station," were now less influential, but that this was compensated for by much improved mail delivery. He thought that successful operations and the announcement that deserving aircrews would be rotated back to the United States also were helpful to good morale. On the negative side, he listed "having to work under the USN, lack of recreational facilities, and the slowness of the procurement of awards, promotions, etc." By August Roberts had to report that the group's morale was generally lower, the result of (accurate) rumors that the AAFAC was going out of business.[37]

The individual problems that concerned Roberts focused mainly on aircrew and more senior officers, in both flying and ground assignments. By late August, Roberts reported that he had a "dire need" to rotate eight crews who had accumulated more than 400 operational hours on overseas duty, and who were showing the strain of continued operations. Illustrating the critical nature of this problem, the group commander reported that "four officer members of these crews . . . are nervous wrecks."[38] The intense action off Cape Finisterre in July, occurring at maximum operational range, presumably had much to do with this.

A somewhat different sort of concern for Roberts was "an intelligence officer about whom I am beginning to worry and would like to replace as early as practicable." The group commander also reported on the case of "an Armament Officer who broke under strain and was hospitalized for a couple of weeks." As the operational strain on a ground armament officer in a unit with the regular operating pattern of the antisubmarine group, based on secure territory, can hardly be described as intense, the suitability of the man for his work and his responsibilities is perhaps suspect. As Roberts frankly told General Larson in early May: "At present my personnel are so restricted in number, and of those some are quite limited in ability, that I have absolutely no flexibility whatsoever." This surely was at the root of some of the personnel problems the group commander faced. Part of his problem was that some of the officers were rather senior for their work, but not sufficiently able that he could recommend them for promotion. This was true of the intelligence officer noted above, "who does not fit into Intelligence very well, and who, therefore, because of his rank, is somewhat a problem."[39]

At a less senior level were two second lieutenants against whom charges were pending for having "provoked a fight with an enlisted man." Here Roberts's problem was getting NATOUSA authorities to move on authorizing a court-martial. There was also the longstanding problem of "one ground officer, a habitual and flagrant offender since before departure from the U.S.," whom Roberts had recommended for reclassification, but he was still awaiting action on his request.[40] These delays were a consequence of the unit's orphan status with regard to higher organizations, being always in the position of temporary guest in another's house. In the case of NATOUSA, in early May all eyes in Algiers were focused on the ground campaign in Tunisia, then in its culminating stage, and the disciplinary concerns of an antisubmarine unit on the Atlantic coast of Morocco must have ranked very low indeed in its priorities. Directly related to this was the problem of convincing rear echelon commanders that the group was "not here for training, rest, or furnishing base services," but to carry out an operational assignment.[41]

The physical distance between Port Lyautey and "the front" as NATOUSA saw it was the primary cause of this misperception. The unsensational character of antisubmarine warfare, which could not be measured in territory gained, and where what action that did occur did so far from newsmen and photographers, only enhanced the lonely position of the group. Roberts did note that one NATOUSA officer who was sympathetic and helpful to the group was the American deputy commander of NACAF, Brig. Gen. Elwood R. "Pete" Quesada.[42] Quesada's estimate of Roberts is worth quoting: "He is, without reservation, one of the finest officers with whom I have had contact. His efficiency, devotion to duty and intellectual honesty are seldom approached."[43] Quesada was anxious to get Roberts, still a lieutenant colonel, promoted to the rank of colonel. Again, the provisional status of the wing (as the 480th Group then still was) proved an impediment to this action, as it was to clearing up various personnel problems that plagued Roberts. Roberts was able to report in mid-April that since the group's arrival in the NATOUSA, there had been only one new case of gonorrhea, and no new cases of syphilis or other venereal diseases. By mid-May there was a rising incidence of venereal disease in the group, although it was "well below the average for this theater." Roberts was seeking to locate the source of the infection. In mid-June, Roberts reported a venereal rate of four per thousand per month in the 480th Group. Venereal disease, then, while it rose somewhat over time, was not a major problem in the group. As the Port Lyautey area was notoriously bad for malaria, a routine was set up in the group for administering quinine to aircrew and atabrine to ground personnel, along with appropriate control measures, including dress regulations. Roberts's greatest problem in this regard was an inadequate supply of mosquito netting. By the middle of May there was one unconfirmed case of malaria in the group, which was after a strict regimen in the use of quinine or atabrine had been followed. This strict regimen had, however, required administering the atabrine hydrochloride more often in smaller dosages in order to avoid undesirable side effects. In late May there was an outbreak of dysentery. This in turn led to increased efforts at fly control, which were hampered by the continuing shortage of screening. There were by mid-June, however, only two diagnosed cases of malaria.[44]

Group Morale in North Africa: The View from Below

The perspective on morale from the lower ranks proved different from that of the group commander. Not surprisingly, food and weather made up a large part of the 2nd Squadron diarist's comments. With regard to diet, the transfer from St. Eval to Craw Field was seen as a positive development, and he noted on April 9 that "we had fried eggs this morning which was quite a treat."[45] As a rule, during the group's stay in North Africa, the food passed muster. Not so the weather. For the first two months, the Moroccan weather, warm and clear, was a delight after the dampness and darkness of a British winter along the windswept coast of Cornwall. By mid-May, however, the diarist complained that it was "unbearably hot," and in tandem with the hot weather arrived the mosquitoes. In June came large quantities of dust, carried in from the desert on strong, dry winds. By mid-August, while the heat remained "oppressive," the diarist noted that "work is being carried on as usual, the greatest part being done at night." On September 7 came the welcome entry that the weather was cooling off. However, this was a prelude to the onset of the rainy season, and by early October the 2nd Squadron diary records that "rain falls most every day," and was even impeding flying operations. The comments are much what one would expect, and never suggest, despite the rhetoric, that weather was a major impediment to good morale.

In the beginning, the lack of enlisted personnel facilities at Craw Field was irritating. (Officers were housed in old French military buildings.) However, steady progress was recorded here. In early April, squadron personnel began the move out of a "drafty hangar" and to a small community of six-man tents. In early May, a self-help project resulted in electricity being supplied to the tent city. This was followed in early June with wood flooring laid down in all the tents, as living conditions steadily improved. Among the improvements was the opening of an Air Corps PX on the base in early June, closely followed by a squadron barber shop.

Two matters, not unrelated, link together to form the main litany of complaint in the squadron diary: the problem of off-base recreation opportunities and the occurrence of courts-martial (too few and too frequent, respectively, to suit the diarist). The cities and towns of Morocco were very different from those of southern England. The religion, culture, social controls, and ethnic differences, and a great range in living standards, from the opulent to dire poverty, were truly foreign experiences for the men of the 480th Group. The mixture contained the makings of morale and discipline problems for the American visitors. A hint of the problem showed up in the 2nd Squadron diary for April 18: "There is nothing much to do here at Craw Field except go to a show every night. The towns around here hold no interest for the men." This may presumably be translated to mean that there were no suitable women available for companionship, and perhaps even a shortage of suitable prostitutes.

By the middle of June, sufficient problems had surfaced that passes to leave the station were limited to 5 percent of the unit's manpower at any one time. The nature of at least some of the problems is highlighted by the July 22 diary entry: "Symptoms of venereal disease have almost disappeared due to the closing of the G.I. houses two months ago." Evidently, then, the June restriction on passes was to limit the men freelancing once organized facilities were no longer available to them. The consequences of these actions is perhaps reflected in the entry for August 6: "The men are beginning to show the strain of being in a locality which is not to their liking. Several of them have been caught leaving the post without a pass."

A step to improve morale occurred in mid-August, when beer became available on base in the squadron day room for enlisted men. The diarist hoped "many of the men will now remain in camp rather than go to town." Shortly thereafter, he wrote that "the morale of the squadron has picked up considerably as a result of having beer for sale on the post." Certain problem areas persisted, however. Fez was placed off limits to men on furlough, because of the high rate of venereal disease being contracted by men who had been there. However, two of the group's men were injured in a jeep accident in Fez, leading the diarist to observe that "since this town has been placed off limits they may be severely punished."

Punishment raises the subject of courts-martial, a topic that seemed increasingly to concern the 2nd Squadron writer. In mid-April the diarist noted without comment that a court-martial board had convened. The next mention is in early July, and this time a 480th Group enlisted man was sentenced to three months at hard labor. In late August the results of another court-martial were one enlisted man receiving four months in the guard house, and the other defendant being found not guilty. This record hardly suggests a discipline of punitive severity. Yet on August 30, 1943, the day after an aircraft of the squadron crashed, killing five members of its crew, the diary entry has only the briefest reference to the funeral of these men. Rather, the diarist records: "Another court-martial was held today. The morale of the men is very low as a result of this epidemic of court-martials."

Perhaps the real explanation for the diarist's obsession with courts-martial is provided in his entry for September 8: "The men are getting restless, having been here since March. A change would be a great help for the morale." By September 1943 Morocco was distinctly a backwater of the war, which had passed on from Tunisia to Sicily, and then to Italy. That stress was developing in the unit is suggested by the fact that Colonel Roberts himself met with the enlisted men of the group on the evening of September 13, and warned them "not to break army regulations as anyone doing so would be court-martialled." The strain was relieved on October 3, when Colonel Roberts informed the group "that we would leave for the states in 30 days."

Some things come through strongly in this comparative survey of morale—from the top and the bottom, so to speak. One notes at once how different the perspective was from these two angles. The group commander focused on the group's operations, with aircrew morale his first concern. Although Colonel Roberts recognized the importance of the efficiency of the whole unit, such topics as food, weather, off-base recreational opportunities, and courts-martial were secondary. Not so for the enlisted diarist in the 2nd Antisubmarine Squadron. For him, these were the very stuff that determined morale.

There is a certain inevitability about these distinctive viewpoints.

However, it seems fair to say that Roberts had a special problem in commanding an operational unit which by the nature of its work was normally based in a location relatively distant from the main battlefronts of the war. For those personnel who did not fly, the temptation to see the war as far away, and not impinging very directly on them, must have been great. In these circumstances, maintaining unit morale acquires a particular sort of difficulty. Colonel Roberts seems to have done as well as could be expected in these circumstances. Discipline problems were never serious in the 480th Group and morale cannot ever be described as bad.

A Disappointing Conclusion

From an administrative standpoint, deploying units on detached service from their wing organizations was not efficient. It was found necessary to give the deployed units "separate, special" group status so that they could be managed effectively. Overseas wings would have been better yet, but this involved a scale of commitment to ASW operations beyond the Western Hemisphere which AAF Headquarters was unwilling to make.[46] This attitude, in fact, foreshadowed the decision of the USAAF to get out of the ASW business altogether and leave that mission to the USN. This was as that service desired, and left the USAAF free to concentrate its energies on the tactical air and strategic bombing missions. A logical division of labor between the two services, it was disappointing for the personnel of the 480th Group who had distinguished themselves in ASW operations.

8

The 479th Antisubmarine Group in the United Kingdom

Coastal Command Seeks Additional Resources

Air Marshal Sir John Slessor, AOC-in-C Coastal Command, had been dismayed to lose the 480th Antisubmarine Group from his order of battle early in March 1943. The same month he proposed an enlarged effort in the U-boat transit area across the Bay of Biscay, requesting from both British and American resources an additional 160 long-range, radar-equipped aircraft to add to the 100 he was then able to deploy for the bay campaign. Slessor's proposal was greeted with restraint by both the RAF and the USAAF, because both air forces saw their primary mission in the ETO as the strategic bombing campaign against Germany. As the types of aircraft Slessor needed for Coastal Command's bay campaign were the same types used in bombing operations, both RAF and USAAF saw antisubmarine warfare as a drain on the resources they wished to commit to the bomber offensive.[1]

Thus Slessor's proposal hung in limbo for a considerable time, during which the crisis of the Battle of the Atlantic was surmounted, in no small measure by a relatively few VLR aircraft supporting the hard-pressed convoys in the mid-Atlantic. Once the convoy crisis had passed in May 1943, a surplus of antisubmarine aircraft developed in place to cover areas where by mid-

June 1943 there were few if any submarines operating. One such location was Newfoundland, which had more than the needed number of LR and VLR aircraft as determined by the Atlantic Convoy Conference of March 1943. This fact was noted by the Cominch, U.S. Fleet, Adm. Ernest J. King, who proposed that some of the surplus aircraft be assigned to Slessor's Bay of Biscay offensive. Accordingly, at the beginning of July, the 4th and 19th Antisubmarine Squadrons, USAAF, which had been operating Liberators from Newfoundland, were transferred to the United Kingdom as the 479th Antisubmarine Group. They would be joined there later by an additional two squadrons, the 6th and 22nd Antisubmarine Squadrons, but these last two came too late to participate more than very briefly in the Biscay battle.[2]

With Admiral Doenitz acknowledging at least temporary defeat on the convoy routes in May, and recalling his U-boats from the convoy battles in which they had been so bloodied, the Bay of Biscay became the area where the German submarines were most likely to be found, just as the Allies were beefing up their own effort there. Thus the stage was set for what would prove to be the climax of the Battle of the Bay in the period from May to the first few days of August 1943. This climax occurred, it should be said, only because of Admiral Doenitz's fatal miscalculation that his U-boats, with their AA guns increased, crossing the bay on the surface in groups, could fight their way through against air attack, with light loss to themselves.

What Doenitz had done was to present RAF Coastal Command with what in modern parlance would be called a target-rich environment. Slessor had every intention of pressing his attack to the utmost while the opportunity for a rich harvest of sunken U-boats remained available to him. Predictably, it would be too good to last, and Doenitz would recede from his folly early in August. But while it lasted it was a grand old donnybrook.

Getting Off to a Better Start

The 479th Antisubmarine Group got off to an easier start than had the 480th. The 4th and 19th Antisubmarine Squadrons had some time to run in their equipment and to work out bugs before they were deployed to the United Kingdom. Further, both they and the British had learned from the problems that had beset the 1st and 2nd Antisubmarine Squadrons in their pioneering deployment to the United Kingdom. Accordingly, things went more smoothly for the 479th Group from the start. But not too smoothly. On June 24, the 4th Antisubmarine Squadron, operating at the time from Gander, Newfoundland, was ordered to transfer to Westover Field, Massachusetts. On arrival there, the squadron was told it was going in the wrong direction; there were new orders to proceed to the United Kingdom by way, of course, of Gander, Newfoundland.[3]

All twenty-four aircraft of the 4th and 19th Squadrons arrived safely at St. Eval, via Prestwick, Scotland, on June 30 (thirteen planes) and July 7 (eleven planes), 1943.[4] They crossed at a better time of year than the 1st and 2nd Squadrons, and the North Atlantic transit route was much better established by mid-1943 than it had been at the end of 1942. The commander of the 4th Squadron recalled that "the hop across had been easy. [The Gander-Prestwick leg] was not as long as an ordinary routine patrol."[5]

As had been the case with the first two antisubmarine squadrons, the 4th and 19th came under Eighth Air Force for administration and supply and under the operational control of 19 Group of Coastal Command. The 479th Group, USAAF, under Col. Howard Moore was activated on July 8, 1943, and its two squadrons began flying operational missions on July 13.[6] Before doing this, an aircrew had to complete a training curriculum of about a week, covering radio procedures, codes, and signals, and to fly a training flight. In response to the sharp increase in Luftwaffe activity over the bay in this period, it was sometimes also possible for the American planes to get some practice maneuvering to best advantage when confronted with enemy long-range fighters. The British Beaufighter played the adversary role for this purpose.[7]

Like the personnel of the 480th Group before them, the men of the 479th came quickly to admire their British allies. One member of an aircrew wrote:

> I had/have great respect for the English civilian population considering the hardships that were placed on them during World War II, and also I feel the same toward the military in the RAF. It looked as though they would take anything they could get into the air and fly their missions . . . against the enemy.[8]

The commander of the 4th Antisubmarine Squadron recalled "the splendid cooperation given us by the RAF and the hospitality with which we were received." He attributed this warm welcome in good part to the groundwork laid at St. Eval by the 1st and 2nd Squadrons. "They . . . had been extremely popular with the RAF personnel at the station."[9]

In the first week of August the two recently arrived squadrons were transferred from St. Eval to a newer RAF station at Dunkeswell in adjacent Devonshire. There the 479th Group had the facility to itself, although at first it was dependent on a good deal of RAF ground support. While the station commander exercised a general supervision, Colonel Moore was largely free to run the 479th Group as he saw fit, according to USAAF customs and practices. Further, many of the administrative and logistical problems that had plagued the 480th Group were avoided by assigning at the outset to the 479th Group the 87th Service Squadron, the 1813th Ordnance Service and Maintenance Company, the 1177th Military Police Company, and the 444th Quartermaster Platoon. These all arrived in England with the ground echelon of the group and the first two squadrons. When the 6th and 22nd Antisubmarine Squadrons arrived in England, they joined the 4th and 19th Squadrons at Dunkeswell.[10]

The chief drawback of Dunkeswell was that it was still incomplete, particularly with regard to the off-runway facilities, and the tracks that passed for roads on the RAF station were inadequate for heavy equipment, broke up under heavy use, and tended to become quagmires in the damp climate. Compared to the difficulties that had beset the first American antisubmarine group, however, this counted as only a minor inconvenience. From the time the 479th flew its first operational missions it was able to maintain a steady tempo of operations. The weather from July to September, when the 479th did most of its flying, was certainly an improvement over what the 480th Group experienced from November to February. However, the longest mission a plane of the 479th Group flew, 13 hours and 59 minutes airborne, was the result of bad weather, making it almost impossible to find an open field where the aircraft could get down safely. On October 18, 1943, K/22 finally found safe haven at St. Eval, where the Americans had started their antisubmarine flying some 11 months earlier.[11]

Operating Conditions

The long missions over the bay imposed their own tempo and their own stress on the aircrews. Each crew hut on the field at Dunkeswell held the enlisted personnel of two aircrews, six on each side of the hut. As most of the group's ASW flights were timed to be in the patrol area by summer daybreak, this meant being turned out as early as 3 A.M., with the aircrew then being "taken to a mess hall for a meal, if we had survived the wild ride in the darkness by the English driver."[12]

After breakfast, the crew also picked up at the mess hall their "picnic lunch" for the long flight upcoming. Next came the flight briefing, followed by checking out all personal and aircraft equipment essential to the flight. The plane would normally be airborne for about 10 hours, "then back to the base and go through the whole thing in reverse. The whole operation would take about fifteen hours, and the crew would be ready to hit the sack when we had returned."[13]

Part of the "equipment" carried on every operational flight was a pair of homing pigeons. These were picked up in their cage before each flight and returned following landing. They were useful for two purposes: to relay messages that were not time-critical when complete radio silence was required, but more essentially, to inform Coastal Command when something had gone badly wrong. A crash landing at sea, particularly if the radio operator had not been able to get off a message informing base of the crew's situation and location, was the prime opportunity for the homing pigeons to be of service. It assumed, of course, that the pigeons survived the crash landing, when their fate was not likely to be uppermost in the minds of the crew. In their less critical use, the pigeons had to be released into the plane's slipstream, apt to be quite turbulent. Further, the airspeed of the B-24 was unlikely to have been much less than 150 MPH. Thus a special procedure was required to get the pigeon safely away, involving some unique equipment: "paper bags—bags of the grocery store type."[14]

If a message was to be sent back during flight, it would be attached to the bird and then the pigeon was stuffed into the bag, head first, of course. One of the gunners at the waist window would carefully set the package outside. The closed end of the bag would be placed into the wind and in this way it was supposed to prevent the wind from stripping the bird's feathers off so quickly. As the package slowed down the pigeon was supposed to free himself and take off in the desired direction.[15]

The B-24D equipped the 479th as well as the 480th Group, but the 479th's aircraft already incorporated many improvements that had come slowly to the 480th Group. By the time the 22nd Squadron left the United States, for example, it was equipped with the improved model D which had a nose turret. Two flexible guns replaced the tail turret, reducing weight aft in the plane.[16] The Liberator, as always, proved to be a dependable aircraft. An examination of twenty-seven missions that had had to be curtailed between August 11 and October 29 (one after nine hours airborne when the plane's instruments failed) shows that the most common reason for an early return (seven occasions) was because of a malfunctioning turret. Given the activity of the Luftwaffe over the bay in this period, this problem understandably would lead to early termination of a mission. Next as a cause of lost mission time were engine problems (five occasions), including one occurrence of an engine bursting into flames only 15 minutes into a flight. This potentially dangerous development had a happy ending in a safe landing, and was fortunately a rare event. Fuel leaks also caused five flights to be curtailed, and unspecified mechanical failures accounted for four abbreviated flights. The 27 flights thus curtailed, of the 346 flown in this period, gives a 7.8 percent early return rate.[17]

In theory, crews were to be kept together, and each crew was to have an individual aircraft assigned to it. While the first of these goals was generally, if imperfectly, achieved in the 479th Group, the second was not. Maintenance and flying schedules did not often match up neatly, and aircrews flew whatever planes were available. In one example, only eight of eighteen operational missions were made in the crew's "regular" aircraft.[18] The goal of a three-day flying cycle was no more achieved by the 479th than it had been by the 480th Group. Something closer to a four-day cycle prevailed, but with notable variations.[19]

Antisubmarine Operations

During their operations over the Bay of Biscay, aircraft of the 479th Antisubmarine Group made twelve sightings and delivered eight attacks. Ten sightings and six attacks came in the period before August 2, when Admiral Doenitz altered his tactics from confronting to avoiding Allied ASW aircraft. Three U-boats were sunk, all before August 2, with credit divided between an American and a British attacking aircraft in two cases and with a Canadian aircraft in the third case.[20]

The group's first attack on a U-boat was a good try, but not quite good enough. Aircraft P/4 (1st Lt. Walter R. Young, pilot), flying a patrol at 5,000 feet in 5/10 cloud on July 18, 1943, obtained a radar contact at 20 miles range. Using cloud to cover his approach, Young established visual contact at 12 miles in position 46.47°N/11.21°W. As the plane descended to attack, the U-boat, unlike most German submarines in this period, submerged. This proved a sound decision by the submarine commander. He was able to get under about 25 to 30 seconds before Young could cross over the vanished U-boat's track, and release a stick of four British Mark XI 250-pound Torpex depth charges. Further, as the pilot saw the U-boat go under while still some distance away, he attempted to cover that distance at maximum speed in a dive, and the Liberator's indicated airspeed when the depth charges were released from 50 feet was 260 MPH, surely a record attack speed for a B-24.

The high attack speed had predictable repercussions on the stick spacing, which photos indicated to be in the vicinity of 250 feet, rather than the desired 50 to 100 feet. The stick fell across the U-boat's estimated track about 65 feet ahead of the swirl. As the submarine would by then have advanced about 300 feet, it was a clear miss behind the U-boat. The pilot was determined, and the plane made a second pass to drop four more depth charges. Again the calculated position was well behind the forward path of the submarine. The chance of hitting the U-boat, which had now been submerged over a minute, was nil. Not surprisingly, there was no sign of a crippled U-boat and the assessment was one of insufficient evidence of damage.[21] Two days later the group would have a chance to improve on this hasty beginning.

July 20, 1943, began with a fatal encounter when aircraft B/19 engaged a U-boat in the bay. "B for Beer" (1st Lt. Harold E. Dyment, pilot) was flying in heavy overcast in 45.30°N/09.45°W when it transmitted an action signal, followed by silence. Communications intelligence revealed that Dyment had attacked a surfaced submarine, whose AA fire brought down the American aircraft, and its ten-member crew was lost with the plane. However, the Liberator succeeded in dropping several depth charges as it passed over the U-boat, which in turn suffered serious damage. The Admiralty assessment, on the basis of this information, was that of severely damaged.[22] But it was the Americans who had paid the higher price in this exchange. B/19 would be the only plane of the 479th Group lost to enemy flak.

U.558 Sunk

The score was quickly evened up. Shortly after B/19's loss, F/19 (1st Lt. Charles F. Gallmeier, pilot) participated in the sinking of U.558. The fate of this U-boat is a good illustration of what German submariners faced while crossing the bay on the surface. U.558 had sailed on its tenth war patrol on May 8, and was now on its way back to port.[23] It was first spotted on July 15 by a Wellington of 179 Squadron, RAF Coastal Command, but its experienced commander, Kapitaenleutnant Guenther Krech, had his AA gunners fight back vigorously. The Wellington was only slightly damaged, but the flak from the U-boat had been sufficient to throw off its aim. U.558 had survived its first encounter with the wall of Allied antisubmarine aircraft deployed across the Bay of Biscay. Two days later, U.558 had its second encounter, this time with a Liberator of 224 Squadron, RAF. Again, Krech stayed on the surface and fought it out with the attacking plane, which was hit several times during its approach, but not deterred from releasing its weapons. But again, both plane and submarine survived the exchange.

On the twentieth, U.558's luck ran out. "F for Freddie" was patrolling at 2,000 feet in 10/10 cloud with its base at 1,000 feet when its SCR-717A radar picked up a contact 24 miles ahead.[24] In fact, F/19 had found two U-boats, with both a Sunderland and a British Liberator circling above, looking for an opening to attack them. But a rain squall enveloped both the aircraft and submarines, and the planes emerged from the squall to find the U-boats gone. They had presumably used the opportunity offered by the weather to submerge, a wise course of action given the increasing air activity over their heads. An hour after the first sighting, "F for Freddie" was still searching when a second radar contact was achieved, this time at 30 miles range. Again Gallmeier closed the indicated target, but the second contact was lost, possibly because it was an aircraft and not a U-boat. Forty-five minutes after the second contact, the American Liberator, still at 2,000 feet, was flying in position 45.18°N/09.58°W when yet a third radar contact was achieved, this time at 13 miles.

It was a case of third time lucky; this radar indication was not lost, and visual contact with a surfaced U-boat was achieved at five miles from a height of 1,000 feet. After so much frustration in finding his quarry, Gallmeier did not delay, but went directly into the attack. The boat was U.558. Krech responded as he had to all previous comers, and the U-boat put up a formidable volume of flak. F/19 was hit several times, the left waist gunner was wounded in both legs, and the port inner engine damaged. Gallmeier passed over the sub at 100 feet while his bombardier released a stick of seven depth charges with an observed spacing of about 50 feet. These fell closely along the port side of

U.558, which was mortally wounded by the attack. As Gallmeier circled for a second attack, his damaged number 2 engine cut out on him. As a British Halifax was seen rapidly approaching, Gallmeier left it to the RAF plane to deliver the *coup de grâce,* jettisoned his remaining depth charges, and headed for home on three engines.

The situation aboard the U-boat was critical. The boat never recovered from the confusion during the attack of the B-24. Gas escaping from a mixture of seawater and ruptured battery plates made it impossible for the crew to stay below. U.558 went into a series of tight turns while it slowed and began to sink from the stern. Halifax E/58 Squadron released eight depth charges, which fell across the U-boat and ensured that there would be no recovery from Gallmeier's attack. Unfortunately, the U-boat's crew was just beginning to abandon ship as the depth charges came down, and casualties were high. In the end, only five of the crew, including the captain, were rescued from a life raft five days later by HMCS *Athabascan.* Forty-one members of U.558's crew perished with their boat. The kill was shared equally between the American and British aircraft.[25]

Krech and his crew had fought hard all the way, receiving attacks from four aircraft in the space of five days. U.558's flak had damaged three of the attacking planes, but had been unable to deter any of them from attacking. All the planes returned safely to their bases. In exchange for slightly wounding one flier, U.558 had forfeited the majority of her crew. The opportunity for two aircraft, both four-engine planes carrying large depth-charge loads, to attack U.558 sequentially sealed her doom. Notable, too, was the fact that Gallmeier's attack on U.558 came some two hours after his first radar contact with an indicated target. The Liberator's ability to carry both a large fuel load and a substantial weapons load made it effective as an ASW aircraft. Perhaps the most remarkable aspect of this episode was that in the face of one U-boat after another undergoing the sort of ordeal U.558 had just endured and failed to survive, Admiral Doenitz persisted in his tactic of fighting his subs across the bay on the surface for yet another two weeks. Certainly, they were weeks of great opportunity to the sub hunters.

U.404 Sunk

Events on July 28 again demonstrated the terrible vulnerability of surfaced U-boats to repeated aerial attacks. The victim on this date was U.404, outbound from St. Nazaire on her seventh war patrol, but with a new CO, Ober-leutnant Adolf Schoenberg.[26] The first Allied aircraft to pick up the German submarine was Y/4, commanded by Maj. Stephen D. McElroy, who was also CO of the 4th Antisubmarine Squadron. The weather was clear that day and Y/4 was at 5,000 feet when radar reported a contact nine miles ahead. This was quickly supplemented with visual contact by both navigator and bombardier. When the plane was still a half mile away the submarine dived. Seven seconds after the U-boat had gone under, the crew attempted to release eight depth charges, but these failed to drop, and U.404 had survived its first attack.

The problem with the depth-charge release was thought to be with a faulty intervalvometer, and McElroy ordered his bombardier henceforth to release the depth charges with his manual toggle. While apt to be less accurate, it was more certain of getting the weapons away. The 4th Squadron commander was also a persistent hunter. Y/4 had released a marine marker to indicate where the attack had occurred, and McElroy continued his search in the area. Two hours later another marker was released to keep the plane oriented as it employed baiting tactics, leaving and then returning to the area. Nearly three hours after the first attack, the bombardier with binoculars in the nose of the plane spotted a surfaced U-boat in 46.09°N/09.35°W. It was U.404, which Schoenberg had unwisely brought to the surface again. This time, the U-boat commander chose to slug it out with the rapidly approaching Liberator. An AA shell entered the cockpit of Y/4, destroyed the copilot's fuse box, and burst further on, damaging the plane's radio equipment. Remarkably, the plane's crew, four of whom were in close proximity to the exploding shell, survived unscathed. Indeed, their return fire appears to have prompted the inexperienced U-boat commander to submerge again.

Determined not to lose his target a second time, McElroy attacked down track toward the rapidly disappearing U-boat. The conning tower was under for just five seconds when the plane dropped its weapons. Eight depth charges were released by toggle, and fell in a long line beside the submerged vessel's course. (The hull of the U-boat was still visible just beneath the water's surface as the plane passed by.) A significant outflowing of black oil was seen rising to the surface of the bay as the aircraft pulled up and away. With his number 3 engine apparently losing oil pressure at this point, McElroy did not remain in the area, but set course for home, having feathered the prop on the damaged engine. The black oil on the water apparently came from a damaged fuel tank, but the U-boat's pressure hull survived the attack. The Admiralty assessors awarded McElroy's attack an *F*, or insufficient evidence of damage, evidently because the photographs taken did not turn out. Cominch evaluated it as a *D*, or probably severely damaged, evidently on the basis of the crew's testimony.[27] The greater significance of the attack was that it fixed the location of the U-boat, and 19 Group of Coastal Command was able to divert other aircraft toward the spot where it had submerged.

Also on July 28, N/4 (1st Lt. Arthur J. Hammer, pilot) was north of Cape Finisterre flying at 4,000 feet in light cloud when a fully surfaced U-boat was seen five miles off to starboard. There had been no radar contact, and it is possible the submarine had just surfaced.[28] Hammer had been attracted to this location by intercepting McElroy's messages, and arrived in the area about half an hour after his squadron's commander had been forced to depart. Schoenberg had not stayed under long this time, suggesting that Major McElroy's attack may have done some damage. On the other hand, Hammer's report does not mention sighting any oil leaking from the surfaced submarine. Hammer promptly attacked, and the U-boat just as promptly opened fire as Schoenberg swung his boat through a series of S-turns to complicate the Liberator's attack. At a thousand yards, the B-24's guns answered the U-boat's fire, and appeared to knock two men into the water. Flying at an altitude of 100 feet, the plane dropped eight depth charges, spaced at 60 feet, five falling short of and three beyond the conning tower in a neat straddle. The Liberator then made a second run, releasing from an altitude of only 50 feet four more depth charges, spaced now at 100 feet apart. All four fell short of the still surfaced sub, the last close to the hull.

As the B-24's nose guns had run out of ammunition and the top turret's guns jammed on the second run in, the plane could not suppress the AA fire coming up at it. Thus U.404's gunners had an undisturbed aim, and they hit back hard, knocking out the B-24's port outboard engine, and inflicting other damage. At this point, a British Liberator, W/224, commanded by Flying Officer R. V. Sweeney, arrived on the scene. He had been attracted by the plumes from Hammer's depth charges, and proceeded to deliver yet another attack on the much-battered U.404. Seven depth charges were released, straddling the U-boat, which now submerged only to surface again abruptly, and then go under for the final time. About ten of the U-boat's crew were left in the water amid the debris. They had continued the fight as long as possible, knocking out the starboard outer engine of Sweeney's aircraft.

Both American and British planes safely reached England to share equally in a certain kill. It was not an easy return flight for Arthur Hammer and his crew. In addition to losing the number 3 engine, there were oil leaks from the number 4 engine and elsewhere caused by the flak. At first, the crew thought that the fuel lines had also been affected, so Hammer made off in the direction of some British ASW ships, about 50 miles away, in case he had to ditch the plane. Happily, this proved not to be necessary, as the fuel lines were undamaged, and Hammer was able to stabilize the plane's altitude on three engines. So the aircraft headed for home, only to encounter bad weather as it approached England, which required a landing on a fighter base near the coast.

The last attack on U.404 came over six hours after Major McElroy's first attack on the submarine. In that space of time, three Liberators had made a total of five passes over the U-boat and released a total of twenty-seven depth charges. Despite the AA fire, which knocked out one engine on each of the three planes, no aircrew members were either killed or wounded, and all three planes brought their crews home safely. Not so fortunate was the crew of U.404, all fifty of whom perished.

Two days later, aircraft A/19 (1st Lt. A. L. Leal, pilot) participated in a massive onslaught against three U-boats attempting to cross the bay together.[29] Leal was unlucky in that during his initial attack on one of the German submarines, flak hit his bomb bay, rendering it impossible to release depth charges. Leal's attack was assessed by Cominch as inflicting no damage; the Admiralty did not assess as no weapon had been released. This was cold comfort for the three submarines, U.461, U.462, and U.504, all of which were sunk that day by a combined air and surface ship assault. Leal's had been one of seven aircraft from six different squadrons of three different nations (American, Australian, British) participating in the attack.[30] Further, the pilot of one of the five British aircraft was a Dutchman. Two of the subs were sunk by aircraft, and the 2nd Escort Group of the Royal Navy finished off the third. By the end of July the only question was how long the U-boats could continue to absorb such punishment.

U.706 Sunk

On August 2 came the 479th Group's last attack during the "open hunting season" in the bay.[31] T/4, piloted by Capt. Joseph L. Hamilton, flying at 2,500 feet above scattered clouds with their base at 1,800 feet, while patrolling some 400 miles due west of St. Nazaire, obtained a radar return 20 miles distant. Five minutes later the copilot, 1st Lt. Robert C. Schmidt, sighted the U-boat 10 miles away, fully surfaced in position 46.27°N/09.59°W. The submarine had just come under attack from a Hampden, A/415 Squadron RCAF, piloted by Squadron Leader C. G. Ruttan. Ruttan had made a rather deliberate attack and dropped six depth charges that may have succeeded in damaging the submarine. The Admiralty assessor was rather critical of this attack, noting that it had been made against the inner side of a turning U-boat, which "is always less likely to be lethal than if made from the outside, as in the latter case the U/B is turning into the stick and making it worse for itself, and in the former case is turning away, and out of [the] stick." The assessor concluded that "if damage was inflicted it had no time to show itself" before the U-boat was destroyed by Hamilton's subsequent attack.

The submarine Hamilton then proceeded to attack was U.706, which had sailed from La Pallice on July 29 on her fifth war patrol. T/4 attacked the sub directly out of the sun. The U-boat was alert, however, and opened fire at one mile's range, scoring a hit that damaged the plane's left main wheel. As the plane closed its target, first the top turret gunner and then the nose gunner began to return the fire. Hamilton pushed on in at 200 MPH some 50 feet above the water, with his bombardier planning to release a stick of eight depth charges, spaced at 50 feet. In fact all twelve dropped, perhaps because he was using his manual release rather than the intervalvometer. (Since that piece of equipment had failed in Major McElroy's attack on the twentieth, the squadron commander had prohibited its use.) In any case, the accuracy of the attack was never in doubt. The tail gunner saw the depth charges straddle the submarine, and an excellent set of photos confirmed his observation. The U-boat proceeded to sink stern first, leaving about fifteen men in the water. The B-24 dropped a rubber life raft to them, and five were observed to climb in. HMS *Waveney* later picked up the survivors of the sunken U-boat.

Both the Admiralty and Cominch evaluated Hamilton's attack as an *A,* or known kill. The sinking of U.706 was shared with the Canadian Hampden, a decision that seems somewhat at odds with the Admiralty assessor's report. It was nonetheless a satisfactory end to a hectic period of operations, for the next day Admiral Doenitz at last abandoned the policy that had cost the lives of so many of his men and changed his tactical instructions for crossing the bay to maximum avoidance of aircraft. It was a long overdue decision on the part of the Grand Admiral. After Doenitz changed his operating procedures, sightings in the Biscay fell off precipitously, and between August 3 and October 31, American aircraft would achieve only two further sightings, both by one plane on what was something of a jinxed flight.

A Damp Squib

Sometimes when opportunity seemed to knock, the experience turned out to be disappointing. That happened to the crew of P/19 (1st Lt. J. O. Bolin, pilot) on September 7, 1943. The Liberator sighted a U-boat on the surface under cannon attack by RAF Beaufighters. Although Bolin pressed on as fast as possible, by the time the B-24 was in a position to drop its depth charges, the U-boat had prudently withdrawn from the increasingly unhealthy surface of the bay to greater privacy underwater. As 75 seconds had elapsed between the disappearance of the submarine and the release of the depth charges, there was almost no chance of success. Given the long famine of sightings, the release of the depth charges was perhaps an understandable act of frustration, although standard operating procedure strongly recommended against doing so. Now quite aroused, the American crew's adrenalin was pumping furiously. Less than two hours after the lost chance, the wake of a U-boat's periscope was spotted. A prompt attack followed, with depth charges descending upon what was identified too late as a smoke-float on the water. There were days like that.[32]

Achievement

If we include Bolin's two attacks on a long-submerged submarine and a non-submarine target, there were eight attacks or attempted attacks by aircraft of the 479th Group during their operations from the United Kingdom. In only three instances, Lieutenant Young's attack on July 18 and Lieutenant Bolin's attacks on September 7, was there an absence of U-boat fire. In the other instances, the U-boats fought back vigorously. One Liberator from the 479th Group was lost to U-boat AA fire. In the remaining cases, flak did significant damage to the American aircraft, knocking out one engine on three separate occasions. Except for the crew of B/19, shot down on July 20, where the

Table 8.1. Attacks on U-boats by 479th Group Aircraft

Date	Aircraft	Pilot	Position	Assessment and Remarks
7/18/43	P/4	Young	46.47°N/11.21°W	F
7/20/43	B/19	Dyment	45.30°N/09.45°W	D; B/19 shot down, crew lost
7/20/43	F/19	Gallmeier	45.18°N/09.58°W	A; U.558 sunk, shared with E/58 Sqn., RAF
7/28/43	Y/4	McElroy	46.09°N/09.35°W	F; Cominch assessed as D
7/28/43	N/4	Hammer	45.53°N/09.25°W	A; U.404 sunk, shared with W/224 Sqn., RAF
7/30/43	A/19	Leal	45.10°N/10.30°W	G; A/19 damaged, could not release depth charges
8/2/43	T/4	Hamilton	46.27°N/09.59°W	A; U.706 sunk, shared with A/415 Sqn., RCAF
9/7/43	P/19	Bolin	45.34°N/10.13°W	N/A; attacked too late
9/7/43	P/19	Bolin	Not recorded	N/A; non-U-boat attacked

Source: Compiled from 479th Group records, USAFHRC.

entire crew of ten perished, the airmen had remarkable good fortune; only one man was wounded in the other actions.

The price to the U-boats was high, with the American aircraft participating in the sinking of three. On one other occasion, Lieutenant Leal's attack was frustrated by a U-boat's flak damaging his bomb bay, but the submarine was itself promptly sunk by another of its multiple attackers. This was, indeed, pretty much the inevitable fate of a U-boat that stayed on the surface and slugged it out. During the window of opportunity Admiral Doenitz's mistaken policy had given them, the aircrews of the 479th Group had been very active and aggressive, as the record shows. The attacks by group aircraft are tabulated in Table 8.1.

The intensity of the struggle in the Bay of Biscay campaign in this period, and the fate of the submarines involved, is reflected in the figures in Table 8.2.

Over half of all sightings were converted into attacks in this period, and one U-boat was sunk for roughly every five attacks. These very high rates changed abruptly after August 2, and only the brief flurry of activity during the first days of the Normandy landings would see anything close to similar rates. Admiral Doenitz may have been a slow learner, but in this regard he seems to have learned well that for his U-boats to survive, they had to avoid

Table 8.2. Aerial ASW Activity in the Bay of Biscay, May–August 1943

Month	Sightings	Attacks	U-boats	
			Sunk	Damaged
May	99	72	8	6
June	67	22	2	6
July	45	27	11	3
August	13	7	4	1
Total	224	128	25	16

Source: Franks,*Conflict over the Bay,* 232.

exposing themselves to ASW aircraft. The 479th Group had participated in attacks represented in the above table only in the last half of the month of July and in August. They had shared in 20 percent of the fifteen U-boats sunk in those two months. Their averages had been rather higher than the general figures in Table 8.2. Eight of twelve sightings had been converted into attacks (seven of eleven, if we exclude Lieutenant Bolin's attack on a smoke-float), and three of eight attacks resulted in U-boats sunk. The primary reason for these high rates was that the American attacks came when the U-boats were most determined to fight it out on the surface, and when it was possible to make multiple aircraft attacks on the submarines, all but assuring their destruction. That the U-boats made themselves available for attack does not detract from the accomplishment, for the intensity of U-boat flak made such attacks dangerous undertakings. The planes of the 479th Group were fortunate to get off as lightly as they did.

Given the debate in RAF Coastal Command over the mandated 100-foot depth-charge spacing, it is interesting to look at the three attacks carried out by the 479th Group which were lethal to German submarines. All three came while the group was using the British Mark XI depth charge, and while the 100-foot spacing instruction was in effect. In its attack on U.558 on July 20, F/19 dropped seven depth charges spaced at 50 feet. Eight days later N/4 helped sink U.404 when it made two attacks. The first was with eight depth charges with a 60-foot spacing between them. The second attack was with four depth charges and the 100-foot spacing. No photographs of these two passes were available, but the crew claimed that the first eight charges straddled the U-boat, five short and three over. With a 60-foot spacing, one if not both of the fifth and sixth charges in the stick should have been fatal. In the

Table 8.3. 479th Antisubmarine Group Operational Statistics

	7/14–8/9/43	8/10–10/29/43	7/14–10/29/43
Patrols flown	95	357	452
Operational hours	868	3,337	4,205
Sightings	10	2[a]	12
Attacks	6	2[a]	8
Hours per sighting	86.8	1668.5	350.4
Hours per attack	144.7	1668.5	525.6
479th Group			
Aircraft lost	3	2	5
Aircraft damaged	4	5	9

[a]Including one nonsubmarine
Source: Compiled from figures in 479th Group records, USAFHRC.

second run, the last of the four charges was seen to fall close by, just short of the hull of the submarine. Presumably, if a shorter spacing than 100 feet had been used in this case, all four weapons would have fallen outside lethal range.

The third sinking of a U-boat by a plane of the 479th Group came on August 2, when T/4 dropped a stick of twelve depth charges spaced at 50 feet which helped sink U.706. It would seem that the American squadrons were not using the 100-foot spacing, except when they dropped fewer than six depth charges in a stick. In the one case where the longer spacing was used, with a stick of four charges, the spacing was demonstrated to have been tactically correct by testimony of the American airmen. However, it was only the *coup de grâce*, as an earlier stick with a shorter spacing probably killed the boat. At least when U-boats stayed up to fight, a spacing of 50 to 60 feet between charges in a stick of eight or more depth charges produced good results. After August 2, opportunities to attack U-boats were never the same, as can be seen in Table 8.3.

The sharp difference between the two periods of 479th Group activity, noted above, was largely the consequence of the change in German policy in early August to one of maximum submergence and evasion of Allied aircraft. The result of this change is clear: a nearly twenty-fold increase in the number of flying hours required to achieve a U-boat sighting. This was the great weakness of aircraft operations against U-boats in World War II; aircraft could attack, and possibly sink, submarines only if they could first find the vessels. And a submarine that did not wish to be found could be very elusive indeed.

This is not to say that the Bay of Biscay campaign after August 1943 was a bust, although it may have consumed more Allied resources after this date than results justified, at least until the D-day landings of June 1944 approached. The great service the bay campaign performed, far more than simply sinking some submarines, was the delay it imposed on the U-boats in reaching and returning from their operational patrol areas. The relatively small diesel-electric submarines of the era were limited in endurance by the amount of fuel they carried, the amount of supplies, especially edible food-stuffs available to the crews, and the level of strain over time placed on the U-boat crews themselves. The bay campaign eroded all of these, shortening U-boat operational time on the convoy lanes. This was the main contribution of the Biscay campaign to the Battle of the Atlantic.

9

The Hunters Become the Hunted
479th Group Aerial Combats

During the summer and early autumn of 1943 the Luftwaffe was more active over the Bay of Biscay than ever before or after. German aircraft took a serious toll of the Allied antisubmarine planes, which were usually caught flying alone by a number of enemy planes flying offensive sweeps against the ASW aircraft. The intensity of these combats can be seen in Table 9.1.

By August the Allied U-boat hunters were turning into the hunted, and as U-boat losses dropped, those of Allied aircraft rose. It is not hard to understand why. Just as a surfaced U-boat made a large and clumsy target for the more nimble ASW aircraft, so these planes were themselves slow and unmaneuverable in comparison with the LR fighters, chiefly JU 88s, which the Luftwaffe sent out over the bay in packs to hunt the lumbering antisubmarine aircraft. Again the principle of multiple attacks on the same target came into play. The more JU 88s that engaged in firing runs at an ASW aircraft, the greater the likelihood of that aircraft suffering fatal damage. The Luftwaffe campaign became a deadly business for the antisubmarine planes from August on. How serious this was for the 479th Group is seen in Table 9.2.

Table 9.1. Aerial Combats over the Bay of Biscay, May–September 1943

	Combats	Allied Losses		Luftwaffe Losses
		ASW Planes	Long-Range Fighters	
May	8	6	0	5
June	16	5	3	9
July	20	5	2	3
August	34	17	6	7
September	25	7	1	6
Total	103	40	12	30

Source: Franks, *Conflict over the Bay*, 233.

Table 9.2. 479th Group Aerial Combat

Date	Aircraft	Pilot	Position	Comments
7/26/43	L/19	Grider	46.16°N/09.39°W	Nine JU 88s; no damage
8/8/43	K/19	Owen	45.30°N/09.20°W	One JU 88; no damage
8/8/43	Q/4	Thomas	45.30°N/09.20°W	B-24 shot down, crew lost
8/16/43	D/19	Barnett	44.12°N/09.25°W	One JU 88 claimed damaged
8/16/43	E/19	Gallmeier	44.10°N/10.10°W	Eight JU 88s; no damage
8/18/43	G/19	Moore	45.09°N/11.28°W	B-24 shot down, four crew killed, six rescued
8/18/43	J/19	Leal	45.55°N/09.42°W	Four-plus JU 88s; B-24 has one engine shot out
8/23/43	V/4	Dustin	46.53°N/09.18°W	Ten JU 88s; 1:47 hour action; B-24 loses one engine, four wounded.
8/25/43	E/19	Bolin	46.26°N/09.30°W	One JU 88; B-24 loses one engine
9/7/43	P/4	Young	45.10°N/11.08°W	Seven JU 88s; little damage
9/8/43	B/4	Finneburgh	48.00°N/10.54°W	B-24 shot down, only three crew rescued; two JU 88s claimed destroyed
9/9/43	K/19	Owen	46.20°N/09.54°W	One JU 88; no damage done
9/18/43	K/22	Van Zyl	43.50°N/08.40°W	Eight JU 88s; B-24 damaged
9/27/43	B/22	Cummings	49.20°N/07.55°W	Six ME 109s/110s; B-24 damaged
10/17/43	C/22	Estes	47.14°N/08.35°W	Twelve JU 88s; no damage

Source: 479th Group records, USAFHRC.

July and August Encounters

It was not until the 479th Group had been operational for about two weeks that an American aircraft encountered the Luftwaffe over the Bay of Biscay. On July 26, aircraft L/19 piloted by 1st Lt. S. M. Grider encountered nine JU 88s. There was only a brief exchange of shots before the B-24 was able to hide itself in cloud cover with no harm done on either side.[1] This good fortune did not last, however. On August 8, Q/4, piloted by Capt. R. L. Thomas Jr., reported that it was under attack by enemy aircraft. Nothing further was heard from the plane, and search efforts failed to find any trace of the plane or its crew, all of whom were lost in the action.[2]

The same day, Capt. E. R. Owen and his crew in K/19 had their own encounter with one JU 88. While flying at 2,000 feet in thin cloud, the Liberator's radar operator reported a plane closing rapidly from six miles astern. The enemy aircraft approached the ASW aircraft, arced around to attack out of the sun, and then dove on the B-24, opening fire at about 700 yards. The Liberator successfully jettisoned its depth charges and put up a stiff fire, which seemed to discourage the JU 88 from coming to close quarters again. After several minutes of sniffing around, the German pilot evidently decided that the Liberator was too well armed and alert for his taste, and he disappeared.[3]

The planes of the group did not encounter the Luftwaffe again until August 16. On that day, D/19, piloted by 1st Lt. D. F. Barnett Jr., had a two-minute engagement with a single JU 88. Again, the enemy aircraft didn't have much success, taking heavy fire from the B-24. Tracers indicated that the German aircraft was being hit, and its starboard engine began to smoke. The JU 88 abruptly broke off the action and appeared to head for home. While his attack did lead the American plane to release its depth charges, it did not contribute much to the security of the U-boats, as by that date they had already turned to a policy of maximum submergence, and seldom encountered any ASW aircraft. Action in the Bay of Biscay campaign was turning more and more into a series of aircraft engagements. It was also on August 16 that 1st Lt. Charles F. Gallmeier and his crew, flying in E/19, encountered eight JU 88s. Seven of these closed to attack, but Gallmeier was able to escape into heavy cloud before they could do so. Although the B-24 fired on them as they approached, the enemy aircraft did not reply, and the brief action was over as quickly as it began. Again, the ASW aircraft jettisoned its depth charges.[4]

Since their success in shooting down Captain Thomas's plane on August 8, the JU 88s had not had much luck against the alert and well-defended Liberators of the 479th Group. On August 18, aircraft G/19, with Lt. Charles H. Moore as pilot and Lieutenant Grider as check pilot, encountered some eight to ten JU 88s. As there was only light cloud cover, and that rather high, around 12,000 feet, the Liberator, which was at 6,000 feet, had to climb to reach what cover was available. Well before it got there, the faster JU 88s were able to close and attack. In fact, it was the first pass by the first JU 88 which was critical. The German pilot, obviously no amateur, made a head-on attack, during which he managed to shoot out two of the Liberator's engines and severely damage the plane's left rudder, leaving the American aircraft in critical straits.

Moore and Grider were barely able to exercise any control over their rapidly descending B-24. A very rough crash landing on the water followed, the plane hitting at a speed of about 130 MPH. It promptly broke in two just behind the radio compartment. Both parts went down almost at once, and as heads came to the surface it was soon clear that four of the crew had not survived the crash landing, including the bombardier and navigator, who evidently never got out of the highly vulnerable nose compartment. The radar operator and assistant engineer were also lost in the crash. That six of the crew survived was above the average for B-24 crash landings at sea, notable in view of how badly the plane was damaged and how violently it had crashed.

The surviving aircrew managed to get two rubber life rafts into the water, which was probably their salvation. The radio operator also had managed to get off an enemy aircraft report before the plane went in, and Coastal Command laid on the usual thorough search procedure for survivors. But not until four days later, on August 22, did a plane of the 4th Antisubmarine Squadron spot the survivors, three in each of the two life rafts. The following day a British ship reached them and effected their rescue. The testimony of the survivors was that Lieutenant Moore's conduct had been remarkable throughout the episode; certainly no less remarkable for a man who had just spent five days in a life raft after a rough crash landing, he and another member of the crew were back on active duty on August 28. The other four survivors were not quite so robust, but were making a good recovery in hospital on that date.[5]

On August 18 another Liberator of the 19th Squadron, with 1st Lt. A. L. Leal as pilot, also encountered enemy aircraft. This time, there were only four

JU 88s, which appeared abruptly about 500 feet above the B-24, as it was flying in clear air at 8,000 feet. The Liberator had unfortunately just emerged from a solid cloud bank, and its crew was now feeling very exposed. The enemy aircraft were not spotted until they were within 800 yards and the leading enemy plane was beginning to peel off to make his attack run from above and to starboard. Both the top turret gunner and starboard waist gunner opened fire on the enemy leader, but no hits on the JU 88 were observed. The other three followed their leader into the attack, passing across the B-24 from starboard to port before breaking away astern of the Liberator after their attack runs. The B-24's starboard inner engine had to be shut down, and bullets thudded into the big plane's fuselage. Leal headed for the nearest cloud cover, which he reached in about a minute's time.

The cloud was not large, and shortly thereafter Leal emerged at 5,000 feet and promptly came under attack again from a single JU 88. Leal turned into his attacker, who could not correct his approach in time and passed over the B-24 without being able to score on it. The Liberator's top turret gunner and tail gunner each got in a good burst at the German aircraft, and smoke was seen emerging from one of its engines as it vanished into the distance. The B-24 was not further attacked. In addition to the starboard inner engine being shot out, the outer engine on that side received minor damage and the hydraulic system also was damaged. A minor fire was started by a 20mm shell exploding some .50-caliber ammunition in the nose compartment, but the navigator was able to extinguish this fire. No one in the crew was injured, and the plane returned safely to base. The crew estimated that seven JU 88s had been sighted in the course of the action, but this may have been a typical case of counting some aircraft more than once.[6]

Five days later, it was the 4th Squadron's turn again. Where most actions with enemy aircraft were relatively brief, this one was exceptional in lasting nearly two hours. V/4, 1st Lt. K. H. Dustin as pilot, was at 5,000 feet when ten JU 88s were sighted two miles ahead, closing directly in groups of three, four, and three. There was only slight cloud available, which promised difficulties for the ASW aircraft. Bullets from the initial attacks entered the cockpit of the Liberator, slightly wounding both the pilot and copilot. The German long-range fighters proceeded to alternate attacks on the Liberator from starboard and port, beginning from ahead and about 500 feet above the B-24 and turning into it. The twin-engine fighters descended swiftly upon the lumbering ASW aircraft, which Lieutenant Dustin was flogging along at

200 MPH. The JU 88s seemed to concentrate their fire on the nose and waist of the American plane. After five runs on the Liberator without producing much in the way of results, one of the German planes turned its attention to the Liberator's wing area, immediately damaging the number 1 engine, which had to be feathered. This cost the B-24 both precious speed and maneuverability.

However, the Liberator's gunners were giving a good account of themselves, and at about this part of the action, a JU 88 was seen by two of the crew to go down in flames, crashing into the bay. At last the American plane gained some cloud cover, which was a welcome relief. This was balanced by the fact that damage to the plane made it impossible to jettison the depth charges, which would have considerably eased the load on the three engines still operating. Indeed, the Liberator was not able completely to hold its altitude on its three operating engines. Accordingly, Dustin took the chance of unfeathering the prop of his number 1 engine and using it briefly to enable the Liberator to climb to 9,000 feet. While he was doing this, the bombardier and one of the waist gunners managed to force open the bomb-bay doors using an ax, and free the depth charges to fall away safely from the plane. However, it was now impossible to close the bomb-bay doors, which also exerted drag on the plane. Happily, no further attacks developed, and the much-battered aircraft limped home successfully. In all, four crew members were slightly injured by fragments. Over 2,000 rounds of .50-caliber ammunition had been fired by the gunners in defense of their plane. The B-24 proved again to be a robust aircraft, able to take considerable punishment and stay aloft so long as it did not lose more than one engine.[7]

Enemy aircraft activity continued to be intense in late August, and there were other close calls. On August 25 1st Lt. J. O. Bolin and his crew of the 19th Squadron had both portside engines damaged by a single JU 88. The inner port engine erupted in flames, which quickly died down and were extinguished. The other portside engine continued to function. Fortunately, the German plane did not renew the action, perhaps assuming from the flaming inner engine that the B-24 was a goner. If so, the German pilot was mistaken, for Bolin managed to nurse his crippled plane back to a safe landing at St. Mawgan, not far from St. Eval in Cornwall. The crew had been very lucky; the JU 88s usually did not work alone over the Bay of Biscay, and if there had been more present the future of the American aircraft could have been bleak.[8]

September and October Actions

The first action in September was prolonged, for on the seventh, aircraft P/4, flown by 1st Lt. W. R. Young and his crew, encountered seven JU 88s and a 15-minute battle ensued. The Liberator suffered damage to both left and right wing flaps before it was able to escape into cloud cover. The crew attributed their getting off so lightly, considering the length of the action, to the fact that only the German leader seemed very aggressive. The other six German planes were reluctant to come within effective range. They may have been discouraged by the 1,175 rounds of .50-caliber ammunition the gunners of the B-24 expended in the combat, although no damage was claimed to any of the JU 88s.[9]

Both Bolin and Young had a certain amount of good fortune in their engagements, which allowed their planes to return home safely. Such luck was too good to last. The law of averages caught up with the 479th Group on September 8, and the victims were 1st Lt. E. T. Finneburgh and his crew in B/4. The American plane was flying at 4,000 feet with unlimited visibility when eight JU 88s appeared and took up their normal pre-attack positions in two parallel lines of four aircraft, about 500 feet above and 3,000 yards to port and starboard of the B-24. The planes to starboard attacked first, pulling slightly ahead of the Liberator, then successively turning into it in a shallow dive. Finneburgh and his copilot, Flight Officer Schneider, turned the B-24 into the attacking JU 88s to shorten their firing time and create as acute a firing angle as possible for them. The first German, as usual, was the most aggressive and the most skillful, shooting out the Liberator's radio and number 1 engine. The following starboard attackers failed to add to the first plane's damaging hits. Although in difficulties, the Americans managed to turn and lose altitude abruptly, frustrating the attack of the port foursome. The depth charges were also successfully jettisoned.

It took the Germans about 10 minutes to get themselves sorted out after the initial passes, while the Liberator plowed on at its best speed on three engines. In the second series of attacks, single JU 88s attacked alternately from starboard and port, evidently to prevent the Liberator from making a violent maneuver to throw off the attack run of an entire set of fighters. The first three runs in this series were ineffective, but the fourth JU 88 shot away the B-24's rudder control and trim tabs and damaged the top turret, whose gunner survived with only a severe chin gash. Despite his and the turret's battered condition, he continued to fire his guns at the enemy aircraft. The next attacker seemed to get off stride, coming in very close without being able to get his guns lined up on the B-24. Evidently a very inexperienced pilot, he fatally bled off speed in an effort to bring his fixed guns to bear by pulling up in front of the Liberator, where nose and top gunners could both get off long bursts into him. The JU 88 nosed over abruptly and went down in flames.

By now, the B-24 was down to 1,500 feet and under continuous attack. A second JU 88 was claimed destroyed during this part of the action. However, cannon fire from the German aircraft ripped open large holes in the Liberator's right wing inboard and outboard fuel tanks. A cannon shell exploded in the cockpit instruments directly in front of the pilot, badly injuring Lieutenant Finneburgh. Flight Officer Schneider struggled to control the damaged plane while the radio operator, with no radio to operate, did what he could for the injured pilot. With fuel streaming away from the starboard tanks, and neither engine on that side getting fuel, their props had to be feathered, leaving only one engine running and a crash landing inevitable. At 1,000 feet, with the copilot attempting a gliding approach to the sea, another JU 88 closed in, ripping up the fuselage with his cannon fire and destroying one of the B-24's life rafts. Just after this attack the Liberator hit the water at a speed of about 90 MPH. While the plane was in shreds, only the pilot had been seriously injured up to the moment of impact with the water.

On hitting the water, the B-24 broke in two at the radar turret position, roughly halfway between the main wing and the tail structure. The tail part of the plane sank at once. The forward part of the plane stayed afloat about a minute, remarkable considering that 20-foot waves were running in a very rough sea. Seven members of the crew got out, but Lieutenant Finneburgh and the bombardier were not among them. Four men, including the copilot and navigator, managed to get into a life raft. They briefly saw three other crew members in the water in their Mae Wests, but in the rough seas the three individual crew members in the water quickly vanished from view. They were never seen again.

The four survivors managed to get through the night of the eighth despite the rough seas. The next day a Catalina was seen and its attention attracted by firing flares. But poor visibility obscured the raft from the searching aircraft. On the tenth a plane again located the raft. The plane signaled that surface craft were in the area to make a pickup, but they could not find the life raft before night fell. It was during the night of September 10/11 that the radio operator, who had been bleeding from the mouth, evidently from internal injuries suffered in the crash landing, died. At midday on the eleventh, a Sunderland found the raft again with its three surviving occupants. Several hours later, a British ship, guided by the Sunderland, picked up the three remaining aircrew.[10]

Only a day after the loss of B/4, it was the turn of the 19th Squadron. K/19 (Capt. E. R. Owen, pilot) encountered a single JU 88, which after a brief exchange of fire disappeared when the B-24 entered cloud cover. This was Captain Owen's second encounter with an enemy aircraft in just over a month. As radio reports indicated numerous German planes between him and England, he decided to fly on to Gibraltar, where he landed safely.[11]

The 22nd Antisubmarine Squadron had joined the 479th Group much later than the 4th and 19th Squadrons, so it was not until September 18 that a plane of the squadron encountered the Luftwaffe. The crew of K/22 (1st Lt. Harold R. Van Zyl, pilot) observed eight JU 88s approaching from port and above the Liberator. While there was good visibility, there were also some clouds about, for which Van Zyl headed. The initial fighter's pass resulted in damage to the B-24's rudder, the plexiglass of the top turret, and a few holes in the fuselage. This was the only damage the Liberator sustained, however. The JU 88s did not seem to coordinate their attacks very well, nor press them home with much vigor. Again, something of a standard pattern seemed repeated here. The first German attacker was normally both skilled and aggressive, and if he inflicted serious damage on his pass, then the Liberator was apt to be in difficulties. If, on the other hand, the B-24 survived the initial attack, there was neither great skill nor energy shown by the remainder of the enemy pilots in their attacks. K/22's gunners claimed to have damaged two of the attackers, which may have discouraged the German LR fighters from becoming overly aggressive. Van Zyl brought his plane safely home with no casualties.[12]

A plane of the 22nd Squadron was again the target of opportunity for what appeared to be one Me 109 and five Me 110s on September 27. While 1st Lt. C. H. Cummings was flying east of 8°W longitude, he came under attack, so the identity of the aircraft is not improbable. Indeed, of twenty-five sightings or combats with enemy aircraft which the 479th Group experienced, this was the farthest east an American plane reached. The German planes managed to inflict scattered damage on the B-24, including hits to the left wing and both portside engines. However, none was serious and the enemy aircraft did not linger to press their attacks. Cummings had no difficulty getting his plane home safely.[13]

The last enemy action for the 479th Group came on October 17, and again a plane of the 22nd Squadron was the target. Capt. J. A. Estes was flying C/22 when he encountered twelve JU 88s. This attack was better coordinated, with the fighters lining up in two cab ranks, to port and starboard of the B-24, from which positions they alternated runs on the Liberator. The starboard outer engine of the B-24 was disabled and the right wing damaged before Estes was able to gain cloud cover. Thereafter he successfully eluded further action and brought his plane home safely on three engines.[14]

In addition to the fifteen occasions when fire was actually exchanged, on another ten occasions the American antisubmarine planes encountered enemy aircraft, but the meetings were so fleeting that no firing took place. The frequent heavy cloud cover over the Bay of Biscay made such encounters fairly common, and the clouds were certainly welcomed by the American aviators, who had the odds against them in any such engagements. A typical experience came on October 7, when 1st Lt. Wilmer L. Stapel was piloting a Liberator of the 22nd Antisubmarine Squadron. He remembered that while flying in and out of cloud cover, four JU 88s "passed within several hundred feet of the nose of my aircraft. All happened so quickly that they were gone before anyone in any of the . . . aircraft could react."[15]

Evaluation of the Aerial Combats

No one in Captain Thomas's crew survived the destruction of their aircraft, so information about aerial combats is limited to fourteen actions. Four of these were encounters with single JU 88s, and on three occasions no damage resulted to the American plane. The fourth time serious damage was inflicted, but the Liberator got home because the individual JU 88 did not renew its attack, and it had no comrades to finish the job it had begun. In general, the odds were against a single German LR fighter being able to bring down a

B-24, although it could and was done. As the number of enemy aircraft present rose, the odds moved steadily against the single antisubmarine aircraft. Yet of the ten remaining actions, in half the cases the American Liberator suffered little or no damage. Partly this was related to the presence of ample cloud cover to hide in, but also on only two of these five occasions did the German planes show much aggressiveness, and then it was usually only the enemy leader who did so.

In the five remaining cases, including two in which the American planes were shot down, the Luftwaffe pilots showed a somewhat more consistent effort. Of the two engagements in which the Liberator was destroyed, the first enemy firing run was critical in the case of lieutenants Moore and Grider's aircraft. After the damage sustained in that first attack, it was just a matter of finishing off a cripple. Lieutenant Dustin's and Lieutenant Finneburgh's aircraft each came under systematic, well-organized attack and the latter's plane was destroyed. To the degree that one can generalize from fourteen actions, it appears that the Luftwaffe was running short on experienced pilots, and that the less experienced ones were also prone to be cautious.

Certainly by the late summer and early autumn of 1943, the German Air Force (GAF) was seriously overextended. The Eastern Front steadily bled away German resources in the air as on the ground. A high level of activity during the spring and summer of 1943 in the Mediterranean Theater had resulted in very high Luftwaffe losses. Finally, by mid-1943 the British-American strategic bombing campaign was imposing its own strain on the GAF. In particular, the RAF night attacks were serious enough to demand allocation of the bulk of the Luftwaffe's twin-engine fighters to try to erode the bomber stream flowing over targets on the continent. This did not leave many aircraft for the Bay of Biscay, and the number of experienced pilots who could be allotted to this task would not have been great. The Luftwaffe was simply stretched too thin. The antisubmarine aircraft had reason to be grateful for this.

In addition to the fifteen combats listed which cost the group three aircraft and twenty-one aircrew killed, one plane was also shot down by U-boat flak, with the loss of all ten crew members. A further aircraft was lost on August 11 when O/4 crashed 15 minutes after takeoff, killing six of the crew. Considering the intensity of operations, losses to the unit were relatively light; the total aircrew lost with the five aircraft destroyed was thirty-seven. An additional five planes were damaged by enemy aircraft, and five were damaged by U-boat flak. Remarkably, the total casualty list in these ten actions was five wounded. The greater danger was clearly that posed by the Luftwaffe, and the U-boat flak was comparatively less dangerous.[16]

Some Operational Problems

Operations were not, nor could they be, error-free. On October 4 a 19th Squadron Liberator expended 100 rounds of .50-caliber ammunition on what it then recognized was a friendly aircraft. On the twenty-ninth of the same month a plane of the 22nd Squadron fired off 250 rounds at a "U-boat," which on second look turned out to be a "friendly surface craft." The vessel, fortunately, was recognized in time not to be depth-charged.[17]

A constant plague to ASW aircraft operating in the bay was the presence of French and Spanish tunny boats in the fishing seasons. Although the British expended a great deal of effort endeavoring to convince these sturdy fishermen to stay in harbor, the pressure of economics prevailed over the risk involved—which was great—of being mistaken for U-boats. Radar sets did not discriminate sufficiently to tell aircraft which was which. In bad weather, or at night, tunny boats were at high risk of attack. While they often fished in groups, which alerted aircrews to their identity, Coastal Command feared that the Germans placed observers on them, and used them as cover for moving U-boats across the bay. While no evidence has ever come to light of the latter practice, the RAF's concern was understandable. Accordingly, efforts were made to discourage the tunny fishermen.

Sometimes the effort was overdone. A plane of the 6th Antisubmarine Squadron, patrolling in the bay on September 9, planned to release one depth charge near a tunny boat to encourage it to go home. Unfortunately, the entire load of twelve depth charges descended near the vessel, which got a wild jolting. The dropping of depth charges was more than an inconvenience as it could effectively scare off the fish the tunnymen sought. Other techniques attempted ranged from dropping leaflets aboard the vessels (a remarkable feat, one would think) to putting machine-gun fire through the sails of some of the fishing boats. As the tunnymen knew perfectly well that the Allied aircrews would not deliberately place them at mortal risk, they were quite prepared to put up with such inconveniences as depth charges and machine-gun fire through their sails (as well as the risk of an occasional fatal mistake) in order to harvest the fish they needed to preserve their livelihood.[18]

Assessment: The End of a Job

July was the golden period of submarine hunting in the Bay of Biscay, with the 479th Group's Liberators achieving sightings at an unparalleled rate. August and September were a very different story, with too many undesired sightings—of enemy aircraft. Open hunting season for the antisubmarine aircraft would not return to the bay until June of 1944, when for a brief period U-boats took great risks to try to reach the D-day landing area and interdict the Normandy invasion. But with that exception, finding U-boats was never again easy in the Bay of Biscay and the large Allied air effort there was no more than a serious nuisance to the U-boat command. Thus the 6th and 22nd Antisubmarine Squadrons came too late to participate in more than a few patrols, the two squadrons arriving at Dunkeswell on August 20–21. Their ground echelons never did join the 479th Group, but rather remained in the continental United States. Operations of the 479th Antisubmarine Group continued until the end of October, when the group stood down from antisubmarine work and was disbanded on November 11, 1943. Most of its aircrews were absorbed into VIII Bomber Command.[19]

10

Conclusions

USAAF Antisubmarine Operations in the Eastern Atlantic

The 479th and 480th Antisubmarine Groups accounted for only 15 percent of the operational flying time of U.S. Army Air Forces Antisubmarine Command, but for 71 percent of its attacks on U-boats.[1] This excludes the record of the AAFAC's precedent organization, the I Bomber Command. The inclusive figures are given in Table 10.1.

The two antisubmarine groups encountered enemy aircraft more often than U-boats, and accounted for all air combats of the USAAF Antisubmarine Command. The results are tabulated in Table 10.2.

The chief contribution of the two ASW groups came in the period July 1–August 2, 1943, when RAF Coastal Command's effort against U-boats in the Bay of Biscay transit area enjoyed maximum opportunities for attack as a result of Admiral Doenitz's order to his submariners to fight their way through the bay on the surface. In that period, eighty-eight U-boats were in the interdicted transit zones, and fifty-five of them were attacked. (Multiple attacks on individual U-boats produced a total of sixty-five individual aircraft attacks; this does not include multiple passes by the same airplane on the same target.) Eighteen U-boats were sunk, fifteen in the bay proper and three

Table 10.1. AAFAC Operational Statistics

	Operational Flying Hours		Attacks		U-boats
	Number	Percentage	Number	Percentage	sunk
I Bomber Command	59,248	38.92%	81[a]	61.4%	1
Antisubmarine Command,					
Western Atlantic	75,879	49.83%	15	11.4%	0
479th and 480th Groups	17,136	11.25%	36[b]	27.3%	8[c]
Total	152,263		132		9

[a]In many of these attacks, in the early months of the war for the United States, the presence of a U-boat is uncertain and even unlikely.
[b]AAFAC includes the actions by Thorne and Easterling on April 7, and by Bolin on September 7, 1943, although these were not assessed by Cominch.
[c]Three shared with RAF Coastal Command aircraft. (Sometimes calculated as $^1/_2$ kills, which would yield a figure of $6^1/_2$.)
Source: "History of AAFAC," 189, completed by author.

in the adjacent Cape Finisterre area. Of the eighteen, all three in the Cape Finisterre region were destroyed by B-24s of the 480th Group; of the fifteen sunk in the bay, the 479th Group participated in the destruction of three. As this group did not begin flying operational sorties until July 13, well into the period, its achievement would surely have been greater had it arrived in the United Kingdom earlier.[2]

As it was, the two USAAF groups were involved in the destruction of a third of all U-boats sunk in this period of maximum intensity. For four squadrons, two of which began operations only in mid-July, this was a

Table 10.2. AAFAC Aerial Combats

	479th Group	480th Group
Number of combats with enemy aircraft	15	16
Estimated number of enemy aircraft encountered	165	55
Enemy aircraft claimed destroyed	3	5
USAAF aircraft lost in aerial combat	3	4
USAAF aircraft damaged in aerial combat	7	3

All the aircraft destroyed by the 479th Group were JU 88s; for the 480th Group all were FW 200s (this excludes three seaplanes destroyed on the surface of the water). All the USAAF aircraft were B-24s.
Source: "History of AAFAC," 192, with some data added by author.

respectable performance. The USAAF squadrons possessed certain advantages, most notably that all were equipped with the B-24D Liberator. While this aircraft was certainly not without its faults, it was the preferred ASW landplane of World War II by both the USAAF and the RAF. Both USAAF groups were experienced, the 479th from flying ASW operations from Newfoundland and American coastal waters, and the 480th in bay operations flown from the United Kingdom before its move to North Africa. All the American aircraft were equipped with 10-cm radar that the U-boats could not detect at the time. The achievement of the two groups was not cost-free. Between July 1 and August 2, fourteen Allied ASW aircraft were lost, four to U-boat flak, six to Luftwaffe attack, and four undetermined. American losses in the period were only two aircraft, one to U-boat flak and one undetermined but probably enemy aircraft. However, losses inflicted on the two groups by the Luftwaffe during the rest of August and the month of September were high, three aircraft from each group.

In the end, what neither group could do, nor could the full efforts of RAF Coastal Command, was to bring the U-boats to battle once they had decided to avoid contact with the Allied aircraft. After August 2 the USAAF squadrons were condemned to join their RAF and USN brethren in patrolling empty seas, flying long hours with seldom a sighting, and only rarely the opportunity for an attack. This was not the result of any lack of effort on the part of the aircrews, but was inherent in the character of antisubmarine warfare as it stood in 1943. It is sufficient to say that they did the best they could with what they had. By any reasonable standard, that was very good indeed.

AAFAC: Stepchild in the Home of Strategic Bombing

In a sense, the AAFAC had been, if not quite an unwanted, then at least something of an unloved child in the Army Air Forces.[3] This had become evident in January of 1943 when General Larson submitted to his Air Force superiors a plan for establishing the authorized strength of his organization at six wings composed of a total number of forty-two squadrons. To equip these squadrons he wanted 544 B-24 aircraft. At the time, he had an organization of two wings composed of nineteen squadrons, but only 20 of his 209 aircraft were B-24s.[4] Larson justified his proposed strength on the need to provide antisubmarine forces on a worldwide basis, covering the Eastern as well as Western Hemisphere, the Pacific as well as the Atlantic.

The response of AAF headquarters indicated that the senior leadership of the Army Air Forces envisioned a significantly more modest force of twenty-four squadrons, and not all equipped with the B-24. Immediate equipment plans were restricted to 228 of these aircraft, 12 for each of the existing nineteen squadrons of the AAFAC. This lesser establishment was based on AAF headquarters' view of the AAFAC as "a highly mobile striking force" that would not become permanently based in any area outside the continental United States, but whose squadrons would move from place to place as the need arose.[5] It was just this conception that the experience of the 480th Antisubmarine Group would demonstrate was unworkable in the prevailing circumstances. As this became clear to AAF headquarters, the already minimal attractiveness of the ASW mission was bound to fade yet further. A larger commitment of bombardment-type aircraft to this activity, at the expense of the strategic bombing mission, was bound to be viewed as a distraction at the top of the USAAF hierarchy.

The status of antisubmarine warfare in the USAAF's priorities is indicated by the aircraft allocations planned for 1943. Construction schedules called for manufacture of 6,400 B-24s in that year. Of this number, 343 were allocated to the USN for all its purposes, including ASW. Adding the 228 for the AAFAC gives a total of 571 B-24s for all maritime purposes. There would be, in addition, some allocations in 1943 to the RAF and RCAF that would go to the ASW mission. Somewhat less than 10 percent of B-24 production, then, would be potentially available for American ASW work, and with the British allocations added in, probably a little more than 10 percent. The bulk of the remaining B-24s would be allocated to strategic bombing.[6]

On February 6, 1943, Maj. Gen. George Stratemeyer summed up the position of the AAF leadership when he wrote that

> use of aircraft and surface forces against submarines at sea can never be expected to effectively reduce the total number of operational submarines. The only way to destroy the submarines is to destroy them at their source by destruction of crucial materials, assembly plants, yards and operating bases.[7]

General Stratemeyer was surely correct in his description of the ideal and most efficient way to stem the submarine problem. The difficulty was that the British and American strategic bombing forces would prove incapable of achieving this goal in 1943. Indeed, not until well into 1944 would the strategic bombing campaign begin to bite heavily into German submarine production programs. Attacks on operating bases were never effective because the Allied bombs could not penetrate the concrete U-boat pens. The AAF headquarters' vision, however ideal, was simply not relevant in the shorter term. But in order to achieve the ideal solution, AAF headquarters did not wish to see the strategic bombing program hobbled by too large an allocation of resources to the war at sea. As General Stratemeyer put it: "Any diversion of a large force of our air effort for the purpose of hunting down the submarines at sea, would be reducing the effective number which can be used against the submarines at the source and is an improper employment of available forces."[8] This analysis kept the objective clearly in view—namely the establishment of an effective strategic bombing force that could cripple at its source the enemy's power to wage war. The problem that remained was what to do in the short term, until the strategic bombing campaign could reach fruition.

In the short term, Stratemeyer admitted, "we must, therefore, divert a certain amount of our effort to protection of our lines of communication." But "the amount diverted," he wrote, "should be sufficient only to fill the need of protecting our shipping and not sufficient to attempt to destroy the submarine at sea."[9] If this were to be taken literally, then the AAFAC was already in peril of elimination, for the AAFAC saw the protection of shipping as an appropriate naval task, while its aircraft carried the offensive to the enemy, ideally in the transit zones such as the Bay of Biscay. Certainly in this ambition the AAFAC shared a vision held in RAF Coastal Command, if perhaps never quite fully embraced at the highest level in the RAF. In short, while the two major Allied air force leaderships saw strategic bombing as their primary mission, by 1943 there existed in both air forces a lower-level organization whose operations at least potentially impinged on the primary strategic mission. The RAF solution to this problem was already clear by early 1943, to allocate a minimum of RAF resources and a maximum of other people's resources to the war at sea. This was the AAFAC's great attractiveness in British eyes.

The Crisis of the U-boat War

While the 480th Group was operating over the Bay of Biscay, and with its parent AAFAC slowly and painfully pressing forward in development, events had quite outrun this evolution. A crisis had developed in the mid-Atlantic, where in March and April Allied shipping losses to the U-boats had reached an unacceptable level. Even as this crisis was unfolding, the pressure of rising U-boat successes against the Atlantic convoys, evident from October 1942 onward, had forced a concentration of minds and resources on the shipping problem. Any review of the problem could not fail to note the disarray of the American services in the area of antisubmarine warfare, and their ongoing disagreements over the allocation, control, and proper use of aviation assets in this arena.

On April 16, 1943, Gen. George Marshall, the U.S. Army Chief of Staff, was sufficiently concerned to write to Admiral King that "I wish to state now that I feel the air operations against submarines can be greatly improved and that complete reorganization of method, particularly as applies to very long range aircraft, is plainly indicated."[10] It was an extraordinary communication. Seventeen months into American participation in the war the head of one American service was informing the head of the other major service that the American antisubmarine effort required "complete reorganization of method." The accuracy of General Marshall's observation was proved by its aftermath; a prolonged period of interservice wrangling followed, not over whether, but rather over how to reorganize the antisubmarine effort.

As time had passed, the views of the USN, and in particular of its formidable chief, Adm. Ernest J. King, had undergone steady evolution. In June 1942, after several months of having fiddled as the Roman emperor of old had done, while American tankers burned like funeral torches in sight of the Atlantic coast, Admiral King had been seized with the true faith. In that month, he announced, with all the zeal of the convert, that convoying was the only solution to the submarine menace.[11] Offensive searches for U-boats he dismissed with scorn as hunting for needles in haystacks, a view he reiterated as late as the opening of the Allied Antisubmarine Conference in Washington at the beginning of March 1943. He was certainly correct in June 1942 when he asserted the centrality of convoy to the security of Allied shipping. It was the only adequate methodology available then. It followed that Cominch had no use for the AAFAC's offensive doctrine.

As circumstances changed, offensive patrolling became a more viable option, if never an entirely adequate substitute for convoying. By May of 1943 the American naval chieftain's views were also changing. While not eschewing the importance of defending the vital transatlantic convoys, an indisputably correct first priority in the circumstances of mid-1943, Admiral King did recognize that a more coherent and integrated approach to the use of aircraft in ASW was required. So on May 1, 1943, King proposed to set up at once in the Navy Department an antisubmarine command to be known as Tenth Fleet.[12] Among his duties, the new fleet's commander would exercise control over all LR and VLR aircraft engaged in ASW work. And the commander of Tenth Fleet would be none other than Cominch himself, Admiral King. This was indeed giving first priority to the submarine menace.

Admiral King's proposal had little if any attraction for the AAF leadership.[13] They saw no reason to believe, given the past record, that Admiral King would put their ASW aircraft to good use, and in view of the state of interservice relations, even doubted if he could be trusted to treat AAF units fairly.[14] The creation of Tenth Fleet by Admiral King on May 19, with or without the blessing of the U.S. Army, forced the issue of the AAFAC's future to the top of the agenda. The historians of the AAFAC put the matter in comprehensive form:

> By the latter part of May, a compromise settlement on the antisubmarine situation was no longer possible. By that time, an issue much larger than that of the land-based antisubmarine air force had been raised, and a solution of the lesser problem would have to wait until the larger issue, of which it constituted a part, could be satisfactorily settled. In other words, control of land-based antisubmarine aircraft raised the issue of the control of all land-based long-range aircraft employed on over-water missions.[15]

By the latter part of May it was also becoming clear that the tide had turned decisively in the long-running Atlantic convoy battles. The U-boats, seemingly so close to victory in March and April, had suffered a catastrophe in the following month. Not only had the U-boat command failed to inflict critical losses on the convoys, but had lost in May the staggering number of forty-one submarines. On May 24, admitting temporary defeat, Admiral Doenitz had withdrawn his vessels from the Atlantic convoy lanes. This stunning reversal of fortune had been long in preparation, and was the result of the cumulative concentration of effort by British, American, and Canadian naval and air forces. But its significance for the AAFAC—which had contributed almost nothing to its achievement—was that suddenly attitudes had shifted in Washington. The USN, heretofore vitally concerned with escort of convoy, began to see offensive efforts against U-boats in a new light. Admiral King, long reluctant to support the Bay of Biscay campaign, was now prepared to urge more resources for it.[16]

The AAFAC Leaves the War

With the USN embracing its own offensive doctrine, and mobilizing its own resources for that purpose, what role was left for the AAFAC? Either it would wastefully duplicate the Navy's effort—and the Navy could hardly be denied primacy in the activity of antisubmarine warfare—or it would become a tail to the Navy's kite, hardly an enviable fate.[17] Worse yet, Admiral King had opened a new front in the interservice war over control of LR aircraft. He was now talking about basing such aircraft, USN aircraft, on Pacific islands and using them for the strategic bombing mission.[18] For the USAAF leadership this was the last straw. They were condemned to a bleak future in antisubmarine warfare and saw the AAF primacy in strategic bombing now coming under threat. On June 10, 1943, generals H. H. "Hap" Arnold and Joseph McNarney for the USAAF concluded an agreement with Vice Adm. John S. McCain, head of naval aviation, to provide a definitive solution to the issue of control of antisubmarine aircraft and finally to secure the AAF role in strategic bombing beyond challenge. The agreement provided that the AAF would withdraw from antisubmarine operations, which would become exclusively a naval responsibility. Army B-24s equipped for antisubmarine warfare would be turned over to the Navy, and the Army would be compensated with naval B-24s not so equipped, which would be transferred to the USAAF. For the AAF leadership, the most important provision in the agreement stated that:

> It is primarily the responsibility of the Army to provide long-range bombing forces (currently called "strategic air forces") for operations from shore bases in defense of the Western Hemisphere and for appropriate operations in other theaters.[19]

While the basic agreement was struck on June 10, there followed some final skirmishing. True to form, Admiral King accepted the part of the agreement that turned over all responsibility for antisubmarine operations to the Navy, but ignored the provision regarding strategic air forces. The American secretary of war, Henry Stimson, was sufficiently incensed to threaten to take the whole matter to the president.[20] This proved unnecessary. General Marshall wrote to Admiral King on June 28, making clear that such an evasion of the June 10 agreement would have serious consequences. As the Army chief of staff observed:

> I feel the present state of procedure between the Army and Navy is neither economical nor highly efficient and would inevitably meet with public condemnation were all the facts known.

He further proposed an additional paragraph nailing down the point under contention:

> This agreement to the transfer of long range aircraft for antisubmarine operations makes it clear that such transfer does not establish a basis for duplication of long range air striking force now in being in the Army.[21]

This warning shot across King's bow did the job. King, who had protested as recently as June 15 that the provision in the original Arnold-McNarney-McCain agreement was "inappropriate" and implied "a lack of confidence in the intentions of the Navy," now on July 3 meekly responded: "I accede to your wish for reassurance on the other air matters raised in your memorandum."[22] On July 9, both military departments formally accepted the June 10 agreement.[23] A schedule was subsequently adopted for transfer of seventy-seven Army B-24s to the Navy, in return for an equal number of combat-equipped B-24s from Navy allocations.[24] Nearly three months had passed since Marshall's April letter to King raising the need for a more efficient management of American ASW resources.

Sir John Slessor, who was head of RAF Coastal Command for most of 1943, believed the AAF leadership had made a serious mistake in surrendering its claim to the ASW mission. "In the interest of the U.S.A.F. and of his country," Slessor wrote, General Arnold should have stuck to the principle that air operations, whether over land or sea, are the job of the USAAF.[25] It is hard to agree with Slessor. In theory, and from the RAF perspective, there was much to be said for Slessor's position. But the development of aviation in the American military in the interwar period had been much different from that in Great Britain. In that period the USN had developed a powerful aviation element that was integrated into its own organization. And most notably, while an independent air force as a separate military service had been in existence in Britain since 1918, the American air force leaders were still struggling to attain that status when World War II began. The AAF leadership correctly saw that the quest for independence as an organization was tied to the independent air mission—strategic bombing. The soundness of their judgment was proved in the aftermath, when the USAF came into existence in 1947. In the June 10 agreement the USAAF had strengthened its claim on the future, not diminished it. To paraphrase the words of an Englishman, never in military history had so little been given up in order to safeguard so much. With the agreement, the strategic bombing mission was securely in the possession of the USAAF. This was the title deed to an independent USAF after the war.

The Last Days of USAAF Antisubmarine Operations

The 479th and 480th Groups were not involved in this transfer of aircraft. The battle in the Bay of Biscay was at its peak in July 1943, and there was acute distress in RAF Coastal Command at the thought of the AAF antisubmarine squadrons standing down when opportunities to attack U-boats were at an all-time high, and the USAAF units were at a peak of efficiency. By the time they could be replaced by Navy units, a golden opportunity might well have passed. After some discussion, it was decided that both USAAF groups would continue to operate until such time as they could be relieved by Navy ASW squadrons. The RAF's concern was sustained by events. By the time Navy units began to deploy to southwest England in October and to North Africa in November to replace the two USAAF groups, the high tide of the Biscay battle had indeed come and gone, and the naval aviators would be left to join their RAF comrades in flying long hours of largely unrewarding patrol, with a U-boat rarely to be found. It was from this prolonged exercise in boredom and frustration that the USAAF had extracted itself for the more stimulating activity of forcing its way into Hitler's *Festung Europa* in the teeth of the Luftwaffe's determined efforts to protect the Third Reich and its captive empire.[26]

By the time the two overseas groups left the antisubmarine war, their parent organization, the AAFAC, was long gone. It was dissolved at the end of August, and its headquarters became the I Bomber Command of the First Air Force. Most of its domestic squadrons went to the Second Air Force as heavy bombardment units. The 479th Group was inactivated, but its squadrons and most of their personnel were transferred to Eighth Air Force for the purpose of developing a pathfinder force for the American strategic bombers. The noted "Carpetbagger" low-altitude intruder force in support of European resistance forces would also emerge from the cadre provided by the 479th Group. The 480th Group, which had been overseas for roughly a year, returned to the United States. Its planes and personnel became widely scattered, with perhaps a majority going to the Second Air Force. A fair number of its personnel later served in the Pacific before the war ended.[27]

With the passage of time, the role of the USAAF in antisubmarine warfare was largely forgotten. The independent U.S. Air Force that came into existence in 1947, with the strategic air mission its foremost concern, had no reason to look back on a role the USAAF had played for only a short time, and then only reluctantly. The AAFAC had gone out of existence before the war ended, and there remained in the new USAF no institutional structure to preserve the memory of what had been a minor function at best. The U.S. Navy, emerging from World War II in sole possession of the antisubmarine mission, had no reason to preserve the memory of the USAAF's activities in that area. Most AAFAC personnel went on to other assignments and developed other loyalties. So the subject has remained largely unexplored, a neglected aspect of the world's last great military conflagration. This account has endeavored to describe the achievement of those who served, largely unsung, in the AAFAC's only two groups to deploy overseas.

Appendix A
Assessments of Antisubmarine Group Attacks on U-boats

Assessments of 480th Antisubmarine Group Attacks on U-boats

Assessment	Date	Location	Pilot (Sqn.)	Remarks
A (Cominch)	3/22/43	30.15°N/18.13°W	Sanford (2)	U.524 sunk
A (Cominch)	7/12/43	42.30°N/16.30°W	Salm (1)	U.506 sunk
B (Adm'ty)	2/10/43	47.05°N/18.34°W	Sanford (2)	U.519 sunk
B (Cominch)	7/7/43	37.40°N/15.30°W	McDonell (1)	U.951 sunk
B (Cominch)	7/8/43	40.37°N/13.41°W	Darden (2)	U.232 sunk
C (Adm'ty)	12/31/42	51.20°N/20.58°W	Thorne (1)	
D (Adm'ty)	2/20/43	49.30°N/21.00°W	Johnson (1)	U.211 damaged[a]
D (Cominch)	7/7/43	37.50°N/14.30°W	Isley (1)	
D (Cominch)	7/9/43	39.20°N/13.00°W	Kuenning (1)	
E (Cominch)	5/7/43	41.20°N/18.05°W	Northrop (2)	
E (Cominch)	5/15/43	31.40°N/21.15°W	Powers (2)	
E (Cominch)	6/19/43	35.31°N/18.20°W	Sanford (2)	
E (Cominch)	7/9/43	38.12°N/13.36°W	Damann (2)	
E (Cominch)	7/14/43	40.03°N/17.57°W	Pennoyer (2)	
F (Adm'ty)	12/29/42	52.12°N/24.00°W	Northrop (1)	
F (Adm'ty)	2/6/43	48.12°N/17.35°W	Sands (1)	Depth charge problem
F (Adm'ty)	2/9/43	48.10°N/20.35°W	Hutto (1)	

Assessment	Date	Location	Pilot (Sqn.)	Remarks
[a]F (Cominch)	5/7/43	41.00°N/18.50°W	Darden (2)	
F (Cominch)	7/11/43	41.24°N/15.00°W	McDonell (1)	
F (Cominch)	7/13/43	39.04°N/20.06°W	Cantrell (2)	
G (Adm'ty)	2/9/43	47.43°N/17.53°W	Jarnagin (2)	
G (Cominch)	6/3/43	33.00°N/21.10°W	Reeve (1)	Depth charge problem
G (Cominch)	7/6/43	39.28°N/14.26°W	Adams (2)	
G (Cominch)	7/9/43	40.15°N/14.05°W	Pomeroy (1)	Depth charge problem
G (Cominch)	7/10/43	39.17°N/13.32°W	Jarnagin (2)	
N/A	2/6/43	Not recorded	Sanford (2)	Depth charge problem
N/A	2/9/43	47.21°N/20.08°W	Jarnagin (2)	Depth charge problem
N/A	2/10/43	47.25°N/14.50°W	Kraybill (2)	Depth charge problem
N/A	4/7/43	34.35°N/24.56°W	Thorne (1)	
N/A	4/7/43	34.35°N/24.56°W	Easterling (1)	
N/A	7/5/43	38.52°N/18.12°W	Damann (2)	Bomb bay damaged by U-boat flak

[a]In fact, a case of under-assessment; U.211 was forced to return to port, which qualifies for a C assessment.

Assessments of 479th Antisubmarine Group Attacks on U-boats

Assessment	Date	Location	Pilot (Sqn.)	Remarks
A (Adm'ty)	7/20/43	45.18°N/09.58°W	Gallmeier (19)	U.558 sunk
A (Adm'ty)	7/28/43	45.53°N/09.25°W	Hammer (4)	U.404 sunk
A (Adm'ty)	8/2/43	46.27°N/09.59°W	Hamilton (4)	U.706 sunk
D (Adm'ty)	7/20/43	45.30°N/09.45°W	Dyment (19)	Aircraft lost
F (Cominch)	7/18/43	46.47°N/11.21°W	Young (4)	Adm'ty did not assess
F (Adm'ty)	7/28/43	46.09°N/09.35°W	McElroy (4)	Cominch assessed as D.
G (Cominch)	7/30/43	45.10°N/10.30°W	Leal (19)	Adm'ty did not assess
N/A	9/7/43	45.34°N/10.13°W	Bolin (19)	U-boat under for 75 sec.
N/A	9/7/43	Not recorded	Bolin (19)	Nonsubmarine

Key: A = U-boat known sunk; B = U-boat probably sunk; C = U-boat damaged severely enough to have to return to port; D = U-boat damaged; E = U-boat slightly damaged; F = Insufficient evidence of damage; G = No damage to U-boat; H = Insufficient evidence of U-boat present; I = Nonsubmarine attacked; J = Too little evidence to assess; N/A = not assessed, usually because of weapons misfunction.

Note: There were two assessment authorities, committees of the British Admiralty (Adm'ty) and the office of the Commander-in-Chief, U.S. Fleet (Cominch).

Sources: Compiled from assessment forms in AAFAC records, MR K1012, USAFHRC; 479th Group records, MR B0637, USAFHRC; assessment forms in 1st and 2nd Squadron records, MR A0522; 480th Group records, MR B0638; and ADM and AIR files in the PRO.

Appendix B
480th Antisubmarine Group Operations

480th Antisubmarine Group Operations from the United Kingdom

	Operational missions	Operational hours flown	U-boats Sighted	U-boats Attacked
November 16–30, 1942	9	77:45	0	0
December 1–31, 1942	30	231:10	2	2
January 1–31, 1943	58	490:10	1	0
February 1–28, 1943	111	1052:05	15	5[a]
March 1–5, 1943	10	116:10	2	1
Totals for 110 days	218	1967:20	20	8[a]

[a]On three occasions in February, depth charges hung up. I have not considered these three as attacks, as RAF Coastal Command and the AAFAC did not do so. However, some documents do include them, which would give figures of 8 and 11, respectively.

480th Antisubmarine Group Operations from North Africa

	Operational missions	Operational hours flown	U-boats Sighted	U-boats Attacked
March 6–31, 1943	N/A	400	1	1
April 1–30, 1943	N/A	1,519	2	2
May 1–31, 1943	N/A	1,407	3	3
June 1–30, 1943	N/A	1,660	2	2
July 1–31, 1943	N/A	2,469	13	12
August 1–31, 1943	N/A	1,678	0	0
September 1–25, 1943	N/A	1,106	0	0
Totals for 204 days	967	10,239	21	20

Cumulative Totals

	Operational missions	Operational hours flown	U-boats Sighted	U-boats Attacked
United Kingdom	218	1,967	20	8
North Africa	967	10,239	21	20
Totals for 314 days	1,185	12,206	41	28

Source: 480th Group records, MR B0638, USAFHRC.

Appendix C
Cumulative Records of the 480th Antisubmarine Group, November 16, 1942–September 25, 1943

		ETOUSA	NATOUSA
Operational missions			
Total number			1,185
Convoy escort			319
Antisubmarine sweeps			847
Air-sea search and rescue			19
Hours			
Operational hours flown			12,206
Longest mission			17:20
Average mission			10:18
U-boats		ETOUSA	NATOUSA
Sighted	41	20	21
Attacked	28	8	20
Sunk	5	1	4
Damaged	9	2	7
Enemy Aircraft			
Combats with enemy aircraft	16	5[a]	11[b]
Enemy aircraft claimed destroyed	8(5 FW 200)		
Group Aircraft Lost			
From enemy aircraft	4		
Accidents/crashes	7		
Missing/unknown	5[c]		

Casualties	Dead	Injured	Total
From enemy aircraft	25	16	41
From U-boat flak	0	5	5
Crashes/accidents	35	10	45
Missing/unknown	51	0	51
Total	111	31	142

[a]One attack by "friendly" nightfighters included.
[b]Excludes attack on three German seaplanes not airborne.
[c]Includes two lost on Atlantic crossing.

Note: The sources do not always agree and it is not always possible to deduce why they do not. I have tried to achieve the most accurate figures, wherever possible by cross-referencing and comparing sources for accuracy of detail and for their completeness. No claim to exact precision is put forward. When in doubt, I have chosen to err on the side of caution.

Source: Compiled from 480th Group records, USAFHRC.

Appendix D
Aircraft Losses and Aircrew Casualties

479th Group Aircraft Losses and Aircrew Casualties

Date	Pilot	Crew lost	Remarks
7/20/43	Dyment	10	U-boat flak
8/8/43	Thomas	10	Enemy aircraft
8/11/43	Not recorded	6	Crash on takeoff
8/18/43	Moore/Grider	4	Enemy aircraft
9/8/43	Finneburgh	7	Enemy aircraft;
			5 aircraft, 37 personnel lost

480th Group Aircraft Losses and Aircrew Casualties

Date	Pilot	Crew lost	Remarks
11/24/42	Tuttle	11	On Atlantic crossing
12/21/42	Enochs	10	On Atlantic crossing
1/6/43	Lolley	10	Unknown
1/10/43	Martin	4	Ground collision
1/22/43	Broussard	10	Crashed in bad weather

480th Group Aircraft Losses and Aircrew Casualties (cont'd)

Date	Pilot	Crew lost	Remarks
2/8/43	Sands	10	Unknown
2/26/43	Tomlinson	10	Enemy aircraft
4/12/43	Rubenstein	0	Crashed on takeoff
5/11/43	Dale/Easterling[a]	6	Crashed on takeoff
7/3/43	Fraser	0	Unknown
7/28/43	Hyde	1	Crashed; field closed[b]
8/17/43	Maxwell	3	Enemy aircraft
8/28/43	McKinnon	1	Enemy aircraft
8/29/43	Damann	5	Crashed on night landing
9/4/43	Kraybill	10	Crashed on takeoff
9/18/43	Jarnagin	10	Enemy aircraft;
			16 aircraft, 111 personnel lost

[a]Copilot was in pilot's seat; copilot (Dale) killed; pilot (Easterling) survived.
[b]Plane lost after crew bailed out; one death was from earlier combat with enemy aircraft.

Breakdown by Cause of Loss

	Aircraft	Crew	Cause of Loss
479th Group	3	21	Enemy aircraft
	1	10	U-boat AA fire
	1	6	Crash following takeoff
480th Group	4	25	Enemy aircraft
	3	30	Unknown causes
	7	35	Crashes/accidents
	2	21	Atlantic crossing
Combined Group Losses			
Combat losses	7	46	Enemy aircraft
	1	10	U-boat flak
Other losses	8	41	Crashes/accidents
	3	30	Unknown causes
	2	21	Atlantic crossing
Total	21	148	

Sources: Compiled from group and squadron records, USAFHRC.

Appendix E
Combats with Enemy Aircraft

479th Group

	Pilot	Enemy Aircraft	Remarks
7/26/43	Grider	9 JU 88s	No damage to any aircraft
8/8/43	Thomas	Unknown	B-24 and 10 crew lost
8/8/43	Owen	JU 88	No damage to either plane
8/16/43	Barnett	JU 88	Damage to JU 88 claimed
8/16/43	Gallmeier	8 JU 88s	B-24 escaped into cloud cover
8/18/43	Grider/Moore	10 JU 88s	B-24 lost, four killed; six survivors picked up 8/23
8/18/43	Leal	4 JU 88s	B-24's starboard engines, nose, hydraulic system damaged
8/23/43	Dustin	10 JU 88s	No. 1 engine and bomb-bay hit; depth charges jettisoned
8/25/43	Bolin	JU 88	Both port engines of B-24 hit; no. 2 engine caught fire
9/7/43	Young	7 JU 88s	Minor damage to B-24; possibly to two JU 88s
9/8/43	Finneburgh	8 JU 88s	B-24 lost; survivors picked up on 9/11
9/9/43	Owen	JU 88	B-24 escaped into cloud; landed at Gibraltar
9/18/43	Van Zyl	8 JU 88s	Extensive damage to B-24; damage to two JU 88s claimed
9/27/43	Cummings	5 Me 110s, 1 Me 109	Both port engines hit; depth charges jettisoned
10/17/43	Estes	12 JU 88s	No. 4 engine of B-24 disabled; possible damage to JU 88s

Note: In addition to these fifteen actions, there were ten other encounters with enemy aircraft when neither side fired on the other, usually because the B-24 escaped into cloud cover before it could be attacked.

480th Group

	Pilot	Enemy Aircraft	Remarks
12/3/42	Lueke	JU 88	No damage to either plane.
1/26/43	Johnson	JU 88	No certain damage JU 88.
1/29/43	Johnson	2 JU 88s	One JU 88 and B-24 damaged.
2/13/43	Johnson	Unknown	B-24 attacked by nightfighters; probably friendly;[a] no damage
2/26/43	Tomlinson	Unknown	B-24 and ten crew missing
7/18/43	Maxwell	FW 200	Damage to FW 200 claimed
7/28/43	Hyde	FW 200	FW 200 destroyed; B-24 returned to base on three engines; fog forced crash; one killed in action, none in crash
7/31/43	Mosier	FW 200	FW 200 destroyed
8/13/43	McKinnon	FW 200	FW 200 claimed destroyed
8/17/43	Maxwell	2 FW 200s	One FW 200 known destroyed; the other probably; B-24 crashed; three crew died in crash
8/25/43	Graham	Numerous	
8/27/43	Jarnagin	Numerous	
8/27/43	Kuenning	FW 200	FW 200 and B-24 damaged
8/28/43	McKinnon	FW 200	B-24 shot down; one killed in crash; no claim on FW 200
9/10/43	McKeown	Do 26, 2 Do 24s	Enemy seaplanes destroyed on the water
9/18/43	Jarnagin	Unknown	B-24 and ten crew missing
10/7/43	Mosier	Numerous	Three JU 88s claimed damaged

[a] I have included the one attack by "friendly" aircraft with the cases of known hostiles on the principle that firing actually took place and, had it been accurate, would have been as fatal as hostile fire.

Sources: Compiled from group and squadron records, USAFHRC.

Appendix F
How Radar Works

The word *radar* is a palindrome for *RA*dio *D*etection *A*nd *R*anging. This accurately conveys both its character and its function. Simply put, radar is a radio device for "seeing" remote objects by means of radio waves rather than the light waves on which simple optical observation devices depend. Radar does this by sending out, in a known direction, very short but powerful pulses of radio energy spaced widely apart and then receiving back weak pulses reflected from objects that the radio energy has illuminated. The distance from the radar equipment to the illuminated object can be accurately measured by the time required for the radio pulses to reach the object and return to the equipment.

Although radar would come to be based on the transmission of pulses of radio energy, the so-called beat method was the first approach to radio detection. It detected moving objects by observing the signal fluctuations in a radio receiver as an object moved through a constant radio propagation field. Although this possibility was recognized as early as 1922, and considerable work expended on it by both the U.S. Naval Research Laboratory and the U.S. Army Signal Corps, it proved a dead end. In the early 1930s a better idea occurred, using pulsed radio energy, which greatly simplified the measurement of distance and determination of direction of the object detected. (In fact, the earliest use of the pulse method was to measure the height of the ionosphere, which was done in 1925.)

By the mid-1930s, working independently of each other, American, British, and German scientists had all identified the potentiality of the pulse method of radio detection which would become the basis for World War II radars. While the pulse method offered great promise, it required far greater amounts of radio energy than the beat method, and this in turn demanded technology that was only emerging at the time. The progress of radar in the 1935–45 period would be heavily dependent on the development of equipment that could handle the high energy requirements of pulse radar systems.

A radar is normally identified or characterized by its wavelength, its pulse repetition frequency, and the radio frequency at which it operates. The main radar bands of the World War II period[1] were:

Band	Frequency (mc/s^2)	Wavelength	Notes
P	200–500	1.5–0.6m	Original U.S. radars
L	500–1,500	60–20cm	
S	1,500–5,000	20–6cm	Early centimeter or shortwave radars like the SCR-517
X	5,000–15,000	6–2cm	Later centimeter radars

Wavelength is an important characteristic of any radar. The sharper a radar beam, the better one can measure the direction of a detected object. Up to the point where wavelengths become so short that they are absorbed by moisture in the atmosphere, the general rule holds that the shorter the wavelength the more precise the accuracy of the radar (the narrower its beam and the more directional it is), and the smaller the object it can detect. Long wavelengths can "wrap themselves around" small objects so that the receiving equipment does not detect the presence of the object; generally, a radar cannot "see" objects smaller than half its wavelength. Further, airborne radar requires a radar antenna and its attached equipment to be as small and light as possible, as weight and space requirements are critical in an aircraft. This consideration places a premium on radars of higher frequencies (shorter wavelengths).[3]

The higher a radar's frequency, the greater the power requirement. Crucial to successful radar equipment, then, is the ability to generate radio pulses at a level of many thousands of watts, that is, kilowatts. This is necessitated by the sharp increase in transmission loss as wavelengths grow shorter. Centimeter radars such as the SCR-517 would have been impossible had not scientists devised valves, the klystron and the magnetron, which could handle the high energy loads required. Although the klystron valve was developed first, it was better suited to receiving than to transmitting equipment. The crucial breakthrough to effect centimeter radar came with the development of the strapped cavity magnetron valve by a pair of British scientists working at Birmingham University in late 1939 and early 1940.

The first British airborne centimeter radars were of the air-interception variety, used in nightfighters to intercept German bombers over Britain. Next in priority for the RAF came sets for British bombers seeking German targets. That left antisubmarine aircraft a poor third. Fortunately, the twelfth strapped cavity magnetron produced went to the United States with the Tizard mission in August 1940. The Americans were under no pressure to fend off enemy bombers over U.S. territory, and American production quickly exceeded that possible in wartime Britain. Thus it was that the first antisubmarine aircraft equipped with centimetric radar to operate from British soil were the planes of the 1st and 2nd Antisubmarine Squadrons, USAAF, using the SCR-517 set.

The SCR-517 set used an early-type radar screen, rather than the plan position indicator (PPI) that later came into general use. The most common early screen, the A-scope, showed the range of a target in the form of a blip, or "pip," that rose above a horizontal line calibrated for distance. Bearing angle had to be separately indicated. The British devised a clever system of two overlapping signal returns, which indicated bearing by how far to either side of a vertical line the pip extended.

The great superiority of the PPI display was that it put the operator and his equipment at the center of the radar screen (a circular cathode ray tube, or CRT). The radar beam swept out a circle around that center point in synchronization with the radar's antenna. It thus "painted" a map of everything around the airplane. At a glance the radar operator could instantly discern where an object was relative to himself. This greatly facilitated speed and accuracy of readings from the radar scope.

By late 1942, German U-boats had responded to the development of metric (1.5m) radar sets in antisubmarine aircraft by carrying a radar detection receiver. A receiver that had only to detect a signal on the initial transmission pulse, and not its much attenuated reflection, was going to pick up the radar wave at a range greater than the receiving equipment next to the radar transmitter in the antisubmarine aircraft could pick up the return from the detected submarine. This gave a U-boat sufficient time to submerge before the aircraft's radar was aware of its presence. By late 1942, all U-boats crossing the Bay of Biscay had such equipment.

However, to receive or "detect" a radar, the receiving or detecting equipment had to be tuned to the appropriate wavelength. German scientists had determined, incorrectly, that it was technically infeasible to develop valves of sufficient power to make possible centimeter-wave radar. Consequently, the detection devices carried aboard German submarines to reveal the presence of a searching radar were designed to detect only metric wavelengths. Until the Germans belatedly reacted to the discovery that the Allies had centimeter radar (from the wreckage of a crashed bomber near Rotterdam, Holland), planes equipped with SCR-517 and similar shortwave radars could catch the German U-boats unawares.

Sources: Brian Johnson, *The Secret War* (London: Methuen, 1978); Norman Friedman, *Naval Radar* (Annapolis, Md.: Naval Institute Press, 1981); Robert Morris Page, *The Origin of Radar* (Garden City, N.Y.: Anchor Books, Doubleday, 1962); John F. Rider and G. C. Baxter Rowe, *Radar: What It Is* (New York: John F. Rider, 1946).

Appendix G
The Dangers of ASW Flying

There is no easy way to analyze the dangers of ASW flying. All one can do is present some data and comment on what they suggest. Comparing apples and oranges only tells one how many apples and oranges he has, yet comparison seems the only way to get some sense of proportion with regard to the risks of antisubmarine flying. Thus I have taken data on missions flown and operational losses for seven Eighth Air Force heavy bombardment groups that flew B-24s and that began operations in the ETO before the end of 1943 as a basis to compare with the operational missions and losses of the 479th and 480th Antisubmarine Groups.

The flaws of this approach will be evident to the reader. The data for the Eighth Air Force bombardment groups run from initial operations in the ETO until the end of the war in Europe. Thus the data span periods of operations that were greatly different in their risks. Bombing missions over Europe were much more dangerous to fly in 1943 and the first quarter of 1944 than they became in the last year of the war in Europe. The bombardment group figures do not show those differences. For the antisubmarine groups, the basis is much shorter in duration—for the 479th Group only some four months of operations, while the figures for the 480th Group cover not quite a year. Even within these constricted time periods, the risks varied greatly, depending on U-boat tactics and the degree of support the Luftwaffe was willing and able to offer the German submarines crossing the Bay of Biscay.

Risk is an individual thing. Eighth Air Force bomber crews were normally expected to complete twenty-five operational missions during 1942 and 1943, and thirty after February of 1944; the point in time of those missions greatly affected a crew member's life expectancy. For the antisubmarine groups, the standard of service was measured not in operational missions but rather by operational hours flown and time spent in the theater. A high percentage of the crews in the 480th Group served long enough to accumulate an Air Medal and one Oak Leaf Cluster, recognition for 400 operational hours flown. A good number had a second Oak Leaf Cluster for having completed 600 hours. Obviously, the longer one flew, the more he was mortgaging his life against the law of averages. Thus the data presented below should be read with all these caveats in mind.

Group	Dates	Sorties	Operational Losses[a]	Sorties per Operational Loss	Sorties per Combat Loss
44th	9/42–5/45	8,009	153 + 39 = 192	41.7	52.3
93rd	9/42–5/45	8,169	100 + 40 = 140	58.4	81.7
389th	6/43–5/45	7,579	116 + 37 = 153	49.5	65.3
392nd	7/43–5/45	7,060	127 + 57 = 184	38.4	55.6
445th	11/43–5/45	7,147	108 + 25 = 133	53.7	66.2
446th	11/43–5/45	7,259	58 + 28 = 86	84.4	125.2
448th	11/43–5/45	6,774	101 + 34 = 135	50.2	67.1
All bombardment groups		51,995	763 + 260 = 1,023	50.8	68.1
479th	7–10/43	446	4 + 1 = 5	89.2	111.5
480th	11/42–10/43	1,185	5 + 9 = 14	84.6	237.0
Both ASW Groups		1,631	9 + 10 = 19	85.8	181.2

[a]Figures are combat losses + other operational losses = all operational losses.

By this rough and ready estimate, a crew member was more likely to survive a tour of duty in antisubmarine operations than in strategic bombing operations over Europe. Calculated by operational hours flown, the numbers would be even more favorable to the antisubmarine units, whose hours per sortie were higher than the bombardment groups.

Sources: All Eighth Air Force data is from Freeman, *The Mighty Eighth*, 240–41, 244, 255–58. I have calculated the figures for the 479th and 480th Groups.

Appendix H
The Risks of Ditching at Sea
in a B-24 Liberator

As the Liberator came into increasing use in RAF Coastal Command as its preferred LR/VLR antisubmarine aircraft, concern began to mount about its safety when it was necessary to ditch into the sea. In May 1943 the RAF and the Ministry of Aircraft Production (MAP) took stock of the situation, found reasons for concern, and put in hand efforts to improve the plane's safety when it had to ditch. While the number of ditchings for RAF Liberators was too small to allow a great deal of confidence in the statistics derived, they were troubling. Accumulated data gave the following figures:

Aircraft	Number Ditched	Total Crew	Crew Saved	Percent Saved
Halifax	29	199	90	45.2%
Whitley	133	716	319	44.6%
Wellington	199	1,112	322	28.9%
Liberator	16	131	8	6.1%

(Coastal Command Liberators in 1943 usually flew with crews of eight or nine, although I have run across cases of only seven crew members. B-24Ds of the 479th and 480th Groups always operated with a crew of ten.)

It is interesting to compare this with the figures for the 479th and 480th Groups:

Aircraft	Number Ditched	Total Crew	Crew Saved	Percent Saved
All ditchings	11	110	25	22.7%
Events known	4	40	25	62.5%

All ditchings, that is, all operational losses over the sea, include those for which there is no evidence as to what happened, and thus no idea how many crew members might have been killed in combat before the plane crashed, or how many survived the crash, but then perished in the sea when rescue efforts failed to locate them. This is consistent with the assumptions used in the British data, above. While the experience of the American squadrons was nearly four times better than that of the RAF, it still leaves the Liberator the most deadly of all ASW aircraft to ditch at sea. The "events known" data concern only those crashes at sea where we know what happened. This gives some idea of survival chances when the ditching is more or less controlled. These were by definition the fortunate ones, and survival rates are much higher, as one would expect.

The British conclusion was clear: "The Liberator is, without exception, the worst type of aircraft in the R.A.F. as regards ditching safety." The reasons for this were identified as:

1. Extreme weakness of the fuselage underbody at the bomb bays;
2. Inadequacy of the emergency exits;
3. "Complete absence of suitable ditching stations in the rear of the aircraft;"
4. No provision to store survival equipment with the plane's dinghies; and
5. Nonautomatic operation of the dinghies (life rafts to the USAAF).

Some of these problems were amenable to quick and relatively easy improvements, but the major structural problem was not. The weakness of the Liberator's underbody produced three unhappy effects. In the first place, "collapse of bomb doors causes a catastrophic dive under water in ditching, with resultant heavy deceleration." Further, the bombardier's sighting window at the bottom of the nose plexiglass and the nose-wheel doors were both inadequately robust to withstand the impact of ditching; their prompt collapse allowed a wave of water to flood into the forward end of the airplane, "which is likely to overwhelm [the] crew." Finally, the general collapse of the underbody destroyed fuselage buoyancy, "hence aircraft sinks almost instantly to wing level, drowning the crew before they have time to escape." Both the bombardier's window and the nose-wheel doors were capable of being strengthened so as to better withstand the shock of a ditching. The British study group in May 1943 recommended a strength able to withstand 10 to 12 pounds per square inch pressures. But "short of radical re-design, there is little that can be done with the existing [bomb bay] doors."

The British study group strongly recommended improvements in exits from the plane. In the forward part of the plane there was only one emergency exit for five (British) or six (American) crew members. Further, as the Liberator was a high-wing type, "this exit is rapidly submerged." In the rear of the aircraft the only openings were the two waist gunners' windows. These the British considered to be too far aft in the plane. As they were side openings and the plane was prone to instant flooding, the crew members in the rear of the plane would have great difficulty reaching the top of the fuselage, "if they are not previously overcome by the rearward rush of the water" entering through the bomb bays. Accordingly, two additional exits were recommended. A second forward exit should be installed above the copilot's position, and an exit through the top of the fuselage from the platform above the bomb bays was recommended for the after part of the plane. Improvements to the crew's ditching stations were also advised.

The two dinghy storage spaces built into the Liberator were too small to accommodate emergency equipment, which the British rightly insisted had to be stored with the dinghies. The crew would be too busy extricating themselves in a ditching to attend to moving such equipment out of the plane and into the dinghies, even if it were feasible. So, too, that there was only manual operation of the dinghy inflation devices was seen as a handicap to aviators who might be hard-pressed to get the rafts inflated in the hectic and critical conditions of a crash at sea. All other modern land aircraft types in RAF use carried automatic-inflating dinghies, and so important was this considered that even RAF seaplanes were being so equipped. The recommendation of the group was that the dinghy storage areas be increased in depth, an emergency pack with essential survival equipment be stored in the compartment and under the dinghy, and that the dinghy itself be a self-inflating model, folded so that the self-inflating process would work to spring-eject the dinghy from its compartment.

Meeting all these recommendations was put in hand by the MAP and the RAF. The AAFAC, before it went out of existence, also took some steps, although not as comprehensive as the RAF and MAP, to improve the chances for Liberator crews to survive a ditching. The fuselage life-raft compartments were being modified so that they would be large enough to hold both the life raft and the emergency equipment necessary for survival at sea. A standard "shipwreck kit" had been developed and in June 1943 was being provided to AAFAC units. At that time, the AAFAC authorized its antisubmarine aircraft to carry an additional life raft. There were also improvements to the individual crew members' standard life-vest ("Mae West") equipment. The AAFAC did not, however, consider structural alterations to the Liberator to improve ditching safety, other than those required to enlarge the life raft compartments.

Sources: All RAF and MAP information is from AVIA 15/3012, PRO. AAFAC improvement program is from "General Program of Aircraft Modification and Assignment in the Antisubmarine Command," June 5, 1943, AAFAC file 424.8613, USAFHRC. I have calculated the USAAF loss percentages.

Appendix I
Awards and Decorations

No comprehensive listing exists of all awards and decorations received for performance of duty in the 479th and 480th Groups. Without such a listing, it would be invidious to include the awards of a few, while omitting many. In any case, much of the service of antisubmarine units consisted of fighting monotony in the performance of an often tedious task with only occasional opportunities for notable achievement. What was achieved on those occasions was meritorious without normally being of a character that would lead to the higher awards for valor. Wayne Johnson, who was awarded a British DFC for his role in finding the German blockade runner, received the decoration from the British Ambassador, Lord Halifax, at the British Embassy in Washington. Of that occasion he wrote: "There were a number of people receiving decorations—some of much higher rank; posthumous; etc. While it was a distinct honor to be included as a recipient, and I wore the decoration proudly, I think we and our feat were among the lesser lights of the occasion."[1] This might serve as a proper assessment for the achievements and recognition that came to the two antisubmarine groups in proportion to the scale of the war as a whole.

Where individuals received awards for more than the routine performance of duty, I have endeavored to note them in the narrative. As a general rule, an Air Medal was awarded to any individual completing 200 hours of operational flying; this normally meant completing about 20 missions. An Oak Leaf Cluster was awarded for each additional 200 hours. Most aircrew in the 480th Group served long enough to receive the Air Medal and one Oak Leaf Cluster. A fair number had two Oak Leaf Clusters. As the medal and cluster were also awarded for outstanding performance of duties, there were men in the 480th Group with at least three Oak Leaf Clusters. One individual is known to have been awarded four Oak Leaf Clusters, but it is not clear whether one or more of these were for flying in the western Atlantic or for distinguished conduct.

Some indication of the number of such awards is a listing for the 2nd Antisubmarine Squadron, which on the last day of September 1943 showed one hundred Air Medals awarded for flying 200 operational hours, and fifty-three more such awards pending. Further, there were sixty-five Oak Leaf Clusters awarded for an additional 200 hours completed, with sixty-two more awards pending. Air Medals and Oak Leaf Clusters were also awarded for participation in attacks on U-boats and for enemy aircraft destroyed. Forty DFCs (Army) and nineteen DFCs (Navy) were pending for attacks on U-boats. There were forty-five Purple Hearts, forty-four of them posthumous, awarded in the squadron. Figures for the 1st Antisubmarine Squadron would likely be quite similar.[2]

With regard to the 479th Group, Maj. Stephen D. McElroy, commanding the 4th Squadron, recorded a presentation of medals to members of the group on October 1, 1943, with Air Medals and Oak Leaf Clusters being awarded to men who had achieved 200, 400, and 600 hours of operational flying. These awards must have included operational flying in the western Atlantic. T. Sgt. William D. Meredith, who was the flight engineer in Captain Hamilton's crew, which sank U.706, logged 180 operational hours in eighteen missions between July 15 and October 29, and his experience was surely typical for the group.[3]

Theoretically, if a crew flew a 10-hour operational sortie every fourth day between July 15 and October 29 they would have accumulated 270 operational hours. However, the 4th Squadron, which flew the most missions, logged only 202 flights of 1,823 hours during its European operations. Assuming an average strength of ten aircrews in the squadron throughout the period, the average number of flights per crew would have been 20 of 9 hours duration, or again 180 hours, which is what Meredith actually logged.[4]

It seems unlikely, then, that many aircrews in the 479th Group reached the 200-operational-hour threshold while flying from the United Kingdom. The DFC was the normal USAAF award for exceptional performance that occasioned risk above that normally involved in any operational mission. On October 5, Lt. Gen. Ira Eaker presented thirty DFCs and thirteen Purple Hearts to members of the 479th Group. Clearly, this did not include all of the awards to this group.[5]

The 480th Group was awarded a Presidential Unit Citation. This cited "outstanding performance of duty in action with the enemy during the period 10 November 1942 to 28 October 1943." The group was honored as "the pioneer organization in the establishment of the Army Air Forces offensive antisubmarine operations in the Eastern Hemisphere." Special notice was taken of the twelve attacks on U-boats in the period July 6–14, 1943, although the conclusion that eight resulted in "the destruction, or probable damage to, the enemy" was slightly optimistic. The citation concluded that "the 480th Antisubmarine Group has contributed with heroism and superior efficiency to the winning of the Battle of the Atlantic. Its record is inspiring and worthy of emulation."[6] The 479th Group did not exist long enough to be in a position to compile a record that would qualify it for consideration for a unit citation.

Abbreviations

AA	Antiaircraft (gun, gunfire, etc.)
AAFAC	Army Air Forces Antisubmarine Command (U.S.)
ADM	Admirality Records, PRO
AIR	Air Ministry Records, PRO
AOC-in-C	Air Officer Commanding-in-Chief (major RAF commands)
A/S	Antisubmarine
ASV	Air-to-surface vessel (radar)
ASW	Antisubmarine warfare
ASWORG	Antisubmarine Warfare Operational Research Group (U.S.)
AVIA	Ministry of Aircraft Production Records, PRO
CAS	Chief of the Air Staff (RAF)
CC	Coastal Command (RAF)
CG	Commanding General (U.S. Army, USAAF)
CO	Commanding officer
Cominch	Commander-in-Chief, U.S. Fleet (may refer to both the person and his office/staff)
COS	Chiefs of Staff (British)

DFC	Distinguished Flying Cross
Do	Dornier, a German aircraft manufacturer
ESF	Eastern Sea Frontier (of the United States)
ETO	European Theater of Operations
FAW	Fleet Air Wing (USN)
Flak	Antiaircraft gun (lit. *Fliegerabwehrkanone*); also used to refer to fire from such guns
FW	Focke-Wulf, a German aircraft manufacturer
GR	General Reconnaissance (type of aircraft, of squadron, etc.)
He	Heinkel, a German aircraft manufacturer
HMCS	His/Her Majesty's Canadian Ship
HMS	His/Her Majesty's Ship (British)
JCS	Joint Chiefs of Staff (U.S.)
JU	Junkers, a German aircraft manufacturer
LR	Long range
MAP	Ministry of Aircraft Production (British)
Me	Messerschmitt, a German aircraft manufacturer
MR	Microfilm reel
MSF	Moroccan Sea Frontier
msn	Military service number (of an aircraft)
NACAF	Northwest African Coastal Air Force
NATOUSA	North African Theater of Operations, U.S. Army
OOW	Officer of the Watch
ORS	Operational Research Section (of a British command)
OTU	Operational Training Unit (RAF)
PLE	Prudent limit of endurance
PPI	Plan Position Indicator, a radar scope that showed the operating aircraft at the center of the screen and portrayed every other indication on the screen relative to it
PRO	Public Record Office, Kew, Surrey, England
RAAF	Royal Australian Air Force
RCAF	Royal Canadian Air Force
RMS	Royal Mail Steamer

TI	Tactical Instruction (issued by RAF)
TM	Tactical Memorandum (issued by RAF)
U-boat	Anglicized form for *Unterseeboot,* or submarine
USAFHRC	U.S. Air Force Historical Research Center, Maxwell Air Force Base, Alabama
USNHC	U.S. Naval Historical Center, Washington Navy Yard
VLR	Very long range
VLR(E)	Very long range (extended)
WAAF	Women's Auxiliary Air Force (British)

Notes

Sources abbreviated at first appearance can be found in full in the Bibliography.

Chapter 1. A Strategic Antisubmarine Force

1. "History of the Army Air Forces Antisubmarine Command" (hereafter "History of AAFAC"), 94, USAFHRC. The phrase "merry massacre" is Samuel Eliot Morison's.

2. Marshall to King, September 14, 1942, copy in AAFAC file 424.549B, USAFHRC. By "area responsibility," Marshall refers to the U.S. Navy's system of organizing coastal areas into sea frontiers. The Anti-Submarine Army Air Command was changed to the Army Air Forces Antisubmarine Command (AAFAC).

3. Craven and Cate, eds., *The Army Air Forces in World War II*, 2:379.

4. Brig. Gen. C. W. Russell to CG, Army Air Forces, November 3, 1942, AAFAC Files, USAFHRC.

5. Brig. Gen. W. T. Larson to Col. G. C. Sweeney Jr., Operations Division, War Department General Staff, June 10, 1943, AAFAC Files, USAFHRC.

6. Ibid.

7. Craven and Cate, eds., *The Army Air Forces in World War II*, 2:379. It was the Liberator's ability to carry a useful weapons load to great ranges which made it so desired as a strategic antisubmarine aircraft.

8. Bernard E. Benson to author, January 8, 1992. Benson was a 1st Antisubmarine Squadron navigator.

9. For a brief account of this contest and its outcome, see Max Schoenfeld, "'First Things Must Come First': Winston Churchill and the Allocation of Aircraft Between Coastal Command and Bomber Command of the RAF, July 1941–November 1942," in Richard M. Langworth, ed., *Proceedings of the Churchill Societies, 1988–1989* (Contoocook, N.H.: International Churchill Society, 1990).

10. The aircraft would at all times belong to the RAF; the Royal Navy's only internal air units were those that went to sea on ships. At issue was whether the long-range aircraft would go to RAF Coastal Command (CC), which operated under the general direction of the British Admiralty in prosecution of the war at sea, or to Bomber Command, pursuing the strategic bombing mission against Germany.

11. Winston S. Churchill to Harry Hopkins, November 20, 1942, message no. 202. My copy is from the Chief of the Air Staff's files, Public Record Office (hereafter CAS and PRO, respectively), AIR 8/1397; it exists in numerous copies and is printed in Kimball, ed., *Churchill and Roosevelt,* 2:26–27 (C-202). Churchill did not disguise his priorities: without this American assistance, he observed, he would have to "make a further diversion from the small force of long range bombers responsible for the air offensive against Germany."

12. RAF Delegation to the Combined Chiefs of Staff, Washington (RAFDEL), to CAS, November 22, 1942, reported that the USAAF had eight, later corrected to nine, centimeter-radar equipped Liberators then en route to North Africa, and another twelve then being so equipped for the same theater. AIR 8/1397, PRO.

13. AGWAR (War Office, Washington, D.C.) to USFOR (U.S. Forces HQ, London), November 24, 1942. Copy in AIR 8/1397, PRO.

14. COS to JCS, November 26, 1942, CAB 105/30, PRO.

15. Hopkins to Churchill, December 2, 1942. Copies in ADM 205/14 (First Sea Lord's files) and AIR 8/1397 (CAS's files), PRO. Churchill promptly responded that the British would "arrange with General Eisenhower for the best use of the 21 American Liberators as you suggest." Churchill to Hopkins, December 3, 1943. Copies in ADM 205/14 and AIR 8/1397, PRO; COS to Eisenhower, December 14, 1942, copy in AIR 8/1397, PRO; Eisenhower to COS, December 15, 1942, copy in AIR 8/1397, PRO.

16. Churchill to First Sea Lord and CAS, December 16, 1942, CAS copy in AIR 8/1397, PRO.

17. Hopkins to Churchill, December 2, 1942.

18. The best introduction to the role of aircraft in ASW is Price, *Aircraft versus Submarine.*

19. It could carry four 100-pound bombs or two 250-pound bombs. AIR 15/305, RAF/CC, TI No. 5, November 20, 1939, PRO.

20. Ibid. TI No. 5 gives the 100-pound bomb a lethal radius of three feet, which was perhaps overly optimistic.

21. Price, *Aircraft versus Submarine,* 43.

22. AIR 15/305, RAF/CC TI No. 5, November 20, 1939, PRO, has pages of esoteric calculations for setting time fuses to sink U-boats which had long since submerged. It was a futile use of paper, for the task was impossible.

23. For some examples, see Price, *Aircraft versus Submarine,* 47.

24. Ibid., 53. The term "depth bomb" is often used for a depth charge dropped from the air, especially by American units. I shall use "depth charge" throughout.

25. This was clear very early in the war: see the comments in AIR 15/305, RAF/CC TI No. 5, November 20, 1939, PRO, on this.

26. It was in fact scientists engaged in analyzing operations who came up with the idea of white camouflage; see Air Ministry (UK), *The Origins and Development of Operational Research in the Royal Air Force,* 80. I am grateful to Prof. Will Jacobs of the University of Alaska–Anchorage for providing me with xeroxes from this publication.

27. Price, *Aircraft versus Submarine,* 54.

28. The Hudson could carry up to ten 100-pound bombs, or four 250-pound bombs. Normally, it carried only five of the 100-pound bombs in order to extend its range. AIR 15/305, RAF/CC TI No. 5, November 20, 1939, PRO.

29. Price, *Aircraft versus Submarine,* 56.

30. Figures are from ibid., 57. They appear to be "optimums," or the best results possible if everything works perfectly. The effective area swept might easily be half the optimum, the consequence of equipment degradation, operator fatigue, and weather conditions, to note the more common causes.

31. American developments can be found in Terrett, *The Signal Corps,* 194–202.

32. Price, *Aircraft versus Submarine,* 78–79.

33. A good account of how the problems of developing the Leigh Light were surmounted appears in ibid., 60–64.

34. Figures are from ibid., 92.

35. Ibid., 94.

36. This difference is hard to overcome. The energy necessary to send out a radar wave impulse, and to enable it to return to the sender, inevitably leads to its detection at a longer range by a device that needed only to detect the radar's initial impulse.

37. Price, *Aircraft versus Submarine,* 95.

38. The Mark XI remained in short supply late into 1942. Its lethal radius was officially given as 19 feet.

39. AIR 15/732, ORS Report No. 248, February 1943, PRO. Operational Research was the British usage of the time; the most common American terminology is Operations Analysis.

40. For all this, see Air Ministry (UK), *The Origins and Development of Operational Research in the Royal Air Force,* 76–77.

41. AIR 15/305, RAF/CC TI No. 31, July 24, 1942, PRO.

42. This was designed to slow the rate at which the Mark VIII sank, as it was thought that an air bubble formed around it as it sank and delayed the action of the water pressure on the hydrostatic pistol, so that it exploded beneath its set depth.

43. AIR 15/305, RAF/CC TI No. 31, July 24, 1942, PRO. As the lethal area of each depth charge was a radius, the outer edges of the lethal area of a stick would vary. The wider the spacing in a stick, the greater the variation.

44. There were two kinds of aiming error, for range and for line. Line was easier to get right than range, and range errors were typically two to three times greater than line errors.

45. All data are from AIR 15/305, RAF/CC, TI No. 31, July 24, 1942, PRO. Attacks as late as 30 seconds after a submarine had disappeared were thought worth making.

46. Data are from AIR 15/304, RAF/CC TM No. 52, March 13, 1943, PRO.

47. Air Ministry (UK), *The Origins and Development of Operational Research in the Royal Air Force*, 88.

48. Figures are from Price, *Aircraft versus Submarine*, 74.

49. The best recent study of this fiasco is Gannon, *Operation Drumbeat*.

50. "History of AAFAC," 12.

51. In December 1941 the USN had 103 aircraft available to the commander of the ESF. However, only 10 were warplanes suitable for the ASW mission; the remainder were chiefly trainers or utility planes. "History of AAFAC," 4. In July 1942 the 1920 ruling was changed to allow allocation of land-based aircraft to the Navy. It had, in fact, long employed some land-based scout planes. For all this, see Morison, *History of United States Naval Operations in World War II*, 1:240.

52. In the first nine months of 1942, aircraft sank six U-boats and participated with surface ships in destroying three others in American-patrolled waters, a rate of one U-boat a month. Of these, the USAAF contribution had been to sink two and aid in the destruction of a third. Morison, *History of United States Naval Operations in World War II*, 1:415.

53. "History of AAFAC," 6.

54. Ibid., 22, 40. Pending detailed arrangements on unity of command for coastal defenses, General Marshall and Admiral King agreed on March 25, 1942, to a temporary measure that placed all Army air units allocated for operations over the sea for the protection of shipping and for antisubmarine warfare under naval sea frontier commanders. See Larry I. Bland, ed., *The Papers of George Catlett Marshall*, vol. 3 (Baltimore: Johns Hopkins University Press, 1991), 146–47.

55. The resistance of Cominch to convoying was paralleled by his reluctance to allocate naval resources to the ESF. When the commander of that organization asked on March 30, 1942, for destroyers to meet an upsurge in U-boat activity off the Cape Hatteras shipping bottleneck, he got back from Admiral King the next day the terse reply: "Your knowledge of other demands for DD's [destroyers] as imperative as your own is not given sufficient credit in your [message]." Quoted in "History of AAFAC," 3. It is hard not to suspect that Admiral King simply did not take shipping losses all that seriously, especially when the merchant ships competed with major warships for scarce naval escorts.

56. Figures from Morison, *History of United States Naval Operations in World War II*, 1:257.

57. Ibid., 1:241.

Chapter 2. The 480th Antisubmarine Group in the United Kingdom

1. "History of the 1st Antisubmarine Squadron," USAFHRC (hereafter 1st Squadron history). Lt. Col. Jack Roberts was a graduate of the USMA class of 1935. He had grown up in the small town of Eastman, Georgia, where his father was a prominent lawyer. His brother, Littleton Roberts, some 10 years older than Jack, had received an appointment to West Point, and was an inspiration to young Jack, who aspired to follow his brother to the USMA. However, when Jack was 14, his father died, and thereafter Jack's hopes for an appointment to the USMA faded. He had about given up hope, despite some years of effort, and gone to work in New York City when an appointment became available. The outgoing and energetic Roberts greatly enjoyed his years at West Point. He rose rapidly in the Air Corps and then the USAAF during the late thirties and early forties. He remained active in the newly established USAF, serving in Military Air Transport Command (MATS) and Strategic Air Command (SAC), and suffering through two Pentagon tours. A brigadier general in 1951, he had just been appointed chief of staff to Gen. Curtis LeMay at SAC headquarters when a sudden fatal heart attack struck while he was vacationing in Colorado. He was 43 years old at the time of his death. Information courtesy of Mrs. Cornelia H. Roberts Kimbrough.

2. Records of the 2nd Antisubmarine Squadron, USAFHRC (hereafter 2nd Squadron records).

3. William W. Pomeroy, diary, undated entry but prior to November 16, 1942. Photocopy of diary in the author's possession. Reproduced courtesy of W. W. Pomeroy. Some idea of Pomeroy's feelings at the time is conveyed by the title for his diary entry: "Desperate Journey."

4. Roberts to Brig. Gen. Westside Larson, CG, AAFAC, December 6, 1942, MR A0522, USAFHRC. (All microfilm reels [MR] are USAFHRC.)

5. Ibid.

6. Pomeroy diary.

7. Information from Pomeroy diary.

8. Samuel B. McGowan to author, February 22, 1988.

9. The aircraft's military serial number (msn) was 41-24007; records of the 1st Antisubmarine Squadron (hereafter 1st Squadron Records); McGowan to author, February 22, 1988.

10. "History of the 2nd Antisubmarine Squadron," USAFHRC (hereafter 2nd Squadron history).

11. War diaries, 1st and 2nd Squadrons, USAFHRC.

12. Roberts to CG, AAFAC, December 28, 1942.

13. Ibid.; "History of AAFAC," 102–102a.

14. Roberts to CG, VIII Bomber Command, January 15, 1943.

15. "History of AAFAC," 99.

16. Ibid., 100.

17. Roberts to CG, AAFAC, December 6, 1942.

18. This author maintains that only those who have experienced that system in years past can understand the meaning of the word "frustration."

19. Roberts to CG, AAFAC, December 27, 1942.

20. Ibid., December 6, 1942.

21. Ibid. He also regretfully informed General Larson at AAFAC that "the standard of cleanliness is far below the worst U.S. mess ever visited by the undersigned."

22. Lt. John Krebs in "Interview of Capt. Benson and Lt. Krebs," July 20, 1943, Office of the Assistant Chief of Staff, 26th Wing, AAFAC file 424.620A, USAFHRC. Exclamation point in the original.

23. 480th Group diary, February 3, 1943, USAFHRC.

24. "History of AAFAC," 100.

25. McGowan to author, February 22, 1988.

26. 1st Squadron history.

27. Roberts to CG, AAFAC, December 6, 1942.

28. Ashworth, *Action Stations,* 5:163–68.

29. "The RAF in the Maritime War," vol. 3, appendix I, and vol. 4, appendix I, USAFHRC. Like the two American squadrons, these units were usually somewhat below their established strengths.

30. Roberts to CG, VIII Bomber Command, January 15, 1943.

31. Roberts to CG, AAFAC, January 9, 1943.

32. Records of the 480th Antisubmarine Group, USAFHRC (hereafter 480th Group records).

33. Roberts to CG, Eighth Air Force, December 27, 1942.

34. Roberts to CG, AAFAC, December 6, 1942; "History of AAFAC," 100.

35. "History of AAFAC," 100.

36. Roberts to CG, AAFAC, December 6, 1942.

37. Ibid.

38. In the World War II USAAF, the unit structure in ascending order was squadron, group, wing; in the RAF it was squadron, wing, group. Roberts showed commendable initiative, but he clearly felt that he was receiving inadequate guidance and support from the AAF's Antisubmarine Command: Roberts to Lt. Col. Dale O. Smith, AAFAC, January 14, 1943. The following day, in a message to the Commanding General, VIII Bomber Command, on the establishment of the 1st Antisubmarine Group (Provisional), Roberts noted with some feeling that "this unit has received only one message, a cablegram [regarding training procedures for the entire ASC], from the parent unit, and has never received any information as to the objective and policies of A/S units in the ETO, the furnishing of replacement personnel . . . etc." This was better than two months after his arrival at St. Eval. It should be noted that AAFAC headquarters in New York was having its own problems in this regard. A letter that Roberts had written on January 8 reached AAFAC only on February 2. Col. G. A. McHenry to Roberts, February 2, 1943. AAFAC file 424.3911, USAFHRC.

39. Roberts to Group Captain W. L. Dawson, RAF Station, St. Eval, January 15, 1943, MR B0638; 1st Squadron records; "History of AAFAC," 99; "History of the 480th Group," USAFHRC. Designated the 1st Antisubmarine Group (Provisional), the unit was renamed the 2037th Wing (Provisional) on March 1, 1943, and finally on June 21, 1943, the 480th Antisubmarine Group (Separate) (Special). "History of AAFAC," 246–47. It will usually be referred to in this account by its last designation.

40. 480th Group records. Note that the USAAF was still using U.S. Army designators, such as S-1, at that time. Roberts carried out this reorganization at least partially from personnel considerations. He urged General Larson as early as December 28, 1942, that

> only young, ambitious, and aggressive personnel be sent to the theatre of operations. The [1st Antisubmarine] squadron is over-burdened with ranking officers at present. . . . Further, several personnel, both commissioned and enlisted, have cracked under the strain.

Roberts to CG, AAFAC, December 28, 1942, MR B0638. As "the strain" was relatively modest for an operational theater, the impression is that the USAAF was still in the process of shaking out long-term peacetime career officers and long-service enlisted personnel who were unsuited to the stresses and strains of military operations overseas. Roberts's recommendations regarding selection of personnel for the ETO is also interesting:

> All crew members should be interviewed and analyzed by unit flight surgeons with reference to their mental attitude toward operations, and doubtful members eliminated. The emotional stress, due to long flights, bad weather, and possible E/A [enemy aircraft] attack, is definitely greater than in the continental U.S.

Roberts to CG, VIII Bomber Command, January 3, 1943, MR A0522. Not all of the old hands were happy to be shunted aside into desk jobs by Roberts. One major enclosed Roberts's reorganization order in a letter to the AAFAC, commenting that his "position has become embarrassing" and noting with regard to the reorganization that "I don't believe it to be for the best interest of the service." Maj. Perroneaux R. Chaplin to the Assistant Chief of Staff at AAFAC, January 18, 1943, MR A0522. Chaplin was assigned as intelligence officer in the second squadron, whose commander and operations officer were both still captains and fairly junior to Chaplin in service seniority.

41. 1st and 2nd Squadron histories.

42. 480th Group diary; 2nd Antisubmarine Squadron war diary, USAFHRC.

43. 480th Group diary.

44. Roberts to CG, AAFAC, December 6, 1942, MR A0522.

45. Lt. John Krebs, "Interview of Capt. Benson and Lt. Krebs."

46. 1st Squadron Report to 19 Group, RAF/CC, December 27, 1942, MR A0522.

47. Roberts to CG, Eighth Air Force, December 27, 1942, MR B0638.

48. "Report of Personnel Missing, 8 January 1943," MR B0638. The msn of the aircraft was 41-23997.

49. Roberts to CG, VIII Bomber Command for transmission to AAFAC, January 3, 1943, MR B0638.

50. Ibid.

51. The American squadrons, operating under CC control, adopted the RAF system of giving each aircraft in a squadron an identifying letter, hence "S/2nd Antisubmarine Squadron," rendered in short form, "S/2 Aron," or simply "S/2." Each RAF squadron normally had assigned a two-letter identifying code. Many photos of the World War II era show British aircraft with three letters painted prominently on the fuselage. The two immediately adjacent (usually but not always the first two) are the squadron letters, and the third is the individual plane's letter. There were variations on this, and it should be noted that squadron letters changed from time to time during the war. Sometimes only the individual plane's letter appeared, as was the case with the two American squadrons operating in CC.

52. 2nd Squadron history. Records of the 480th Group show fourteen operational missions (including Broussard's) terminated early or aircraft diverted to alternate landing fields because of weather, or 6.42 percent of all missions flown from the United Kingdom. This does *not* include missions scrubbed because of weather conditions. As the records of the group while operating from St. Eval are less comprehensive than for the period when operating from North Africa, or the 479th Group's records, it is not certain if these are all that were terminated early. It is worth noting that according to the 480th Group's records only six missions were terminated early because of equipment malfunction—in five cases engine trouble—or 2.75 percent of all missions. This is notably lower than the 7.8 percent figure for the 479th Group operating the same equipment. Notable, too, is the fact that the single largest reason for curtailing of 479th Group missions, gun turret failure, never occurs in the records of the 480th Group. Was there none? Or was it the case that at a time of low Luftwaffe activity over the Bay of Biscay and Atlantic such a problem was not considered sufficient cause to curtail a mission? Or are the records simply incomplete?

53. "Fatal Aircraft Crash," January 24, 1943, MR B0638. The aircraft's msn was 41-24019. Broussard had completed four local training flights from St. Eval, and one operational patrol before the fatal one. He had 460 hours total pilot time, 250 of which were in the B-24D. His radio operator requested homing assistance from the 19 Group Controller seven times in the space of 38 minutes, four times prefaced immediate or priority.

54. "Missing Aircraft, 27 February 1943," MR B0638. Sands had some 640 hours time as a pilot, 340 of them in the B-24D. The aircraft's msn was 41-11937.

55. Roberts to CG, VIII Bomber Command, January 23, 1943, MR B0638. The B-24D's msn was 41-23923.

56. Samuel B. McGowan to author, March 3, 1988.

57. William W. Pomeroy to author, May 1992.

58. 1st Squadron history. The Soldier's Medals were awarded April 3, 1943, in North Africa.

59. Roberts to CG, VIII Bomber Command, January 23, 1943, MR B0638.

60. Roberts to CG, AAFAC, December 6, 1942, MR A0522.

61. "The RAF in the Maritime War," 3:71, 81.

62. "History of AAFAC," 103.

63. Roberts to CG, AAFAC, December 6, 1942, MR A0522.

64. Report of 1st Antisubmarine Squadron, November 25, 1942, MR A0522.

65. Roberts to CG, AAFAC, December 6, 1942, MR A0522.

66. Ibid.

67. Ibid., December 28, 1942, MR B0638.

68. Roberts to CG, VIII Bomber Command, January 15, 1943.

69. Ibid., December 27, 1942.

70. Ibid.

71. Roberts to Air Marshal Sir John Slessor, AOC-in-C, RAF/CC, February 15[?], 1943, MR B0638. "Failure" was defined in this report as "any period during which the equipment functioned below 75 percent of its demonstrated sensitivity." The report tabulated twenty-three "failures" in 354.5 hours of operational flying, seven of them complete breakdowns of the equipment.

72. Roberts to Slessor, March 6, 1943, MR B0638.

73. "Radar Performance Report, 1 January–21 February 1943," enclosed in Roberts to Slessor, March 6, 1943, MR B0638.

74. Roberts to Slessor, March 6, 1943, MR B0638. It is difficult to know quite what to make of a report that ascribes fully one-third of all problems with the equipment to "undetermined" causes. The least one can say is that it makes it difficult to assess with confidence what the real problems were.

75. Roberts to Slessor, February 15, 1943. With the arrival of the 2nd Squadron, Roberts had one aircraft in his group with the experimental SCR-517B radar that used a PPI screen. By February he had also seen the British ASV Mark III equipment with a PPI screen. There is no question about the superiority of the PPI screen over the A-scope. The PPI screen is a simple cathode-ray tube, not unlike that in a television set. Its presentation, however, was circular, rather than the squared-off screen of a TV set tube. The aircraft is always in the center of the presentation on the screen, and all phenomena reproduced on the screen are thus relative to the position of the aircraft, greatly simplifying the operator's ability to determine relative position and movement.

Chapter 3. 480th Group Operations from the United Kingdom

1. Roberts to CG, AAFAC, December 6, 1942, MR A0522.

2. The very long range (VLR) version, a *rara avis* in late 1942, and entirely dedicated to convoy coverage, flew out even further. The British designated this type in

RAF service the Liberator I. The USAAF considered the standard B-24D to be VLR, and its extended range version was designated VLR(E). To the British, the standard B-24D was only a long-range (LR) aircraft, a fruitful source of confusion in records.

3. ORS/CC Report No. 264, December 11, 1943. My copy is from USAFHRC file 512.310C. All following material is from this source until otherwise noted.

4. AIR 15/732, ORS/CC Report No. 245, November 15, 1943, PRO. Data was compiled from the period January 1–May 31, 1943.

5. See, for example, Chaz Bowyer, *Sunderland at War* (London: Ian Allan, 1976); Bowyer, *The Short Sunderland* (Bourne End, Bucks.: Aston 1989); Baff, *Maritime Is Number Ten.*

6. ORS/CC Report No. 245.

7. There is ample evidence of the physical difficulties that could occur on long flights. Samuel McGowan remembered that it was often impracticable to leave one's station—in his case as navigator, in the nose of the plane—"to journey to the rear of the aircraft to use the toilet (if it was installed). Constipation (and later, hemorrhoids) was a constant problem." McGowan to author, February 22, 1988.

8. See, for example, the "RAF Coastal Command Manual of A/U Warfare," AIR 15/294, PRO.

9. AAFAC Antisubmarine Manual, SOP III-1, July 29, 1943, AAFAC file 424.205, USAFHRC.

10. Roberts to CG, Eighth Air Force, December 27, 1942, MR B0638.

11. This gives just eight hours per flight, but it is an average of all operational flights, including those terminated early. Roberts to CG, Eighth Air Force, December 27, 1942, MR B0638.

12. For the extra burdens imposed on flying personnel, especially officers, as a result of the shortage of ground personnel, see Roberts to CG, AAFAC, December 6, 1942, paragraph 4.d, MR B0638.

13. Ibid.

14. Roberts to CG, AAFAC, December 28, 1942, MR B0638. One can only agree with Roberts that for Coastal Command to use the tiny handful of aircraft it controlled which were equipped with centimetric radar for expensive shipping strikes close to the coast of occupied Europe was most unwise, and risked compromising the top secret equipment. It also raises questions about the RAF's "need" for American assistance in ASW operations.

15. "Notes on Briefing," November 20, 1942, 1st Antisubmarine Squadron (Prov.), copy courtesy of W. W. Pomeroy; "History of AAFAC," 103; "Report of 1st Squadron," November 25, 1942, MR A0522.

16. The description that follows in based on UBAT No. STE.85 and Admiralty Assessment No. 396. My copies of these documents are from AAFAC files, USAFHRC.

17. It had been intended to release only six depth charges, but twelve fell by error. As all attacks on U-boats by the 480th Group while based in the United Kingdom used the British Mark XI 250-pound Torpex depth charge, I have omitted these specifics from further descriptions of attacks.

18. See n. 16, above.

19. Description is based on UBAT No. STE.84 and Admiralty Assessment No. 382. My copies are from AAFAC files, USAFHRC.

20. Ibid.

21. The two areas consisted of a pair of boxes, with the boundaries of Inner Gondola at 45°N and 48.5°N, and 8°W and 10°W; and for Outer Gondola, 45.5°N and 50°N, and 15°W and 22°W. "The RAF in the Maritime War," 4:84–85.

22. "History of AAFAC," 98; "The RAF in the Maritime War," 4:85.

23. "The RAF in the Maritime War," vol. 4, appendix VII. The British Admiralty did not consider an attack to have been made if no weapon was released, hence the "four attacks" credited to USAAF aircraft. Below, I have described an additional American "attack" where depth charges failed to release, bringing my number to five.

24. Description of attack is from UBAT No. STE.89 and Admiralty Assessment No. 433, in AAFAC files, USAFHRC.

25. Admiralty Assessment No. 433. The assessor noted that an investigation was underway into the causes of the depth charge failures to release and explode. I have not been able to find any report of this investigation in either British or American files.

26. Description from UBAT No. STE.90 and accompanying documents in AAFAC files, USAFHRC; Admiralty Assessment No. 439 from AIR 15/134, PRO.

27. Ibid.

28. Assessment No. 439.

29. Description based on UBAT No. STE.93 and Admiralty Precis WA-526-5b, AAFAC files, USAFHRC.

30. Ibid.

31. Description from UBAT STE.91 and Admiralty Assessment No. 450. My copies from AAFAC files, USAFHRC. The assessor commented, "I take it that the cause of failure of armament to release is being investigated." Unfortunately, I have been unable to find any reports on the causes of this or the other failures.

32. I have found no report on why the depth charges failed to release on this occasion.

33. Fred A. Pribble to author, February 20, 1992.

34. Befehlshaber der U-Boote (BdU), war diary, February 11, 1943, USNHC; information on U.519 from Hoegel, *Embleme, wappen, malings deutscher U-Boote*, 277.

35. Description from UBAT No. STE.92 and Admiralty Assessment No. 452, AAFAC file 424.332, USAFHRC; Bernard E. Benson, "small notebook," February 20, 1943 entry, and "large notebook," same day's entry; AAFAC Monthly Intelligence Review, February 1943, p. 15; "History of AAFAC," 165–66.

36. The "baiting tactic" involved flying away from the position of the attack for about 30 minutes, executing a 180-degree turn, and returning to the spot to see if the U-boat captain, after looking around to see if a plane was still present and spotting none, had brought his boat back to the surface.

37. BdU, war diary, February 20 and 25, 1943. Information on U.211 from Hoegel, *Embleme, wappen, malings deutscher U-Boote*, 227.

38. Description from AIR 15/134, UBAT No. STE.96 and Admiralty Assessment No. 467, PRO.

Chapter 4. Transition

1. AIR 28/470, St. Eval Operations Log (hereafter St. Eval Ops. Log), February 26, 1943, PRO. For details of the ship and its experiences, see Brice, *Axis Blockade Runners of World War II*, 110, 117–18.

2. Bernard E. Benson, "large notebook," for February 26, 1943. Benson kept a "small notebook" on his flights, into which he jotted vital events and data; back at St. Eval he then filled in the details of the flights while they were still fresh in his memory in his "large notebook." He generously loaned both of these to the author. The operations log at St. Eval gives 0340 for takeoff time.

3. Benson, large notebook, February 26, 1943; St. Eval Ops. Log; 1st Squadron history.

4. 1st Squadron history.

5. Duration of encounter from ibid.; details from W. W. Pomeroy, diary entry for December 3, written up on December 5, 1942.

6. Benson, large notebook, January 26, 1943. Time of takeoff is from St. Eval Ops. Log, January 26, 1943.

7. Benson, large notebook. Time of attack was given as 1020, in 47.42°N/08.15°W, 200 miles west-southwest of Brest. The Liberator landed at St. Eval at 1657.

8. Benson, small and large notebooks for January 29, 1943; Pomeroy diary, January 29, 1943; St. Eval Ops. Log, January 29, 1943.

9. Benson, large notebook.

10. Pomeroy diary, January 29, 1943.

11. Ibid.

12. Benson, large notebook; St. Eval Ops. Log.

13. Pomeroy diary. Bill Pomeroy's diary comments on the conduct of the right waist gunner leave nothing to the imagination.

14. St. Eval Ops. Log.

15. Benson, large notebook.

16. Ibid.; St. Eval Ops. Log. Actions such as attacking friendly aircraft were regularly charged against the small number of intrepid and courageous Polish squadrons flying in the RAF, and should be taken with a grain of salt.

17. Benson flight log; St. Eval Ops. Log.

18. "History of AAFAC," 105. The AAFAC history calls them depth bombs, but the documents are so inconsistent in this usage that I have stayed with "depth charges," to distinguish these thin-cased weapons that could be released only at relatively low altitudes from the heavier-cased true aviation bombs.

19. "The RAF in the Maritime War," 3:489 n. 1.

20. Ibid., vol. 4, appendix VII.

21. "History of AAFAC," 106.

22. 1st Squadron history.

23. Price, *Aircraft against Submarines,* 119.

24. Doenitz was prepared for such news. His war diary notes for March 5, 1943: "The enemy is using carrier frequencies beyond the range of the present search receiver. So far the only confirmation of this comes from an enemy aircraft shot down over Holland." Quoted in Ministry of Defence (Navy, UK), *The U-Boat War in the Atlantic,* 2:87. This was indeed the "Rotterdamgeraete" or ten-centimeter radar (H2S) extracted from a crashed Bomber Command plane. It did not, as Doenitz thought, have a 5.7-cm wavelength, but rather one closer to 9.7 cm. It would be a considerable time before the German U-boats could reliably detect such transmissions. The deployment of the snorkel in 1944 would go far in restoring the submarine's security from easy aircraft detection and attack. When World War II ended, it was still difficult for an airplane to find a snorkel-equipped U-boat, despite the introduction of 3-cm radar.

25. A report compiled from oral statements by Capt. D. V. Peyton-Ward, RN of the Coastal Command headquarters staff, and Mr. Lardner of ORS/CC immediately following the operation's completion indicated the value of the 10-cm radar. Of 180 sorties flown, 123 were by centimeter-radar equipped aircraft. All the attacks and all but one of the sightings were by these planes. The 57 sorties flown by planes with ASV Mark II produced only one sighting. Report is in AAFAC file 424.421A, USAFHRC.

26. Figures are from Price, *Aircraft versus Submarine,* 155.

27. Ministry of Defence (Navy, UK), *The U-Boat War in the Atlantic,* 3:12.

28. Data compiled by March 1943 from earlier attacks that could be adequately documented by photographs suggested a normal range error of 150 to 180 feet and an average line error of about 60 to 90 feet, or almost three times what aircrews believed. Data is from AIR 15/304, RAF/CC TM No. 52, March 13, 1943, PRO.

29. AIR 15/305, RAF/CC TI No. 41, June 12, 1943, PRO.

30. Ibid., para. 42.

31. Antisubmarine Manual SOP III-1, July 29, 1943, AAFAC file 424.205, USAFHRC.

32. Both British and Americans were developing other airborne ASW weapons, but they were just entering service in mid-1943. Among the more promising were solid-head rockets that punched through a U-boat's pressure hull, an acoustic homing torpedo, and retrobombs used in conjunction with an airborne magnetic anomaly detector.

33. Antisubmarine Manual SOP III-1, July 29, 1943.

34. Price, *Aircraft versus Submarine,* 97–99.

35. AIR 15/305, RAF/CC TI No. 42, August 20, 1943, PRO.

36. Price, *Aircraft versus Submarine,* 160.

37. See ibid., 164–65, for details.

38. Ministry of Defence (Navy, UK), *The U-Boat War in the Atlantic,* 3:13, 3:14.
39. Ibid., 3:11.

Chapter 5. The 480th Antisubmarine Group in North Africa

1. General Eisenhower's original request in mid-February had been for two radar-equipped B-24 squadrons from the United States, one to operate at Casablanca, and the other in the Mediterranean. Pending their arrival, he asked that seven planes of the 1st Squadron be sent at once to the Casablanca area. See message no. 1051 of February 16, 1943, in AAFAC file 424.311, USAFHRC. The War Department then recommended that "the most effective use of the 1st and 2nd Antisubmarine Squadrons can be obtained by basing both squadrons in North West Africa." Maj. Gen. Thomas Handy, memo in above file. General Andrews in England concurred that sending one squadron would leave the other squadron and group headquarters "occupying without equipment the facilities that will be needed by British for replacement of these units," and he recommended moving the entire American group (USFOR to Allied Forces HQ, North Africa, February 22, 1943, in above file). This was done. Andrews further noted that the British hoped any movement would be deferred until after the Atlantic Convoy Conference scheduled for Washington at the beginning of March, where they could make a case for retaining the American squadrons in the United Kingdom (AAFAC file 424.311, USAFHRC). Port Lyautey is modern-day Kenitra, Morocco.
2. "History of AAFAC," 249, 120.
3. Hugh D. Maxwell Jr. to author, August 3, 1988.
4. "History of AAFAC," 120.
5. Maxwell to author.
6. Roberts to CG, AAFAC, May 18, 1943, MR B0638; 1st Squadron records.
7. "History of AAFAC," 121.
8. 1st Squadron history.
9. ORS/CC Report No. 222, March 21, 1943, AAFAC file 512.310C, USAFHRC. The actual average range of seven U-boat detections which the ORS report recorded was only six miles, but the ORS calculated a longer series of sightings would produce about an eight-mile average.
10. At the time the ASWORG report was prepared, there had been only one U-boat detection by radar while the group was operating in North Africa, and that was at 30 miles.
11. "Performance of SCR-517 Radar in Africa," ASWORG report, May 24, 1943, AAFAC file 424.906, USAFHRC.
12. Report and comments are in AAFAC file 424.8613, USAFHRC. Initial report is dated March 23, 1943, and response and commentary from USAAF Hqrs Requirements Division is dated April 14, 1943.

13. Ibid. Presumably, this helps explain some of the group's problems in the United Kingdom with depth charges hanging up.

14. Ibid., "Modification in Design of B-24 Type Radar Airplane," dated April 11, 1943.

15. Ibid., "General Program of Aircraft Modification," dated June 5, 1943. For a discussion of safety considerations, see appendix H.

16. The pilot and copilot were the CO of the 1st Squadron and the deputy CO of the 480th Group. 480th Group diary.

17. "History of AAFAC," 117.

18. Ibid.

19. 480th Group diary.

20. Quoted in "History of AAFAC," 118.

21. "History of AAFAC," 119.

22. Roberts's papers, MR B0638.

23. Ibid.

24. Ibid.

25. Were the main British participants in the Gibraltar meeting as innocent as Lieutenant Colonel Roberts? He was a convenient lever for them to attempt to prize the USN out of the MSF, but the arrangements had little if any chance of success without support from higher American authority. Did the British anticipate that Roberts could muster that support? It all seems a bit murky and ill thought out.

26. Roberts to CG, AAFAC, May 8, 1943, and May 15, 1943, MR B0638. Roberts continues: "All progress that is made here comes only after relentless plugging on our part. It is most difficult to try to raise them up to our operating standards when they have control over us."

27. Roberts to CG, AAFAC, June 23, 1943, MR B0638.

28. "Analysis of Anti-Submarine Operations in the Moroccan Sea Frontier Area," ASWORG Report, July 22, 1943, AAFAC file 424.310C, USAFHRC.

29. "History of AAFAC," 119.

30. 480th Group diary.

31. "Analysis of Anti-Submarine Operations in the Moroccan Sea Frontier Area."

32. The Catalinas were the PBY-5A amphibians. "History of AAFAC," 122–23.

33. Ibid., 123–24.

34. "Report of Anti-Submarine Action," courtesy of Lt. Col. John H. Shaw, USAF (Ret.), with comments by Colonel Shaw. Maj. Isaac J. Haviland Jr., 2nd Squadron CO, commented that "the crew's technique was faultless except that they failed to fire the forward nose gun on the run in." Colonel Shaw, who was the plane's navigator, later observed that the reason for not firing the forward gun was "because we did not want to negate our element of surprise." As the effective range of the .50-cal. machine gun in the nose was not more than 600 yards, at which range only the blind, deaf, and dumb would be unaware of the B-24 intending mayhem thundering down on them, Haviland's view would seem valid. At 200 MPH, the plane would travel 600 yards in about 5 seconds; the Type VII U-boat required about 25 to 30 seconds to crash dive

from the moment a threat was sighted, so the gunfire could not alert a U-boat crew soon enough for them to escape from their peril.

35. See "History of AAFAC," 164–65.

36. Description from Annex I of AAFAC files, USAFHRC.

37. AAFAC files, USAFHRC.

38. Description of the attack from AAFAC files, USAFHRC.

39. Ibid.

40. Ibid.

41. Photos are printed in AAFAC Monthly Intelligence Review, May 1943, p. 37, AAFAC Box 10, USAFHRC.

42. Description of attack from AAFAC files, USAFHRC.

43. Roberts to CG, AAFAC, June 18, 1943, MR B0638.

44. Roberts to Col. G. A. McHenry, June 18, 1943, MR B0638. Emphasis in the original.

45. Sanford himself would follow them home in early July, as part of the group's rotation policy.

46. Roberts to CG, AAFAC, June 23, 1943, MR B0638.

47. Description from AAFAC files; AAFAC Monthly Intelligence Review, June 1943, pp. 47–48; and "History of AAFAC," 173.

Chapter 6. Climax in July

1. German intentions and movements are from Ministry of Defence (Navy, UK), *The U-Boat War in the Atlantic,* 3:10.

2. Description from AAFAC files, USAFHRC. This was not counted as an attack by AAFAC.

3. Several photos are printed in the AAFAC Monthly Intelligence Review, July 1943, p. 56.

4. Description from AAFAC files.

5. No explanation appears in the records for the failure of the weapons to release.

6. Description from AAFAC files; "History of AAFAC," 174.

7. Description from AAFAC files; "History of AAFAC," 175–76. McDonell's was a replacement crew, sent out from the United States to join the 480th Group in May.

8. U.951 information from Hoegel, *Embleme, wappen, malings deutscher U-Boote,* 279; and Lenton, *German Warships of the Second World War,* 230.

9. Description from AAFAC files; "History of AAFAC," 176–78; Monthly Intelligence Review, July 1943, pp. 51–52.

10. U.232 information from Hoegel, *Embleme, wappen, malings deutscher U-Boote,* 275, and Lenton, *German Warships of the Second World War,* 170.

11. Description from AAFAC files; AAFAC Monthly Intelligence Review, July 1943, pp. 54–55.

12. Description from AAFAC files; AAFAC Monthly Intelligence Review, July 1943, p. 53.

13. Description from AAFAC files; AAFAC Monthly Intelligence Review, July 1943, p. 54; "History of AAFAC," 178–79.

14. There is some question about the type of depth charge. The attack report says "Mk 17-250 lb. Torpex," a nonexistent type. Was it the British Mark XI 250-pound Torpex or the American Mark 47 350-pound Torpex weapon? As the plane was carrying eight, the American type seems the more likely; on all recorded occasions when the planes of the group carried the British Mark XI, they carried twelve.

15. Description from AAFAC files.

16. Ibid.

17. Description from ibid.; AAFAC Monthly Intelligence Review, July 1943, p. 31; "History of AAFAC," 179–80.

18. U.506 information from Hoegel, *Embleme, wappen, malings deutscher U-Boote*, 142, and Lenton, *German Warships of the Second World War*, 191.

19. Description from AAFAC files.

20. Description from AAFAC file 424.332 and letter, J. M. Pennoyer to author, October 25, 1992.

21. This reduced the attack speed to about 160 MPH from the more common 200 MPH.

22. Figures from "The RAF in the Maritime War," vol. 4, appendix VII.

23. Figures derived from reports in AAFAC files and "History of AAFAC."

24. "The RAF in the Maritime War," 4:134 n. 1.

25. "History of AAFAC," 126. An unthreatened convoy was defined as one where no U-boat was plotted by Allied intelligence as being within 100 miles of the convoy's position, or within 100 miles of the convoy's course over the next 24 hours.

26. An area of high probability was defined as an area enclosed by the arc of a circle, 80 miles in radius, drawn about the position of a U-boat as plotted by Allied intelligence. The U-boat's plotted position was normally determined by direction-finding the submarine's radio transmissions.

27. "History of AAFAC," 123.

28. Ibid., 128.

Chapter 7. Final Innings

1. A variety of usages occur here: *Condor, Kondor,* and *Kurier* all being in use. I have used the most common form.

2. It may be somewhat unfair to impute the characteristics of a pachyderm to Kurt Tank's FW 200, originally designed by this gifted aircraft engineer as a civilian passenger plane. The addition of a "bathtub," that is, a ventral gondola, to the military version rather detracted from the plane's graceful lines, but it was certainly even then not as "pudgy" as the Liberator. The two planes were rather close in dimensions and weights. The FW 200.C3 had a wingspan of almost 108 feet and an area of 1,290 square feet, while the B-24D's wingspan was 110 feet and its area 1,048 square feet. Fuselage length of the

German and American planes were almost 77 feet and over 66 feet respectively. Empty weights were about 37,000 pounds for the Condor FW 200.C3 and 34,000 pounds for the early model B-24Ds; maximum weights were about 50,000 pounds for the Condor and 56,000 pounds for the Liberator. Speeds are too dependent on such factors as weight and altitude to be worth quoting; that the Liberator was the faster plane under most conditions seems clear, however.

3. "History of AAFAC," 125.

4. Twelfth Air Force General Order No. 86, November 6, 1943, courtesy Hugh D. Maxwell Jr.; 1st Squadron diary, USAFHRC; 480th Group records. The description of the developments at Craw Field when Hyde arrived there is courtesy of Col. A. J. Hanlon, USAF (Ret.), Hanlon to author, April 9, 1992.

5. Twelfth Air Force, General Order No. 86; AAFAC Monthly Intelligence Review, July 1943; 480th Group records.

6. Twelfth Air Force, General Order No. 86; AAFAC Monthly Intelligence Review, August 1943, pp. 32–33.

7. Hugh D. Maxwell Jr. to author, July 1, 1988. Subsequent quotes by him are from this letter.

8. "History of AAFAC," 184–86; Twelfth Air Force General Order No. 86; Maxwell to author, July 1, 1988.

9. AAFAC Monthly Intelligence Review, August 1943.

10. Ibid.; 480th Group records; press release, December 10, 1943, in AAFAC file 424.309, USAFHRC.

11. 2nd Squadron records.

12. NACAF file 618.204, USAFHRC.

13. Missing Air Crew Report, 480th Group records; the plane's msn was 42-40398.

14. "Aircraft Loss," MR B0638.

15. 2nd Squadron history.

16. Ibid.; Report of Aircraft Accident, MR B0638. The plane's msn was 42-24233.

17. Bernard E. Benson to author, January 8, 1992. The information in Benson's 1992 letter is identical to that in an interview he gave on July 20, 1943: see "Interview of Capt. Benson and Lt. Krebs." Flight times and routing are confirmed in the 480th Group diary. Gen. George C. Marshall's recollection in old age of General Smith is interesting: "hatchet-man. Did the dirty work for Eisenhower. Amazing to me to see how he is acceptable to many people now." Larry I. Bland, ed., *George C. Marshall: Interviews and Reminiscences for Forrest C. Pogue* (Lexington, Va.: George C. Marshall Research Foundation, 1991), 627.

18. 480th Group records. Ten aircraft of the 1st Squadron were assigned to this operation. One plane had engine trouble en route and had to be replaced by a plane from the 2nd Squadron. There were also some rotation of planes and crews during the stay at Protville. 1st Squadron diary.

19. Operations Report, 480th Group, September 13, 1943; Aircraft D/1, 1st Lt. Elbert W. Hyde, pilot, and Capt. Benjamin Wyche, navigator. This crew had done well in the past and Lieutenant Hyde was awarded a well-earned DFC for his conduct in combat on July 28, 1943, with an FW 200, which the American crew shot down.

20. Description of Protville 1 is from 2nd Squadron diary, USAFHRC.

21. Pilot Lt. Henry S. Cantrell and navigator Lt. Ray W. Crook. 480th Group records.

22. Ibid. Italy had surrendered to the Allies on September 3, 1943.

23. Report of Captain (S), Eighth Submarine Flotilla, to CinCMed, September 23, 1943, courtesy of Capt. Richard Gatehouse, DSC**, RN (Retd.), then CO of HMS *Sportsman*. I also wish to thank Commander Richard Compton-Hall, MBE, RN (Retd.) and Gus Britton of the Royal Navy Submarine Museum for documents and for putting me in touch with appropriate individuals.

24. Operational log of HMS *Sportsman*, September 12, 1943, courtesy of Capt. Richard Gatehouse, DSC**, RN (Retd.).

25. Its normal complement was forty-four, so the rescued seamen doubled its normal population.

26. HMS *Sportsman* log. The OOW, Lt. A. H. Anderson, RNR, survived his burns to return to active duty. He was the only casualty. Information courtesy of D. C. R. Webb, Dartford, Kent, to author, March 12, 1988.

27. The equipment suffered shock damage from a depth-charge explosion while submerging. This was thought at the time to be from the aircraft's second run. However, as the plane dropped no charges on the second run, it appears that the detonation was from a charge that had fallen on the submarine, and that had its hydrostatic pistol activated by the water's depth as the sub went down. This was later thought to be a second depth charge, yet the odds against it are very high. The chance of two charges from the same stick falling aboard the submarine were almost nil, and the explosion of an intact charge should have ruptured the submarine's pressure hull and sunk it with all hands. Information is in the log of *Sportsman* and the report of the Captain (S), Eighth Submarine Flotilla, noted above.

28. *Sportsman* log; report of Captain (S), Eighth Submarine Flotilla; 480th Group records. When approaching Algiers harbor, *Sportsman* was fired on by a U.S. Coast Guard cutter, which missed. After identities were straightened out, the sub chided the USCG cutter for its bad shooting. The response was that they'd do better next time. Information from J. W. Pryce, Morecombe, Lancashire, a crewmember of HMS *Sportsman*, to author, c. June 1988.

29. Report of Captain (S), Eighth Submarine Flotilla.

30. Ibid.; letter of Col. Alfred J. Hanlon to author, February 10, 1992. Colonel Hanlon was CO of the 1st Antisubmarine Squadron and sat on the inquiry into the attack on HMS *Sportsman*. The American aircraft does seem to have been in violation of USAAF Antisubmarine Command's operational procedure as laid out in its SOP III-1 of July 29, 1943. This prescribed (paragraph 4.b.) that: "No submarines shall be attacked in a sanctuary unless and until it [*sic*] has been identified as hostile *beyond possibility of doubt*" (emphasis in the original).

31. 1st Squadron history. The history begins this section with the heading "On D[etatched] S[ervice]!!!" The exclamation points seem appropriate. While NACAF was an Allied organization, 328 Wing was an all-British unit. When the 1st Squadron

arrived at Protville, they were given a station briefing by Group Captain Tuttle, RAF, the 328 Wing Commander, Flight Lieutenant Gould, of Wing Intelligence, and Flight Lieutenant Leroux, the Wing's signals officer, early on September 4. There was a briefing for U-boat hunting later that same day. Individual flight briefings are not mentioned in the 1st Squadron diary, but it does describe communications as "satisfactory with many navigational aids available."

32. 1st Squadron diary.

33. 480th Group diary.

34. 2nd Squadron diary. All diary quotes below are from this source. Internal evidence makes clear that the diarist was an enlisted man.

35. Roberts to CG, AAFAC, April 18, 1943, MR B0638.

36. Ibid.

37. Ibid., May 18, 1943, and August 31, 1943. As Roberts and Larson were able to confer personally in July, we unfortunately lack any letters from Roberts to AAFAC between June 18 and August 31.

38. Ibid., May 3 and August 31, 1943.

39. Ibid., May 8 and 15, 1943.

40. Ibid., May 3 and 15, 1943. This officer, the engineering officer for the 1st Squadron, was reclassified and transferred out of the group in mid-May.

41. Ibid., June 18, 1943.

42. Ibid., May 8, 1943.

43. Quesada to Larson, June 29, 1943, MR B0638.

44. Roberts to CG, AAFAC, April 18, May 18, and June 18, 1943.

45. This, and all following quotes, are for the day given in the text, and can be found under those dates in the 2nd Squadron diary.

46. "History of AAFAC," 129.

Chapter 8. The 479th Antisubmarine Group in the United Kingdom

1. "History of AAFAC," 107–8.

2. Ibid., 108.

3. "Major McElroy's Narrative," USAFHRC. McElroy commanded the 4th Antisubmarine Squadron.

4. "History of AAFAC," 110.

5. McElroy narrative.

6. "History of AAFAC," 110; McElroy narrative; "The RAF in the Maritime War," 4:119.

7. Wilmer L. Stapel to author, August 11, 1988.

8. William D. Meredith to author, July 21, 1988.

9. McElroy narrative.

10. "History of AAFAC," 110.

11. 479th Group records, USAFHRC.

12. Meredith to author, July 21, 1988.

13. Ibid.

14. Meredith to author, August 11, 1988.

15. Ibid. Meredith noted that no crew he was on ever used this method, but "I'm sure that it must have worked. It was the Coastal Command's idea and they had a lot of experience before we arrived."

16. Stapel to author, July 20, 1988.

17. 479th Group records.

18. Comparison of William D. Meredith's AAF Form No. 5, which he kindly provided to the author, with the flying records of the 479th Group. Meredith was engineer/gunner in the crew of 1st Lt. (later Capt.) Joseph L. Hamilton. On one of the eighteen missions the pilot was not Hamilton but Major McElroy, the squadron commander.

19. Meredith's AAF Form No. 5 provides some idea of this: a four-day cycle was maintained for much of September, with operational missions on September 2, 6, 10, 14, and 18. August, however, had been notably erratic, with flights on August 2, 11, 23, and 26. Along with the eighteen missions he flew between July 15 and October 29, Meredith also flew twenty-two training missions. His eighteen operational flights totaled 180 hours, an average of 10 hours; his last two operational flights were the longest and shortest, of 12 hours and 7.8 hours respectively. Data from Meredith's AAF Form No. 5.

20. AIR 15/136, PRO; "History of AAFAC," 111. One sighting and one attack were on a nonsubmarine target.

21. AIR 15/136, PRO, UBAAF No. 802; AAFAC files, USAFHRC. As was the case with the 480th Group in the United Kingdom, so too the 479th Group used only the British Mark XI 250-pound Torpex depth charge in its attacks on U-boats. Thus I shall not repeat that information in the remaining descriptions of 479th Group attacks.

22. AAFAC files, USAFHRC.

23. The account of U.558's bay crossing is from Franks, *Conflict over the Bay*, 158–62.

24. Description of Gallmeier attack is from AAFAC files, USAFHRC, and AIR 15/136, Assessment nos. 799 and 801, PRO. There are also accounts in Franks, *Conflict over the Bay*, cited above, and his *Search, Find and Kill*, 93.

25. Sources cited above, and "The RAF in the Maritime War," 4:125.

26. Description from AIR 15/136, UBAAF No. 810, PRO; AAFAC files, USAFHRC; Franks, *Conflict over the Bay*, 173–74.

27. Which assessment is correct? The short answer is we don't know, as the entire crew of U.404, who were best placed to say, perished with the loss of their boat or soon after. I suspect the truth this time falls exactly between the two assessments, an *E*, or probably slight damage, which was sufficient for the inexperienced commander

of U.404 to bring his boat back to the surface only a half-hour after McElroy's second attack, when Hammer found it. However, I have not attempted to second-guess the judgment of the very experienced assessors, and in compiling the attack data have opted for the more conservative assessment.

28. Description from AIR 15/136, UBAAF No. 811, PRO; AAFAC files, US-AFHRC; "History of AAFAC," 180–82; "The RAF in the Maritime War," 4:127; Franks, *Search, Find and Kill,* 94; Franks, *Conflict over the Bay,* 173–75; Arthur J. Hammer to author, April 21, 1992.

29. Description from 479th Group records. For a full account of the July 30 battle, see Franks, *Conflict over the Bay,* 183–200.

30. Namely: two Liberators from 19th Antisubmarine Squadron, USAAF, and 53 Squadron, RAF; two Sunderlands from 228 Squadron, RAF, and 461 Squadron, RAAF; two Halifaxes, both from 502 Squadron, RAF; and a Catalina from 210 Squadron, RAF.

31. Description from AIR 15/136, UBAAF Nos. 823 and 831, PRO; "History of AAFAC," 182–83; AAFAC Monthly Intelligence Review, July 1943, pp. 32–33; "The RAF in Maritime War," 4:131; Franks, *Conflict over the Bay,* 207; Franks, *Search, Find and Kill,* 97.

32. Records of the 19th Antisubmarine Squadron, USAFHRC.

Chapter 9. The Hunters Become the Hunted

1. 479th Group records.
2. Ibid.
3. AAFAC Monthly Intelligence Review, August 1943, p. 32; 479th Group records.
4. Ibid.
5. "History of the 19th Antisubmarine Squadron," USAFHRC; 479th Group records; AAFAC Monthly Intelligence Review, August 1943, pp. 33–34.
6. Ibid.
7. Ibid.
8. 19th Squadron history.
9. 479th Group records.
10. Ibid.; 4th Antisubmarine Squadron records, USAFHRC.
11. 479th Group records.
12. Ibid.
13. Ibid.
14. Ibid.
15. Stapel to author, July 20, 1988.
16. 479th Group records.
17. Ibid.

18. Ibid.

19. "History of the 479th Group," USAFHRC.

Chapter 10. Conclusions

1. "History of AAFAC," 188.

2. "RAF in the Maritime War," 4:119, 122–23, 125, 127, 131, 134 n. 1.

3. This was the view of the secretary of war, Henry Stimson, who used the term "stepchild." Stimson and Bundy, *On Active Service in War and Peace*, 512.

4. "History of AAFAC," 45.

5. Ibid., 46.

6. Figures are from ibid., 241 n. 57.

7. Ibid., 49.

8. Ibid.

9. Ibid.

10. Marshall to King, April 16, 1943. Quoted in "History of AAFAC," 64.

11. King quotes extensively from his letter of June 21, 1942, to General Marshall, including his views on convoy, in King and Whitehill, *Fleet Admiral King*, 456–59.

12. "History of AAFAC," 69.

13. The USAAF did make an offer to establish within Tenth Fleet a single command for all LR and VLR ASW aircraft, with an USAAF general in charge, exercising full operational control over these aircraft, subject only to the oversight of Admiral King. This concept of command King firmly rejected, arguing that operational control would have to be exercised by "Sea Frontiers, the Atlantic Fleet," or special task forces. King and Whitehill, *Fleet Admiral King*, 464. Not surprisingly, this was unacceptable to the USAAF.

14. "History of AAFAC," 70.

15. Ibid., 72.

16. "History of AAFAC," 75, and chap. 2, n. 82.

17. For a discussion of this, see "History of AAFAC," 75.

18. It is not entirely clear what Admiral King's motivation was in this. Was it a serious attempt at expanding the Navy's missions by King, superb military empire-builder that he was? Or was it only a tactical move in his guerrilla war with the USAAF? Or was it simply sheer cussedness? With King, it is not easy to say. General Marshall, who had the closest association with King, recalled in old age something of the admiral's character: "I had trouble with King because he was always sore at everybody. He was perpetually mean." Bland, ed., *George C. Marshall*, 593.

19. "History of AAFAC," 78.

20. This was made clear to King by Marshall in his letter of June 28, 1943. See King and Whitehill, *Fleet Admiral King*, 469 n. 12.

21. Marshall to King, June 28, 1943, quoted in "History of AAFAC," 81.

22. For King's views, and his remarkable retreat on July 3, 1943, see King and Whitehill, *Fleet Admiral King,* 468–70.

23. "History of AAFAC," 82.

24. Craven and Cate, eds., *The Army Air Forces in World War II,* 2:408–9.

25. Slessor, *The Central Blue,* 494–95.

26. See appendix G for an estimate of the price of this activity.

27. "History of AAFAC," 82–83; Craven and Cate, eds., *The Army Air Forces in World War II,* 2:408–10.

Appendix F. How Radar Works

1. These are different from modern-day radar bands.

2. I have adhered to World War II practice of using megacycles per second (mc/s). Modern practice is to replace the term *cycle* with *herz*. Megacycles thus become megaherz (MHz) in present-day usage.

3. Wavelength is given as the speed of light divided by the frequency. In centimeters this is roughly 30,000 divided by the frequency in megacycles. Frequency and wavelength are inversely proportional. Thus the 200mc frequency of early American and British radars had a wavelength of about 1.5m.

Appendix I. Awards and Decorations

1. Wayne S. Johnson to author, January 19, 1992.

2. Some perspective on flying hours by 480th Group members is provided by the remarkable Squadron Leader Ivan Podger, DFC, RAAF, who amassed 1,688 hours in 121 operational sorties flown in Sunderlands of 10 Squadron, RAAF. In the same squadron, a navigator, Flight Lieutenant John H. Portus, had completed 740 operational hours, which was thought worthy of recognition with the DFC. Information is from Baff, *Maritime Is Number Ten,* 182, 300.

3. McElroy narrative; Meredith AAF Form No. 5.

4. Data from 4th Squadron Records, USAFHRC.

5. McElroy narrative.

6. War Department General Order No. 1 of January 4, 1944.

Bibliography

Archival Sources

USAF Historical Research Center, Maxwell Air Force Base, Alabama

AAFAC Monthly Intelligence Review
"Major McElroy's Narrative" (AAFAC file 424.309C)
"The RAF in the Maritime War"
Records of the 26th Wing, USAAFAC
Records of the USAAF Antisubmarine Command

Microfilm Reel A0522

Diary of the 1st Antisubmarine Squadron
Diary of the 2nd Antisubmarine Squadron
"History of the 1st Antisubmarine Squadron"
"History of the 2nd Antisubmarine Squadron"
Records of the 1st Antisubmarine Squadron
Records of the 2nd Antisubmarine Squadron
Records of the 4th Antisubmarine Squadron
Records of the 6th Antisubmarine Squadron

Microfilm Reel A0523

"History of the 19th Antisubmarine Squadron"
Records of the 19th Antisubmarine Squadron
Records of the 22nd Antisubmarine Squadron

223

"History of the 479th Group"
Records of the 479th Antisubmarine Group

Diary of the 480th Group
"History of the 480th Group"
Records of the 480th Antisubmarine Group

"History of the Army Air Forces Antisubmarine Command"

Operational Archives, U.S. Naval Historical Center, Washington Navy Yard

Commander-in-Chief, U-Boats, *War Diary* (ONI translation of Befehlshaber der
U-Boote, *Kriegstagebuch*)

Public Record Office, Kew, Surrey, England

ADM 205, First Sea Lord's Files
AIR 8, Chief of the Air Staff's Files
AIR 15, RAF Coastal Command Files
AIR 28, RAF Station Records
AVIA 15, Ministry of Aircraft Production Files
CAB 105, Cabinet Office Files

Royal Navy Submarine Museum, Gosport, Hampshire, England

Documents relating to the attack on HMS *Sportsman*

Personal Interviews and Correspondence

479th Antisubmarine Group

Arthur J. Hammer
William D. Meredith
Wilmer L. Stapel

480th Antisubmarine Group

Bernard E. Benson
Alfred J. Hanlon
Wayne S. Johnson
Ralph E. Jones
Cornelia H. Roberts Kimbrough (widow of Gen. Jack Roberts)
John L. Krebs
Samuel B. McGowan
Hugh D. Maxwell Jr.
Jordan M. Pennoyer
William W. Pomeroy
Fred A. Pribble
John H. Shaw
Maurice S. Smithberg

Relating to HMS Sportsman

Richard Gatehouse
J. W. Pryce
D. C. R. Webb

Books

Air Ministry (UK). *The Origins and Development of Operational Research in the Royal Air Force,* Air Publication3368. London: HMSO, 1963.

Ashworth, Chris. *Action Stations.* Vol. 5, *Military Airfields of the South-West.* N.p.: Patrick Stephens, Ltd., n.d.

Baff, Kevin C. *Maritime Is Number Ten: The Sunderland Era.* Netley, South Australia: Griffen Press, 1983.

Brice, Martin. *Axis Blockade Runners of World War II.* Annapolis, Md.: Naval Institute Press, 1981.

Craven, Wesley Frank, and James Lea Cate, eds. *The Army Air Forces in World War II.* Vol. 2, *Europe: TORCH to POINTBLANK, August 1942 to December 1943.* Chicago: University of Chicago Press, 1949.

Franks, Norman L. R. *Conflict over the Bay.* London: William Kimber, 1986.

———. *Search, Find and Kill: Coastal Command's U-Boat Successes.* Bourne End, Buckinghamshire: Aston, 1990.

Freeman, Roger A. *The Mighty Eighth.* Rev. ed. London: Jane's, 1986.

Gannon, Michael. *Operation Drumbeat.* New York: Harper and Row, 1990.

Hoegel, Georg. *Embleme, wappen, malings deutscher U-Boote, 1939–1945.* Herford: Koehler, 1987.

Kimball, Warren F., ed. *Churchill and Roosevelt: The Complete Correspondence*. 3 vols. Princeton: Princeton University Press, 1984.

King, Ernest J., and Walter Muir Whitehill. *Fleet Admiral King: A Naval Record*. New York: W. W. Norton, 1952.

Lenton, H. T. *German Warships of the Second World War*. New York: Arco, 1976.

Ministry of Defence (Navy, UK). *The U-Boat War in the Atlantic*. London: HMSO, 1989.

Morison, Samuel Eliot. *History of United States Naval Operations in World War II*. Vol. 1. Rev. ed. Boston: Houghton Mifflin, 1954.

Price, Alfred. *Aircraft versus Submarine: The Evolution of Antisubmarine Aircraft, 1912 to 1980*. New ed. London: Jane's, 1980.

Slessor, John. *The Central Blue*. London: Cassell, 1956.

Stimson, Henry L., and McGeorge Bundy. *On Active Service in Peace and War*. New York: Harper and Bros., 1948.

Terrett, Dulany. *The Signal Corps: The Emergency*. Washington, D.C.: Office of the Chief of Military History, 1956.

Index

All aircraft, squadrons, groups, and depth charge types are listed under their generic headings. Rank indexed for each individual is the highest recorded in the book.